Microsoft Dynamics AX 2012 Development Cookbook

Solve real-world Microsoft Dynamics AX development
problems with over 80 practical recipes

Mindaugas Pocius

BIRMINGHAM - MUMBAI

Microsoft Dynamics AX 2012 Development Cookbook

First published: December 2009

Second edition: May 2012

Production Reference: 1270412

Published by Packt Publishing Ltd.
Livery Place
35 Livery Street
Birmingham B3 2PB, UK.

ISBN 978-1-84968-464-4

www.packtpub.com

Cover Image by David Gutierrez (bilbaorocker@yahoo.co.uk)

Credits

Author

Mindaugas Pocius

Reviewers

Angela McClelland

Yev Taranovs

Acquisition Editor

Kerry George

Lead Technical Editor

Meeta Rajani

Azharuddin Sheikh

Technical Editors

Merin Jose

Lubna Shaikh

Mehreen Shaikh

Copy Editor

Brandt D'Mello

Project Coordinators

Alka Nayak

Proofreader

Kelly Hutchinson

Indexer

Tejal Daruwale

Rekha Nair

Hemangini Bari

Production Coordinator

Arvindkumar Gupta

Cover Work

Arvindkumar Gupta

About the Author

Mindaugas Pocius is currently a freelance Dynamics AX technical and functional consultant and trainer at DynamicsLab Limited (www.dynamicslab.com). The company specializes in providing development, consulting, and training services for Microsoft Dynamics AX resellers and customers.

Mindaugas started his IT consulting career back in 2001 while still in his Information Technology Master Studies at a Lithuanian university. Since then he has become a recognized Microsoft Certified Professional for AX in all major areas: Development, Configuration and Installation, Financials, Projects, and Trade and Logistics. He is also a Certified Microsoft Trainer for Dynamics AX and has delivered numerous Dynamics AX training courses across Europe.

From 2001 to 2012, Mindaugas has participated in over 20 Dynamics AX implementations. He has had a wide range of development, consulting, and leading roles, while always maintaining a significant role as a business application developer.

In December 2009, Mindaugas released his first book, "*Microsoft Dynamics AX 2009 Development Cookbook*", *Packt Publishing*, which is the predecessor of this book.

First of all, I would like to thank my wife Rasa and my two boys Dominykas and Augustas for their support and understanding during my long hours spent on this book. I also want to apologize for the time I have stolen from them to make this book real.

Secondly, I wish to thank the reviewers—Angela and Yev—my colleagues, very experienced Dynamics AX developers, and good friends.

And lastly, special thanks should be given to the Packt Publishing team who made this book possible.

About the Reviewers

Angela McClelland is a Software Developer and Technical Consultant for Dynamics AX (AX) currently working as a freelance consultant in the United Kingdom.

Angela began working with AX in 2001, while completing a Computer Science degree at The University of Waikato in New Zealand. After a successful implementation of version 2.5, and a later upgrade to 3, the spouse and bags were packed up and moved over to England to seek out bigger project challenges, and for a taste of world travel.

Since this move, Angela has worked on many AX implementations, specializing in business solutions design, X++ programming, reporting, and business intelligence. She is a Microsoft Certified Professional for AX: Development, Installation and Configuration, as well as key modules: Finance, Projects, Production, and Trade and Logistics. She is also a Microsoft Certified Trainer for AX.

> A big thanks to Mindaugas for his efforts in writing this book, and for inviting me to be one of the reviewers. I have learned a lot, and already have plans to make use of some of these handy recipes.

Yev Taranovs is an experienced Dynamics AX consultant. Yev has been working with AX since 2002 and has a wide angle of expertise, both technical and functional. Apart from Dynamics AX, Yev is also working with other Microsoft technologies including Microsoft CRM, SharePoint, Reporting Services, Analysis Services, and Visual Studio.

Yev's home town is Riga, Latvia. He started his Dynamics career there and moved to the United Kingdom in 2005. Yev is currently working for Hitachi Solutions.

www.PacktPub.com

Support files, eBooks, discount offers and more

You might want to visit www.PacktPub.com for support files and downloads related to your book.

Did you know that Packt offers eBook versions of every book published, with PDF and ePub files available? You can upgrade to the eBook version at www.PacktPub.com and as a print book customer, you are entitled to a discount on the eBook copy. Get in touch with us at service@packtpub.com for more details.

At www.PacktPub.com, you can also read a collection of free technical articles, sign up for a range of free newsletters and receive exclusive discounts and offers on Packt books and eBooks.

http://PacktLib.PacktPub.com

Do you need instant solutions to your IT questions? PacktLib is Packt's online digital book library. Here, you can access, read and search across Packt's entire library of books.

Why Subscribe?

- ▶ Fully searchable across every book published by Packt
- ▶ Copy and paste, print and bookmark content
- ▶ On demand and accessible via web browser

Free Access for Packt account holders

If you have an account with Packt at www.PacktPub.com, you can use this to access PacktLib today and view nine entirely free books. Simply use your login credentials for immediate access.

Instant Updates on New Packt Books

Get notified! Find out when new books are published by following @PacktEnterprise on Twitter, or the *Packt Enterprise* Facebook page.

Table of Contents

Preface

As a Dynamics AX developer, your responsibility is to deliver all kinds of application customizations, whether it is a small adjustment or a bespoke module. Dynamics AX is a highly customizable system and requires a significant amount of knowledge and experience to deliver quality solutions. One goal can be achieved in multiple ways and there is always the question of which way is the best.

This book takes you through numerous recipes to help you with daily development tasks. Each recipe contains detailed step-by-step instructions along with application screenshots and in-depth explanations. The recipes cover multiple Dynamics AX modules, so at the same time the book provides an overview of the functional aspects of the system for developers.

What this book covers

Chapter 1, Processing Data, focuses on data manipulation. It explains how to build data queries, how to check and modify existing data, how to read and write external files, and how to use date effectiveness.

Chapter 2, Working with Forms, covers various aspects of building forms in Dynamics AX. In this chapter, dialogs and their events are explained. Also, various useful features such as splitters, tree controls, checklists, and others are explained.

Chapter 3, Working with Data in Forms, basically supplements the previous chapter and explains data organization in forms. Examples in this chapter include instructions on how to build form data filters, process multiple records, and work with images and colors.

Chapter 4, Building Lookups, covers all kinds of lookups in the system. The chapter starts with a simple automatically-generated lookup, continues with more advanced ones, and finishes with standard Windows lookups such as the file selection dialog and color picker.

Chapter 5, Processing Business Tasks, explains the usage of the Dynamics AX business logic API. In this chapter, we cover topics on how to process journals, purchase orders, and sales orders. Other features such as modifying transaction text and creating electronic payment formats are included too.

Chapter 6, Integration with Microsoft Office, shows how Word, Excel, Outlook, and Microsoft Project applications could be integrated with Dynamics AX.

Chapter 7, Using Services, explains how to use services in Dynamics AX. The chapter covers standard query, metadata, and document system services. It also demonstrates how to create custom services and how to consume external services.

Chapter 8, Improving Development Efficiency, presents a few ideas about how to make daily development tasks easier. This chapter demonstrates how to build code templates, modify the tools and the right-click context menus, use search in development projects, and how to customize the personalization form.

Chapter 9, Improving Dynamics AX Performance, discusses how system performance could be improved by following several simple rules. This chapter explains how to calculate code execution time, how to write efficient SQL statements, how to properly cache display methods, and how to use Dynamics AX Trace Parser and SQL Server Database Engine Tuning Advisor.

What you need for this book

All coding examples were done using a virtual Microsoft Dynamics AX 2012 Image from the Microsoft Learning Download Center. The following list of software from the virtual image was used in this book:

- ▶ Microsoft Dynamics AX 2012 (kernel: 6.0.947.0, application: 6.0.593.0)
- ▶ Microsoft Dynamics AX Trace Parser (version: 6.0.947.0)
- ▶ Microsoft Windows Server 2008 R2 Enterprise
- ▶ Microsoft SQL Server 2008 R2
- ▶ Microsoft Office Excel 2010
- ▶ Microsoft Office Word 2010
- ▶ Microsoft Office Outlook 2010
- ▶ Microsoft Office Project 2010
- ▶ Microsoft Visual Studio 2010
- ▶ Microsoft Internet Explorer 8
- ▶ Notepad

Although all recipes were tested on the mentioned software, they might work on older or newer software versions without any implications or with minor code adjustments.

Who this book is for

This book is for Dynamics AX developers primarily focused on delivering time proven application modifications. Although new X++ developers could use this book alongside their beginner guides, this book is more focused on people who are willing to raise their programming skills above beginner level and at the same time learn functional aspects of Dynamics AX. So, some Dynamics AX coding experience is expected.

Conventions

In this book, you will find a number of styles of text that distinguish between different kinds of information. Here are some examples of these styles, and an explanation of their meaning.

Code words in text are shown as follows: "Dynamics AX contains a list of `NumberSeqApplicationModule` derivative classes, which holds the number sequence setup data for the specific module."

A block of code is set as follows:

```
static void CustAccountRename(Args _args)
{
    CustTable custTable;

    select firstOnly custTable
        where custTable.AccountNum == '1103';

    if (custTable.RecId)
    {
        custTable.AccountNum = '1103_';
        custTable.renamePrimaryKey();
    }
}
```

New terms and **important words** are shown in bold. Words that you see on the screen, in menus or dialog boxes for example, appear in the text like this: "Run the number sequence wizard by clicking on the **Generate** button in **Organization administration | Common | Number sequences | Number sequences**."

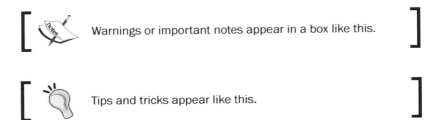

Warnings or important notes appear in a box like this.

Tips and tricks appear like this.

Reader feedback

Feedback from our readers is always welcome. Let us know what you think about this book—what you liked or may have disliked. Reader feedback is important for us to develop titles that you really get the most out of.

To send us general feedback, simply send an e-mail to feedback@packtpub.com, and mention the book title through the subject of your message.

If there is a topic that you have expertise in and you are interested in either writing or contributing to a book, see our author guide on www.packtpub.com/authors.

Customer support

Now that you are the proud owner of a Packt book, we have a number of things to help you to get the most from your purchase.

Downloading the example code

You can download the example code files for all Packt books you have purchased from your account at http://www.packtpub.com. If you purchased this book elsewhere, you can visit http://www.packtpub.com/support and register to have the files e-mailed directly to you.

Errata

Although we have taken every care to ensure the accuracy of our content, mistakes do happen. If you find a mistake in one of our books—maybe a mistake in the text or the code—we would be grateful if you would report this to us. By doing so, you can save other readers from frustration and help us improve subsequent versions of this book. If you find any errata, please report them by visiting http://www.packtpub.com/support, selecting your book, clicking on the **errata submission form** link, and entering the details of your errata. Once your errata are verified, your submission will be accepted and the errata will be uploaded to our website, or added to any list of existing errata, under the Errata section of that title.

Piracy

Piracy of copyright material on the Internet is an ongoing problem across all media. At Packt, we take the protection of our copyright and licenses very seriously. If you come across any illegal copies of our works, in any form, on the Internet, please provide us with the location address or website name immediately so that we can pursue a remedy.

Please contact us at `copyright@packtpub.com` with a link to the suspected pirated material.

We appreciate your help in protecting our authors, and our ability to bring you valuable content.

Questions

You can contact us at `questions@packtpub.com` if you are having a problem with any aspect of the book, and we will do our best to address it.

1
Processing Data

In this chapter, we will cover the following topics:

- Creating a new number sequence
- Renaming the primary key
- Merging two records
- Adding a document handling note
- Using a normal table as a temporary table
- Copying a record
- Building a query object
- Using a macro in an SQL statement
- Executing a direct SQL statement
- Enhancing the data consistency check
- Exporting data to an XML file
- Importing data from an XML file
- Creating a comma-separated value file
- Reading a comma-separated value file
- Using the date effectiveness feature

Introduction

This chapter focuses on data manipulation exercises. Here, we will discuss how to work with query objects from X++ code. We will also discuss how to reuse macros in X++ SQL statements and how to send SQL statements directly to the database. This chapter will explain how to rename primary keys, how to merge and copy records, how to add document handling notes to selected records, and how to create and read XML and comma-separated files. The chapter ends with a recipe about the date effectiveness feature.

Creating a new number sequence

Number sequences in Dynamics AX are used to generate specifically formatted numbers for record identification. It could be anything from voucher numbers or transaction identification numbers to customer or vendor accounts.

When developing custom functionality, very often one of the tasks is to add a new number sequence to the system to support newly created tables. Dynamics AX contains a list of `NumberSeqApplicationModule` derivative classes, which holds the number sequence setup data for the specific module.

These classes are read by the number sequence wizard, which detects existing number sequences and proposes to create the missing ones or newly added ones. The wizard is normally run as part of the application initialization. It can also be rerun at any time later when expanding the Dynamics AX functionality used, where a setup of additional number sequences is required. The wizard also has to be rerun if new custom number sequences are added to the system.

In this recipe, we will add a new number sequence to the system. In a standard application, the customer group number is not driven by any number sequence, so we will enhance this by creating it.

How to do it...

Carry out the following steps in order to complete this recipe:

1. Open the `NumberSeqModuleCustomer` class in the Application Object Tree (AOT), and add the following code to the bottom of the `loadModule()` method:

Downloading the example code

You can download the example code files for all Packt books you have purchased from your account at http://www. packtpub.com. If you purchased this book elsewhere, you can visit http://www.packtpub.com/support and register to have the files e-mailed directly to you.

```
datatype.parmDatatypeId(extendedTypeNum(CustGroupId));
datatype.parmReferenceHelp("Customer group ID");
datatype.parmWizardIsContinuous(false);
datatype.parmWizardIsManual(NoYes::No);
datatype.parmWizardIsChangeDownAllowed(NoYes::Yes);
datatype.parmWizardIsChangeUpAllowed(NoYes::Yes);
datatype.parmWizardHighest(999);
```

```
datatype.parmSortField(20);
datatype.addParameterType(
    NumberSeqParameterType::DataArea, true, false);
this.create(datatype);
```

2. Create a new job with the following code and run it:

```
static void NumberSeqLoadAll(Args _args)
{
    NumberSeqApplicationModule::loadAll();
}
```

3. Run the number sequence wizard by clicking on the **Generate** button in **Organization administration** | **Common** | **Number sequences** | **Number sequences**, and click on the **Next** button, as shown in the following screenshot:

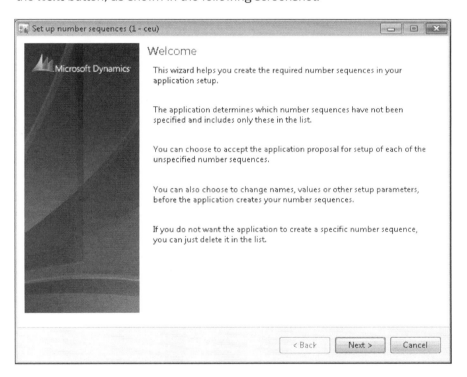

4. Click on **Details** to view more information. Delete everything apart from the lines where **Area** is **Accounts receivable** and **Reference** is **Customer group**. Note the number sequence codes, and click on the **Next** button:

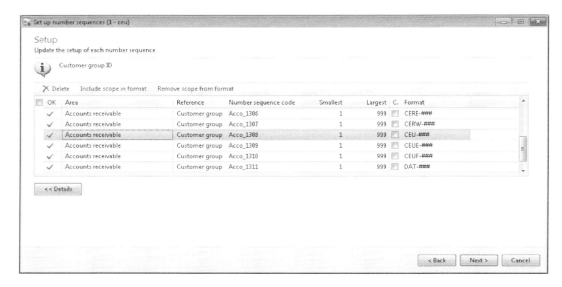

5. On the last page, click on the **Finish** button to complete the set up:

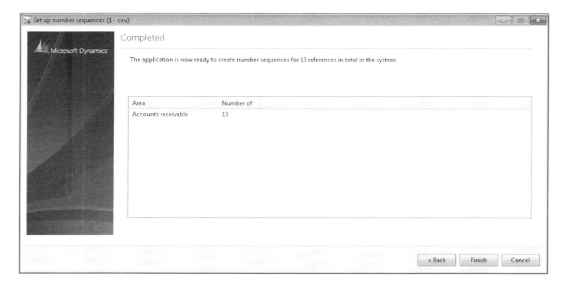

6. The newly created number sequences can now be found in **Organization administration | Number sequences | Number sequences**, as shown in the following screenshot:

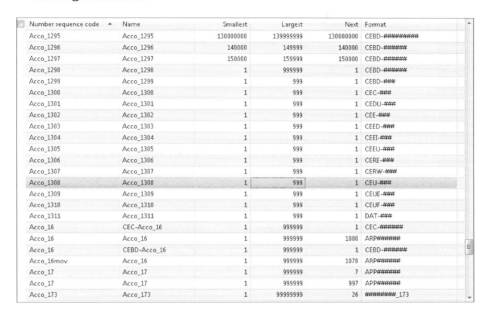

7. Open **Organization administration | Number sequences | Segment configuration** and notice the new **Customer group** reference:

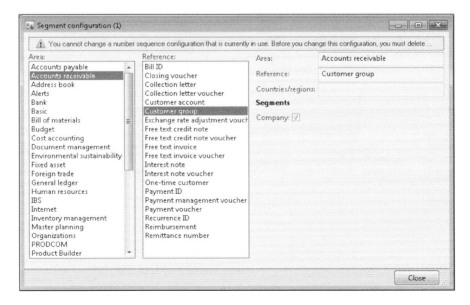

8. Open **Accounts receivable | Setup | Accounts receivable parameters** and go to the **Number sequences** tab page. Here we should see the new number sequence code:

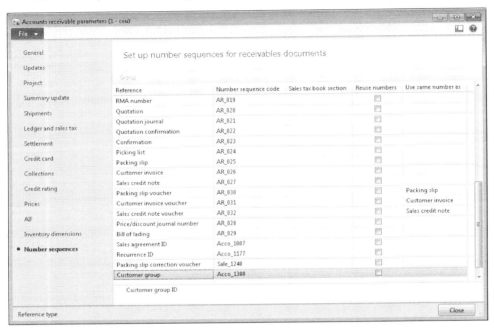

9. The last thing to do is to create a helper method for this number sequence. Locate the **CustParameters** table in the AOT and create the following method:

```
public server static NumberSequenceReference numRefCustGroupId()
{
    return NumberSeqReference::findReference(
        extendedTypeNum(CustGroupId));
}
```

How it works...

We start the recipe by adding a number sequence initialization code into the `NumberSeqModuleCustomer` class. As we can understand from its name, it holds the initialization of all number sequences that belong to the **Accounts receivable** module.

The code in the `loadModule()` method defines the default number sequence settings to be used in the wizard, such as data type, description, highest possible number, and so on. Additional options, such as starting sequence number, number format, and others could also be added here. All mentioned options could be changed while running the wizard. The `addParameterType()` method is used to define number sequence scope. In the example we created a separate sequence for each Dynamics AX company.

Before we start the wizard, we need to initialize number sequence references. This is normally done as a part of the Dynamics AX initialization checklist, but in this example we have to execute it manually by calling the `loadAll()` method of the `NumberSeqApplicationModule` class.

Next, we will run the wizard. We will skip the welcome page and in the second step of the wizard, the **Details** button can be used to display more options. The options can also be changed later in the **Number sequences** form before or even after the number sequence is actually used. The last page shows an overview of what will be created. Once completed, the wizard creates new records in the **Number sequences** form for each company.

The newly created number sequence reference appears in the **Segment configuration** form. Here we can see that the **Data area** checkbox is checked, meaning that we will have separate number lists for each company. The number sequence setup can normally be located in the module parameter forms.

See also

See *Chapter 3, Working with Data in Forms*:

▸ *Using a number sequence handler*

Renaming the primary key

Most of you, who are familiar with the Dynamics AX application, have probably used the standard **Rename** function. This function allows us to rename the primary key of almost any record. It is irreplaceable if a record was saved by mistake or simply needs renaming. The function ensures data consistency that is, all related records are renamed too. It can be accessed from the **Record information** form (shown in the following screenshot), which can be opened by selecting **Record info** from the right-click menu on any record:

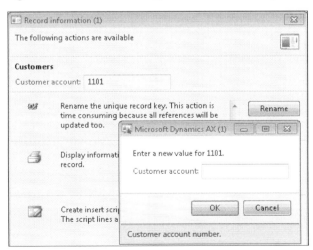

When it comes to manual mass renaming, this function might be very time-consuming. An alternative way of doing that is to create a job that automatically runs through all required records and calls this function automatically.

This recipe will explain how the record primary key can be renamed through the code. As an example, we will create a job that renames a customer account.

How to do it...

Carry out the following steps in order to complete this recipe:

1. Open **Accounts receivable | Common | Customers | All customers** and find the account that has to be renamed:

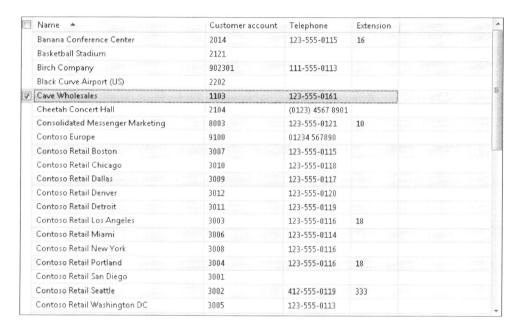

Name ▲	Customer account	Telephone	Extension
Banana Conference Center	2014	123-555-0115	16
Basketball Stadium	2121		
Birch Company	902301	111-555-0113	
Black Curve Airport (US)	2202		
Cave Wholesales	1103	123-555-0161	
Cheetah Concert Hall	2104	(0123) 4567 8901	
Consolidated Messenger Marketing	8003	123-555-0121	10
Contoso Europe	9100	01234 567890	
Contoso Retail Boston	3007	123-555-0115	
Contoso Retail Chicago	3010	123-555-0118	
Contoso Retail Dallas	3009	123-555-0117	
Contoso Retail Denver	3012	123-555-0120	
Contoso Retail Detroit	3011	123-555-0119	
Contoso Retail Los Angeles	3003	123-555-0116	18
Contoso Retail Miami	3006	123-555-0114	
Contoso Retail New York	3008	123-555-0116	
Contoso Retail Portland	3004	123-555-0116	18
Contoso Retail San Diego	3001		
Contoso Retail Seattle	3002	412-555-0119	333
Contoso Retail Washington DC	3005	123-555-0113	

2. Click on **Transactions** in the action pane to check the existing transactions:

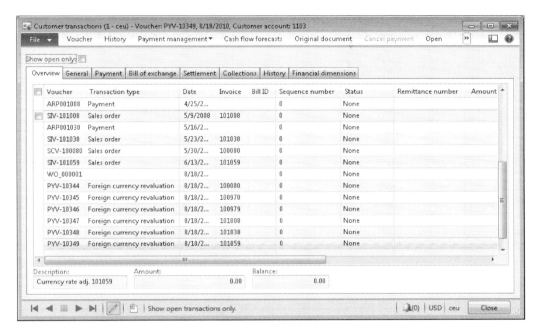

3. Open the AOT, create a new job named `CustAccountRename`, and enter the following code. Use the previously selected account:

```
static void CustAccountRename(Args _args)
{
    CustTable custTable;

    select firstOnly custTable
        where custTable.AccountNum == '1103';

    if (custTable.RecId)
    {
        custTable.AccountNum = '1103_';
        custTable.renamePrimaryKey();
    }
}
```

4. Run the job and check if the renaming was successful, by navigating to **Accounts receivable | Common | Customers | All customers** again, and finding the new account. The new account should have retained all its transactions and other related records, as shown in the following screenshot:

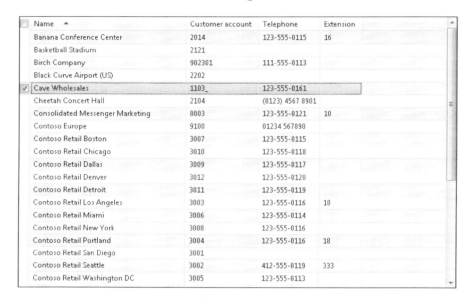

5. Click on **Transactions** in the action pane in order to see if existing transactions are still in place:

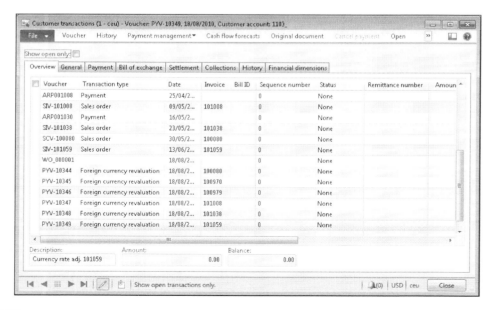

How it works...

In this recipe, first we will select the desired customer account that is, **1103**. Here we can easily modify the select statement to include more accounts for renaming, but for demonstration purposes, let's keep it simple. Note that only fields belonging to a table's primary key can be renamed in this way.

Then we call the table's `renamePrimaryKey()` method, which does the actual renaming. The method finds all the related records for the selected customer account and updates them with the new account. The operation might take a while depending on the volume of data, as the system has to update multiple records located in multiple tables.

Merging two records

For various reasons, data in the system such as customers, ledger accounts, configuration settings, and similar data may become obsolete. This could be because of changes in the business or it could simply be a user input error. For example, two salespeople could create two records for the same customer, start entering sales orders and post invoices. One of the ways to solve that is to merge both records into a single one.

In this recipe, we will explore how to merge one record into another one, including all related transactions. For this demonstration, we will merge two ledger reason codes into a single one.

How to do it...

Carry out the following steps in order to complete this recipe:

1. Open **General ledger | Setup | Ledger reasons** to find two reason code records to be merged. In this example we will use **COUNTER** and **AUCTION**:

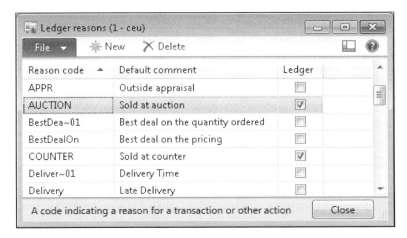

2. Open the AOT, create a new job named `LedgerReasonMerge` with the following code:

```
static void LedgerReasonMerge(Args _args)
{
    ReasonTable reasonTableDelete;
    ReasonTable reasonTable;

    ttsBegin;

    select firstOnly forUpdate reasonTableDelete
        where reasonTableDelete.Reason == 'COUNTER';

    select firstOnly forUpdate reasonTable
        where reasonTable.Reason == 'AUCTION';

    reasonTableDelete.merge(reasonTable);
    reasonTable.doUpdate();
    reasonTableDelete.doDelete();

    ttsCommit;
}
```

3. Run the job to merge the records.

4. Open the **Ledger reasons** form again and notice that one of the reasons were deleted and all related transactions have also been updated to reflect the change:

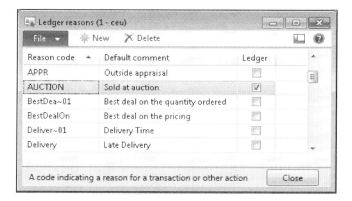

How it works...

First, we retrieve both records from the database and prepare them for updating.

The key method in this recipe is the `merge()` method. It will ensure that all data from one record will be copied into the second one and all related transactions will be updated to reflect the change.

Finally, we save changes on the destination record and delete the first one.

All code has to be within the `ttsBegin/ttsCommit` pair as we perform several database update operations in one go.

Such a technique could be used to merge two, or even more, records of any type.

Adding a document handling note

It is good practice to add some kind of note to the record when doing data renaming, merging, or any other data manipulation task, whether it's manual or automatic. Dynamics AX allows adding a note or a file to any record by using the so-called **Document handling** feature.

By default, it is enabled for all tables, but can be restricted to fewer tables by changing its configuration parameters.

Document handling can be accessed from the form action pane by clicking on the **Attachments** button, choosing **Document handling** from the **File | Command** menu or selecting the **Document handling** icon from the status bar. Document handling allows adding text notes or files to any currently selected record.

Dynamics AX also allows adding document handling notes from the code too, which helps developers or consultants to add additional information when doing various data migration or conversion tasks.

In this recipe, we will add a note to a vendor account.

How to do it...

Carry out the following steps in order to complete this recipe:

1. Open **Accounts payable | Common | Vendors | All vendors**, and locate the vendor account that has to be updated:

	Vendor account	Name ▲	Vendor hold	Phone	Extension	
	3008	A. Datum Corporation	No	987-555-0119		
	3106	A. Datum Electronics	No			
✓	3001	Adventure Services	No			
	3107	Alpine Electronics	No			
	3005	Alpine Ski House	No	987-555-0126		
	8500	April Stewart	No	999-555-5555	555	
	4203	Beetle Electronics	No			
	3113	Blue Yonder Repair	No			

2. Open the AOT, create a new job named `VendAccountDocu`, and enter the following code. Use the previously selected vendor account:

```
static void VendAccountDocu(Args _args)
{
    DocuRef     docuRef;
    VendTable vendTable;

    vendTable = VendTable::find('3001');

    docuRef.RefCompanyId = vendTable.dataAreaId;
    docuRef.RefTableId   = vendTable.TableId;
    docuRef.RefRecId     = vendTable.RecId;
    docuRef.TypeId       = 'Note';
    docuRef.Name         = 'Imported';
    docuRef.Notes        = 'This vendor was imported.';
    docuRef.insert();
}
```

3. Run the job to create the note.

4. Click on the **Attachments** button in the form's action pane or select **Document handling** from the **File | Command** menu to view the note added by our code:

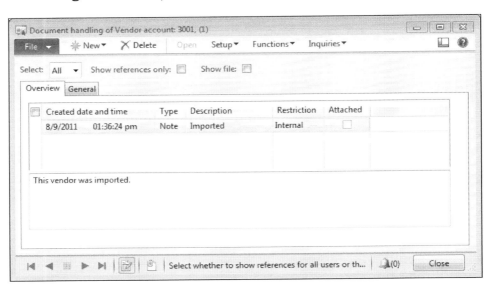

How it works...

All the document handling notes are stored in the **DocuRef** table, where the three fields **RefCompanyId**, **RefTableId**, and **RefRecId** are used to identify the parent record. In our recipe, we will set those fields to the vendor company ID, vendor table ID, and vendor account record ID, respectively.

Next, we will set note type, name, and description, and insert the document handling record. In this way, we will add a note to the record. The code in this recipe could also be added to a separate method for further reuse.

Using a normal table as a temporary table

Standard Dynamics AX contains numerous temporary tables, which are used by the application and could be used in custom modifications too. Although new temporary tables can also be easily created using the AOT, sometimes it is not effective. One of the cases could be when the temporary table is very similar or exactly the same as an existing one. The goal of this recipe is to demonstrate an approach for using standard non-temporary tables to hold temporary data.

As an example, we will use the vendor table to insert and display a couple of temporary records without affecting the actual data.

How to do it...

Carry out the following steps in order to complete this recipe:

1. In the AOT, create a new class named `VendTableTmp` with the following code:

```
class VendTableTmp
{
}

server static void main(Args _args)
{
    VendTable    vendTable;

    vendTable.setTmp();

    vendTable.AccountNum = '1000';
    vendTable.Blocked    = CustVendorBlocked::No;
    vendTable.Party      = 1;
    vendTable.doInsert();
```

```
vendTable.clear();
vendTable.AccountNum = '1002';
vendTable.Blocked     = CustVendorBlocked::All;
vendTable.Party       = 2;
vendTable.doInsert();

while select vendTable
{
    info(strFmt(
        "%1 - %2",
        vendTable.AccountNum,
        vendTable.Blocked));
}
}
```

2. Run the class and check the results:

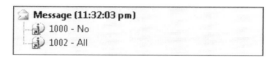

How it works...

The key method in this recipe is in the `setTmp()` method. It is available on all tables, and it declares the current table instance to behave as a temporary table in the current scope. So in this recipe, we will first call the `setTmp()` method on the `vendTable` table to make it temporary in the scope of this method. That means any data manipulations will be lost once the execution of this method is over and actual table content will not be affected.

Next, we will insert a couple of test records. Here, we use the `doInsert()` method to bypass any additional logic, which normally resides in the table's `insert()` method.

The last thing to do is to check for newly created records by listing the `vendTable` table. We can see that although the table contains many actual records, only the ones which we inserted were displayed in the Infolog. Additionally, the two we inserted do not appear in the actual table records.

Copying a record

One of the tasks often used when manipulating data is record copying. For various reasons, an existing record needs to be modified and saved as a new one. The most obvious example could be when a user requires a function that allows him or her to quickly duplicate records on any of the existing forms.

There are several ways of copying one record into another in X++. In this recipe, we will explain the usage of the table's `data()` method, the global `buf2buf()` function, and their differences. As an example, we will copy one of the existing ledger account records into a new one.

How to do it...

Carry out the following steps in order to complete this recipe:

1. Open **General ledger | Common | Main accounts**, and find the account to be copied. In this example, we will use **211100**:

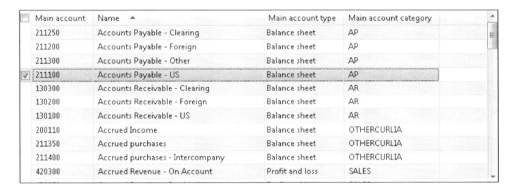

Main account	Name	Main account type	Main account category
211250	Accounts Payable - Clearing	Balance sheet	AP
211200	Accounts Payable - Foreign	Balance sheet	AP
211300	Accounts Payable - Other	Balance sheet	AP
211100	Accounts Payable - US	Balance sheet	AP
130300	Accounts Receivable - Clearing	Balance sheet	AR
130200	Accounts Receivable - Foreign	Balance sheet	AR
130100	Accounts Receivable - US	Balance sheet	AR
200110	Accrued Income	Balance sheet	OTHERCURLIA
211350	Accrued purchases	Balance sheet	OTHERCURLIA
211400	Accrued purchases - Intercompany	Balance sheet	OTHERCURLIA
420300	Accrued Revenue - On Account	Profit and loss	SALES

2. Open the AOT, create a new job named `MainAccountCopy` with the following code, and run it:

```
static void MainAccountCopy(Args _args)
{
    MainAccount mainAccount1;
    MainAccount mainAccount2;

    mainAccount1 = MainAccount::findByMainAccountId('211100');

    ttsBegin;

    mainAccount2.data(mainAccount1);

    mainAccount2.MainAccountId = '211101';

    if (!mainAccount2.validateWrite())
    {
        throw Exception::Error;
    }

    mainAccount2.insert();

    ttsCommit;
}
```

3. Open **General ledger | Common | Main accounts** again, and notice that there are two identical records now:

Main account	Name ▲	Main account type	Main account category	
211250	Accounts Payable - Clearing	Balance sheet	AP	
211200	Accounts Payable - Foreign	Balance sheet	AP	
211300	Accounts Payable - Other	Balance sheet	AP	
✓ 211100	Accounts Payable - US	Balance sheet	AP	
✓ 211101	Accounts Payable - US	Balance sheet	AP	
130300	Accounts Receivable - Clearing	Balance sheet	AR	
130200	Accounts Receivable - Foreign	Balance sheet	AR	
130100	Accounts Receivable - US	Balance sheet	AR	
200110	Accrued Income	Balance sheet	OTHERCURLIA	
211350	Accrued purchases	Balance sheet	OTHERCURLIA	
211400	Accrued purchases - Intercompany	Balance sheet	OTHERCURLIA	

How it works...

In this recipe, we have two variables—mainAccount1 for original record and mainAccount2 for the new one. First, we will need to find the original record by calling findByMainAccountId() on the **MainAccount** table.

Next, we will copy it to the new one. Here, we will use the data() table member method, which copies all data fields from one variable to another.

After that, we will set a new ledger account number, which is a part of a unique table index and must be different.

Finally, we call the insert() method on the table, if validateWrite() is successful. In this way, we have created a new ledger account record, which is exactly the same as the existing one apart from the account number.

There's more...

As we saw before, the data() method copies all table fields, including system fields such as record ID, company account, created user, and so on. Most of the time, it is OK because when the new record is saved, the system fields are overwritten with the new values. However, this function may not work for copying records across companies. In this case, we can use another function called buf2Buf(). It is very similar to the table's data() method with one major difference. The buf2Buf() function copies all data fields excluding the system ones. The code in the function is as follows:

```
static void buf2Buf(Common _from, Common _to)
{
    DictTable    dictTable = new DictTable(_from.TableId);
    FieldId      fieldId   = dictTable.fieldNext(0);
```

```
    while (fieldId && ! isSysId(fieldId))
    {
        _to.(fieldId)    = _from.(fieldId);
        fieldId          = dictTable.fieldNext(fieldId);
    }
}
```

We can clearly see that during the copying process, all the table fields are traversed, but the system fields are excluded. We can also see that this function is slower than the internal `data()` method, as it checks and copies each field individually.

In order to use the `buf2Buf()` function, the code of the `MainAccountCopy` job could be amended as follows:

```
static void MainAccountCopy(Args _args)
{
    MainAccount mainAccount1;
    MainAccount mainAccount2;

    mainAccount1 = MainAccount::findByMainAccountId('211100');

    ttsBegin;

    buf2Buf(mainAccount1, mainAccount2);

    mainAccount2.MainAccountId = '211101';

    if (!mainAccount2.validateWrite())
    {
        throw Exception::Error;
    }

    mainAccount2.insert();

    ttsCommit;
}
```

Building a query object

Query objects are used to visually build SQL statements, which can be used by Dynamics AX reports, views, forms, and other objects. Normally, queries are stored in the AOT, but they can also be dynamically created from code. This is normally done when visual tools cannot handle complex and dynamic queries.

In this recipe, we will create a query dynamically from the code to retrieve project records from the project management module. We will select only the projects of type fixed price, starting with **2** in its number and containing at least one hour transaction.

How to do it...

Carry out the following steps in order to complete this recipe:

1. Open the AOT, create a new job named `ProjTableQuery`, and enter the following code:

```
static void ProjTableQuery(Args _args)
{
    Query                   query;
    QueryBuildDataSource    qbds1;
    QueryBuildDataSource    qbds2;
    QueryBuildRange         qbr1;
    QueryBuildRange         qbr2;
    QueryRun                queryRun;
    ProjTable               projTable;

    query = new Query();

    qbds1 = query.addDataSource(tableNum(ProjTable));
    qbds1.addSortField(
        fieldNum(ProjTable, Name),
        SortOrder::Ascending);

    qbr1 = qbds1.addRange(fieldNum(ProjTable,Type));
    qbr1.value(queryValue(ProjType::FixedPrice));

    qbr2 = qbds1.addRange(fieldNum(ProjTable,ProjId));
    qbr2.value(queryValue('2') + '*');

    qbds2 = qbds1.addDataSource(tableNum(ProjEmplTrans));
    qbds2.relations(true);
    qbds2.joinMode(JoinMode::ExistsJoin);

    queryRun = new QueryRun(query);

    while (queryRun.next())
    {
        projTable = queryRun.get(tableNum(ProjTable));
        info(strFmt(
            "%1, %2, %3",
            projTable.ProjId,
            projTable.Name,
            projTable.Type));
    }
}
```

2. Run the job and the following screen should appear:

How it works...

First, we create a new `query` object. Next, we add a new **ProjTable** data source to the `query` object by calling its `addDataSource()` member method. The method returns a reference to the `QueryBuildDataSource` object—`qbds1`. Here, we call the `addSortField()` method to enable sorting by project name.

The following two blocks of code create two ranges. The first is to show only projects of type fixed price and the second one is to list only records, where the project number starts with **2**. Those two filters are automatically added together using the SQL `and` operator. `QueryBuildRange` objects are created by calling the `addRange()` member method of the `QueryBuildDataSource` object with the field ID number as argument. The range value is set by calling `value()` on the `QueryBuildRange` object itself. It is a good practice to use the `queryValue()` function to process values before applying them as a range. More functions such as `queryNotValue()`, `queryRange()`, and so on can be found in the `Global` application class. Note that these functions are actually shortcuts to the `SysQuery` application class, which in turn have even more interesting helper methods that might be handy for every developer.

Adding another data source to an existing one connects both data sources using the SQL `join` operator. In this example, we are displaying projects that have at least one posted hour line. We start by adding the **ProjEmplTrans** table as another data source.

Next, we need to add relations between the tables. If relations are not defined on tables, we will have to use the `addLink()` method with relation field ID numbers. In this example, relations on the tables are already defined so it is enough only to enable them by calling the `relations()` method with `true` as an argument.

Calling `joinMode()` with `JoinMode::ExistsJoin` as a parameter ensures that a record from a parent data source will be displayed only if the relation exists in the attached data source.

The last thing to do is to create and run the `queryRun` object and show the selected data on the screen.

There's more...

It is worth mentioning a couple of specific cases when working with query objects from code. One of them is how to use the `or` operator and the other one is how to address array fields.

Using the OR operator

As you have already noted, regardless of how many ranges are added, all of them will be added together using the SQL `and` operator. In most cases it is fine, but sometimes complex user requirements demand ranges to be added using SQL `or`. There might be a number of workarounds, such as using temporary tables or similar tools, but we can use the Dynamics AX feature that allows passing a part of raw SQL string as a range.

In this case, the range has to be formatted in a similar manner as a fully qualified SQL `where` clause, including field names, operators, and values. The expressions have to be formatted properly before using them in a query. Here are some of the rules:

▶ The expression must be enclosed within single quotes.

▶ Inside, the whole expression has to be enclosed in parenthesis.

▶ Each subexpression must be enclosed in parentheses too.

▶ String values have to be enclosed within double quotes.

▶ For enumerations use their numeric values.

▶ For value formatting use various Dynamics AX functions, such as `queryValue()`, `Date2StrXpp()`, or methods from the `SysQuery` class.

Let us replace the code from the previous example:

```
qbr1.value(queryValue(ProjType::FixedPrice));
```

with the new code:

```
qbr1.value(strFmt(
    '((%1 = %2) || (%3 = "%4"))',
    fieldStr(ProjTable,Type),
    ProjType::FixedPrice+0,
    fieldStr(ProjTable,ProjGroupId),
    queryValue('TM1')));
```

Notice that by adding zero to the enumeration in the previous code, we can force the `strFmt()` function to use the numeric value of the enumeration.

Now, the result will also include all the projects belonging to the group **TM1** regardless of their type:

Using arrays fields

Some table fields in Dynamics AX are based on extended data types, which contains more than one array element. An example in a standard application could project sorting based on a **ProjSortingId** extended data type. Although such fields are very much the same as normal fields, in queries they should be addressed in a slightly different manner. In order to demonstrate the usage, let us modify the example by filtering the query to list only those projects containing the value **South** in the field labelled **Sort field 2**, which is the second value in the array.

First, let us declare a new `QueryBuildRange` object in the variable declaration section:

```
QueryBuildRange qbr3;
```

Next, we add the following code, right after the `qbr2.value(...)` code:

```
qbr3 = qbds1.addRange(
    fieldId2Ext(fieldnum(ProjTable,SortingId),2));
qbr3.value(queryValue('South'));
```

Notice that we use the global `fieldid2ext()` function, which converts the field ID and the array number into a valid number to be used by the `addRange()` method. This function can also be used anywhere, where addressing the dimension fields is required.

Now, we can run this job, as the project list based on previous criteria will be reduced even more to match projects having only a specific **Sort field 2**:

See also

See *Chapter 3, Working with Data in Forms*:

▸   *Creating a custom filter*

See *Chapter 4, Building Lookups*:

▸   *Using a form for building a lookup*

Using a macro in an SQL statement

In a standard Dynamics AX application, there are macros such as `InventDimJoin` and `InventDimSelect`, which are reused numerous times across the application. These macros are actually full or partial X++ SQL queries, which can be called with various arguments. Such approach saves developing time by allowing you to reuse pieces of X++ SQL queries.

In this recipe, we will create a small macro, which holds a single `where` clause to display only active vendor records. Then we will create a job, which uses the created macro for displaying a vendor list.

How to do it...

Carry out the following steps in order to complete this recipe:

1. Open the AOT, and create a new macro named `VendTableNotBlocked` with the following code:

    ```
    (%1.Blocked == CustVendorBlocked::No)
    ```

2. In the AOT, create a new job called `VendTableMacro` with the following code:

    ```
    static void VendTableMacro(Args _args)
    {
        VendTable    vendTable;

        while select vendTable
            where #VendTableNotBlocked(vendTable)
        {
            info(strFmt(
                "%1 - %2",
                vendTable.AccountNum,
                vendTable.name()));
        }
    }
    ```

3. Run the job and check the results, as displayed in the following screenshot:

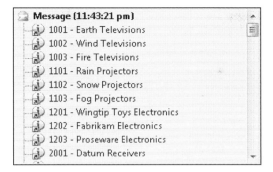

How it works...

First, we define a macro that holds the `where` clause. Normally, the purpose of defining SQL in a macro is to reuse it a number of times in various places. We use `%1` as an argument. More arguments could be added here.

Next, we create a job with the `select` statement. Here, we use the previously created macro in a `where` clause and pass `vendTable` as an argument.

The query works like any other query, but the advantage is that the code in the macro can be reused elsewhere.

Note that although using a macro in a SQL statement can reduce the amount of code, too much code in it might decrease the SQL statement's readability for other developers. So keep it balanced.

Executing a direct SQL statement

Dynamics AX allows developers to build X++ SQL statements that are flexible enough to fit into any custom business process. However, in some cases, the usage of X++ SQL is either not effective or not possible at all.

One of the cases is when we run data upgrade tasks during an application version upgrade. The standard application contains a set of data upgrade tasks to be completed during the version upgrade. If the application is highly customized, then most likely the standard tasks have to be modified to reflect data dictionary customizations, or even a new set of tasks have to be created to make sure data is handled correctly during the upgrade.

Normally at this stage, SQL statements are so complex that they can only be created using database-specific SQL and executed directly in the database. Additionally, running direct SQL statements dramatically increases data upgrade performance because most of the code is executed on the database server where all data resides. This is very important while working with large volumes of data.

Another case when we would need to use direct SQL statements is when we want to connect to an external database using the ODBC connection. In this case, X++ SQL is not supported at all.

This recipe will demonstrate how to execute SQL statements directly. We will connect to the current Dynamics AX database directly using an additional connection and will retrieve the list of vendor accounts.

How to do it...

Carry out the following steps in order to complete this recipe:

1. In the AOT, create a new class named `VendTableSql` with the following code:

```
class VendTableSql
{
}

server static void main(Args _args)
{
    UserConnection                    userConnection;
    Statement                         statement;
    str                               sqlStatement;
    SqlSystem                         sqlSystem;
    SqlStatementExecutePermission     sqlPermission;
    ResultSet                         resultSet;
    DictTable                         tblVendTable;
    DictTable                         tblDirPartyTable;
    DictField                         fldParty;
    DictField                         fldAccountNum;
    DictField                         fldDataAreaId;
    DictField                         fldBlocked;
    DictField                         fldRecId;
    DictField                         fldName;

    tblVendTable    = new DictTable(tableNum(VendTable));
    tblDirPartyTable = new DictTable(tableNum(DirPartyTable));

    fldParty = new DictField(
        tableNum(VendTable),
```

```
        fieldNum(VendTable,Party));

    fldAccountNum = new DictField(
        tableNum(VendTable),
        fieldNum(VendTable,AccountNum));

    fldDataAreaId = new DictField(
        tableNum(VendTable),
        fieldNum(VendTable,DataAreaId));

    fldBlocked = new DictField(
        tableNum(VendTable),
        fieldNum(VendTable,Blocked));

    fldRecId = new DictField(
        tableNum(DirPartyTable),
        fieldNum(DirPartyTable,RecId));

    fldName = new DictField(
        tableNum(DirPartyTable),
        fieldNum(DirPartyTable,Name));

    sqlSystem = new SqlSystem();

    sqlStatement = 'SELECT %3, %4 FROM %1 ' +
        'JOIN %2 ON %1.%5 = %2.%6 ' +
        'WHERE %7 = %9 AND %8 = %10';

    sqlStatement = strFmt(
        sqlStatement,
        tblVendTable.name(DbBackend::Sql),
        tblDirPartyTable.name(DbBackend::Sql),
        fldAccountNum.name(DbBackend::Sql),
        fldName.name(DbBackend::Sql),
        fldParty.name(DbBackend::Sql),
        fldRecId.name(DbBackend::Sql),
        fldDataAreaId.name(DbBackend::Sql),
        fldBlocked.name(DbBackend::Sql),
        sqlSystem.sqlLiteral(curext(), true),
        sqlSystem.sqlLiteral(CustVendorBlocked::No, true));

    userConnection = new UserConnection();
    statement      = userConnection.createStatement();

    sqlPermission = new SqlStatementExecutePermission(
        sqlStatement);

    sqlPermission.assert();
```

```
    resultSet        = statement.executeQuery(sqlStatement);

    CodeAccessPermission::revertAssert();

    while (resultSet.next())
    {
        info(strFmt(
            "%1 - %2",
            resultSet.getString(1),
            resultSet.getString(2)));
    }
}
```

2. Run the class to obtain the list of vendors retrieved directly from the database:

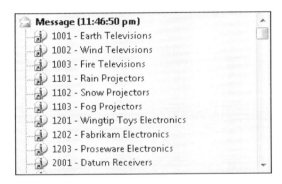

How it works...

We start the code by creating DictTable and DictField objects for handling the vendor table and its fields used later in the query. **DirPartyTable** table is used to get additional vendor information.

A new SqlSystem object also has to be created. It will be used to convert Dynamics AX types to SQL types.

Next, we set up an SQL statement with a number of placeholders for table or field names and field values to be inserted later.

The main query creation happens next when the query placeholders are replaced with the right values. Here we use the previously created DictTable and DictField type objects by calling their name() methods with the DbBackend::Sql enumeration as an argument. This ensures that we pass the name exactly how it is used in the database—some of the SQL field names are not necessary the same as field names within the application.

We also use the sqlLiteral() method of the previously created sqlSystem object to properly format SQL values to make sure they do not have any unsafe characters.

Once the SQL statement is ready, we initialize a direct connection to the database and run the statement. The results are returned into the `resultSet` object, and we get them by using the `while` statement and calling the `next()` method until the end of the `resultSet` object.

Note that we create an `sqlPermission` object of type `SqlStatementExecutePermission` here and call its `assert()` method before executing the statement. This is required in order to comply with Dynamics AX trustworthy computing requirements.

Another thing to mention is that when building direct SQL queries, special attention has to be paid to license, configuration, and security keys. Some tables or fields might be disabled in the application and may contain no data in the database.

The code in this recipe can be also used to connect to the external ODBC databases. We only need to replace the `UserConnection` class with the `OdbcConnection` class and use text names instead of the `DictTable` and `DictField` objects.

There's more...

The standard Dynamics AX application provides an alternate way of building direct SQL statements by using a set of `SQLBuilder` classes. By using those classes, we can create SQL statements as objects as opposed to text. Next, we will demonstrate how to use the `SQLBuilder` classes. We will create the same SQL statement as before.

First in AOT, we create another class named `VendTableSqlBuilder` with the following code:

```
class VendTableSqlBuilder
{
}

server static void main(Args _args)
{
    UserConnection                  userConnection;
    Statement                       statement;
    str                             sqlStatement;
    SqlStatementExecutePermission   sqlPermission;
    ResultSet                       resultSet;
    SQLBuilderSelectExpression      selectExpr;
    SQLBuilderTableEntry            vendTable;
    SQLBuilderTableEntry            dirPartyTable;
    SQLBuilderFieldEntry            accountNum;
    SQLBuilderFieldEntry            dataAreaId;
    SQLBuilderFieldEntry            blocked;
    SQLBuilderFieldEntry            name;
```

```
selectExpr = SQLBuilderSelectExpression::construct();
selectExpr.parmUseJoin(true);

vendTable = selectExpr.addTableId(
    tablenum(VendTable));

dirPartyTable = vendTable.addJoinTableId(
    tablenum(DirPartyTable));

accountNum = vendTable.addFieldId(
    fieldnum(VendTable,AccountNum));

name = dirPartyTable.addFieldId(
    fieldnum(DirPartyTable,Name));

dataAreaId = vendTable.addFieldId(
    fieldnum(VendTable,DataAreaId));

blocked = vendTable.addFieldId(
    fieldnum(VendTable,Blocked));

vendTable.addRange(dataAreaId, curext());
vendTable.addRange(blocked, CustVendorBlocked::No);

selectExpr.addSelectFieldEntry(
    SQLBuilderSelectFieldEntry::newExpression(
        accountNum,
        'AccountNum'));

selectExpr.addSelectFieldEntry(
    SQLBuilderSelectFieldEntry::newExpression(
        name,
        'Name'));

sqlStatement    = selectExpr.getExpression(null);

userConnection = new UserConnection();
statement       = userConnection.createStatement();

sqlPermission = new SqlStatementExecutePermission(
    sqlStatement);

sqlPermission.assert();
```

```
    resultSet = statement.executeQuery(sqlStatement);

    CodeAccessPermission::revertAssert();

    while (resultSet.next())
    {
        info(strfmt(
            "%1 - %2",
            resultSet.getString(1),
            resultSet.getString(2)));
    }
}
```

In this method, we first create a new `selectExpr` object, which is based on the `SQLBuilderSelectExpression` class. It represents the object of the SQL statement.

Next, we add the **VendTable** table to it by calling its member method `addTableId()`. The method returns a reference to the `vendTable` object of type `SQLBuilderTableEntry`, which corresponds to a table node in an SQL query. We also add `DirPartyTable` as a joined table.

Then, we create a number of field objects of type `SQLBuilderFieldEntry` to be used later and two ranges to show only this company account and only active vendor accounts.

We use `addSelectFieldEntry()` to add two fields to be selected. Here we use the previously created field objects.

The SQL statement is generated once the `getExpression()` method is called, and the rest of the code is the same as in the previous example.

Running the class would give us results, which are exactly similar to the ones we got before.

Enhancing the data consistency check

It is highly recommended to run the standard Dynamics AX data consistency check from time to time, that is located in **System administration | Periodic | Database | Consistency check**, to check the system's data integrity. This function finds orphan data, validates parameters, and does many other things, but it does not do everything. The good thing is that it can easily be extended to match different scenarios.

In this recipe, we will see how we can enhance the standard Dynamics AX consistency check to include more tables in its data integrity validation.

Getting ready

Before we start, we need to create an invalid setup to make sure we can simulate data inconsistency. Open **Fixed assets | Setup | Value models** and create a new model, for instance, **TEST**:

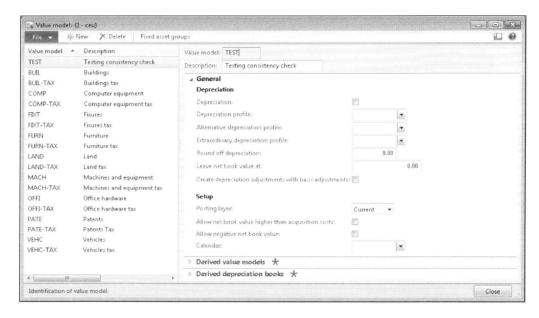

Open **Fixed assets | Setup | Fixed asset posting profiles** and under the **Ledger accounts** group, create a new record with the newly created value model for any of the posting types:

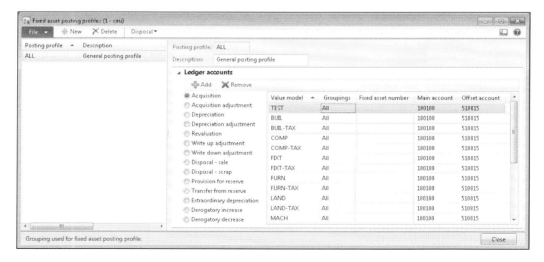

Go back to the **Value models** form, and delete the previously created value model.

Now, we have a non-existing value model in the fixed asset posting settings.

How to do it...

Carry out the following steps in order to complete this recipe:

1. In the AOT, create a new class AssetConsistencyCheck with the following code:

```
class AssetConsistencyCheck extends SysConsistencyCheck
{
}

client server static ClassDescription description()
{
    return "Fixed assets";
}

client server static HelpTxt helpText()
{
    return "Consistency check of the fixed asset module";
}

public Integer executionOrder()
{
    return 1;
}

public void run()
{
    this.kernelCheckTable(tableNum(AssetLedgerAccounts));
}
```

2. Open **System administration | Periodic | Database | Consistency check**, select the newly created **Fixed assets** option in the **Module** drop-down, and click **OK** to run the check:

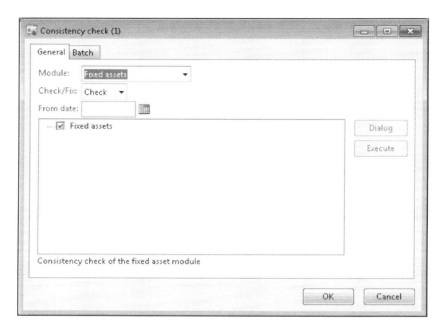

3. Now the message displayed in the Infolog should complain about the missing value model in the fixed asset posing settings:

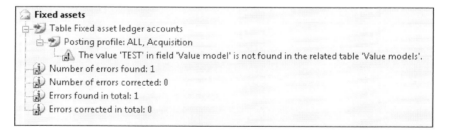

How it works...

The consistency check in Dynamics AX validates only the predefined list of tables for each module. The system contains a number of classes derived from `SysConsistencyCheck`. For example, the `CustConsistencyCheck` class is responsible for validating the **Accounts receivable** module, `LedgerConsistencyCheck`—for **General ledger,** and so on.

In this recipe, we created a new class named `AssetConsistencyCheck`, extending the `SysConsistencyCheck` class for the fixed asset module. The following methods were created:

- ▶ `description()` provides a name on the consistency check form.
- ▶ `helpText()` displays some explanation about the check.
- ▶ `executionOrder()` determines where in the list the check is located.
- ▶ `run()` holds the code to perform actual checking. Here we use the `kernelCheckTable()` member method, which validates the given table.

There's more...

The classes we just mentioned can only be executed from the main **Consistency check** form. Individual checks could also be invoked as stand-alone functions. We just need to create an additional method to allow running of the class:

```
static void main(Args args)
{
    SysConsistencyCheckJob consistencyCheckJob;
    AssetConsistencyCheck   assetConsistencyCheck;

    consistencyCheckJob = new SysConsistencyCheckJob(
        classidget(assetConsistencyCheck));

    if (!consistencyCheckJob.prompt())
    {
        return;
    }

    consistencyCheckJob.run();
}
```

Exporting data to an XML file

Briefly, eXtensible Markup Language (XML) defines a set of rules for encoding documents electronically. It allows the creation of all kinds of structured documents to exchange between systems. In Dynamics AX, XML files are widely used across the application. For example, user profiles can be exported as XML files. Business data, such as financial statements can also be exported as eXtensible Business Reporting Language (XBRL) files, which are based on XML.

Probably, the main thing that is associated with XML in Dynamics AX is the Application Integration Framework. It is an infrastructure that allows exposing business logic or exchanging data with other external systems. The communication is done by using XML formatted documents. By using the existing XML framework application classes prefixed with Axd, you can export or import data from or to the system in an XML format to be used for communicating with external systems. It is also possible to create new Axd classes using the **AIF Document Service Wizard** from the **Tools** menu to support the export and import of newly created tables.

Dynamics AX also contains a set of application classes prefixed with Xml, such as XmlDocument and XmlNode. Basically, those classes are wrappers around the System.XML namespace in the .NET framework.

In this recipe, we will create a new simple XML document by using the latter classes, in order to show the basics of XML. We will create the file with the data from the chart of the accounts table and will save it as an XML file.

How to do it...

Carry out the following steps in order to complete this recipe:

1. Open the AOT and create a new class named CreateXmlFile with the following code:

```
class CreateXmlFile
{
}
public static void main(Args _args)
{
    XmlDocument doc;
    XmlElement  nodeXml;
    XmlElement  nodeTable;
    XmlElement  nodeAccount;
    XmlElement  nodeName;
    MainAccount mainAccount;
    #define.filename(@'C:\Temp\accounts.xml')

    doc     = XmlDocument::newBlank();

    nodeXml = doc.createElement('xml');

    doc.appendChild(nodeXml);

    while select RecId, MainAccountId, Name from mainAccount
    {
        nodeTable = doc.createElement(tableStr(MainAccount));

        nodeTable.setAttribute(
```

```
                fieldStr(MainAccount, RecId),
                int642str(mainAccount.RecId));

        nodeXml.appendChild(nodeTable);

        nodeAccount = doc.createElement(
            fieldStr(MainAccount, MainAccountId));

        nodeAccount.appendChild(
            doc.createTextNode(mainAccount.MainAccountId));

        nodeTable.appendChild(nodeAccount);

        nodeName = doc.createElement(
            fieldStr(MainAccount, Name));

        nodeName.appendChild(
            doc.createTextNode(mainAccount.Name));

        nodeTable.appendChild(nodeName);
    }

    doc.save(#filename);

    info(strFmt("File %1 created.", #filename));

}
```

2. Run the class. The XML file `accounts.xml` should be created in the specified folder. Open it using any XML editor or viewer, such as Microsoft Internet Explorer, and review the created XML structure:

```
<?xml version="1.0" encoding="utf-8" ?>
- <xml>
  - <MainAccount RecId="5637145792">
      <MainAccountId>110100</MainAccountId>
      <Name>Cash and Cash Equivalents</Name>
    </MainAccount>
  - <MainAccount RecId="5637145793">
      <MainAccountId>110110</MainAccountId>
      <Name>110110</Name>
    </MainAccount>
  - <MainAccount RecId="5637145794">
      <MainAccountId>119000</MainAccountId>
      <Name>TOTAL CASH & CASH EQUIVALENTS</Name>
    </MainAccount>
  - <MainAccount RecId="5637145795">
      <MainAccountId>120100</MainAccountId>
      <Name>Bonds and marketable securities</Name>
    </MainAccount>
  - <MainAccount RecId="5637145796">
      <MainAccountId>120300</MainAccountId>
      <Name>Bill of Exchange (BOE)</Name>
    </MainAccount>
  - <MainAccount RecId="5637145797">
      <MainAccountId>120400</MainAccountId>
      <Name>Misc. Securities</Name>
    </MainAccount>
  - <MainAccount RecId="5637145798">
      <MainAccountId>129900</MainAccountId>
```

How it works...

We start the recipe by creating a new XmlDocument using its newBlank() method, which represents an XML structure. Then we create its root node named xml using the createElement() method, and add the node to the document by calling the document's appendChild() method.

Next, we go through the MainAccount table and do the following for each record:

1. Create a new XmlElement node, which is named exactly as the table name, and add this node to the root node.

2. Create a node representing the account number field and its child node representing its value. The account number node is created using createElement(), and its value is created using createTextNode(). The createTextNode() method basically adds a value as text with no XML tags.

3. Add the account number node to the table node.

4. Create a node representing the account name field and its child node representing its value.

5. Add the account name node to the table node.

Finally, we save the created XML document as a file.

In this way, we can create documents having virtually any structure.

Importing data from an XML file

In Dynamics AX, XML file importing is done in a very similar way as exporting. In this recipe, we will continue using the System.XML wrapper application classes. We will create a new class which reads XML files and displays the content onscreen. As a source file, we will use the previously created accounts.xml file.

How to do it...

Carry out the following steps in order to complete this recipe:

1. Open the AOT, and create a new class named ReadXmlFile with the following code. Use the document created in the previous recipe:

```
class ReadXmlFile
{
}
public static void main(Args _args)
{
```

```
XmlDocument doc;
XmlNodeList data;
XmlElement   nodeTable;
XmlElement   nodeAccount;
XmlElement   nodeName;
#define.filename(@'C:\Temp\accounts.xml')

doc  = XmlDocument::newFile(#filename);

data = doc.selectNodes('//'+tableStr(MainAccount));

nodeTable = data.nextNode();

while (nodeTable)
{
    nodeAccount = nodeTable.selectSingleNode(
        fieldStr(MainAccount, MainAccountId));

    nodeName = nodeTable.selectSingleNode(
        fieldStr(MainAccount, Name));

    info(strFmt(
        "%1 - %2",
        nodeAccount.text(),
        nodeName.text()));

    nodeTable = data.nextNode();
}
}
```

2. Run the class. The Infolog should display the contents of the accounts.xml file on the screen:

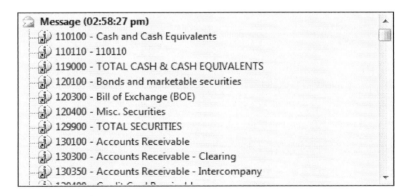

How it works...

In this recipe, we first create a new `XmlDocument`. We create it from the file and hence we have to use its `newFile()` method. Then we get all the document nodes of the table as `XmlNodeList`. We also get its first element by calling the `nextNode()` method.

Next, we loop through all the list elements and do the following:

1. Get an account number node as an `XmlElement`.
2. Get an account name node as an `XmlElement`.
3. Display the text of both nodes in the Infolog.
4. Get the next list element.

In this way, we retrieve the data from the XML file. A similar approach could be used to read any other XML file.

Creating a comma-separated value file

Comma-Separated Value (CSV) files are widely used across various systems. Although nowadays modern systems use XML formats for data exchange, CSV files are still popular because of the simplicity of their format.

Normally, the data in the file is organized so one line corresponds to one record, and each line contains a number of values normally separated by commas. Record and value separators could be any other symbol, depending on the system requirements.

In this recipe, we will learn how to create a custom comma-separated file from code. We will export a list of ledger accounts—the CSV format.

How to do it...

Carry out the following steps in order to complete this recipe:

1. Open the AOT, and create a new class named `CreateCommaFile` with the following code:

```
class CreateCommaFile
{
}
public static client void main(Args _args)
{
    CommaTextIo        file;
    container          line;
```

```
MainAccount              mainAccount;
#define.filename(@'C:\Temp\accounts.csv')
#File

file = new CommaTextIo(#filename, #io_write);

if (!file || file.status() != IO_Status::Ok)
{
    throw error("File cannot be opened.");
}

while select MainAccountId, Name from mainAccount
{
    line = [
        mainAccount.MainAccountId,
        mainAccount.Name];
    file.writeExp(line);
}

info(strFmt("File %1 created.", #filename));
}
```

2. Run the class. A new file named `accounts.csv` should be created in the specified folder. Open that file with Notepad or any other text editor to view the results:

```
accounts.csv - Notepad
File  Edit  Format  View  Help
"110100","Cash and Cash Equivalents"
"110110","110110"
"119000","TOTAL CASH & CASH EQUIVALENTS"
"120100","Bonds and marketable securities"
"120300","Bill of Exchange (BOE)"
"120400","Misc. Securities"
"129900","TOTAL SECURITIES"
"130100","Accounts Receivable"
"130300","Accounts Receivable - Clearing"
"130350","Accounts Receivable - Intercompany"
"130400","Credit Card Receivable"
"130500","Interest Receivable"
"130600","Notes Receivable"
"130700","Other Receivables"
"130900","TOTAL ACCOUNTS RECEIVABLE"
"131100","Prepaid Expenses and Insurance"
"131300","Advances and Prepaid Commissions"
"139990","TOTAL OTHER CURRENT ASSETS"
"140120","Inventory - Car audio"
"140220","Inventory - DVD player"
"140320","Inventory - DVR"
```

How it works...

In the variable declaration section of the `main()` method of the newly created `CreateCommaFile` class, we define a name for the output file, along with other variables. Normally, this should be replaced with a proper input variable. Here, we also define a standard `#File` macro, which contains a number of file-handling modes, such as `#io_read`, `#io_write`, `#io_append`, and so on, file types, delimiters, and other things.

Next, we create a new CSV file by calling the `new()` method on a standard `CommaIo` class. It accepts two parameters—filename and mode. For mode, we use `#io_write` from the `#File` macro to make sure a new file is created and opened for further writing. If a file with the given name already exists, then it will be overwritten. In order to make sure that a file is created successfully, we check if the `file` object exists and its status is valid, otherwise we show an error message.

In multilingual environments, it is better to use the `CommaTextIo` class. It behaves the same way as the `CommaIo` class does plus it supports Unicode, which allows us to process data with various language-specific symbols.

Finally, we loop though the **MainAccount** table, store all account numbers and their names in a container, and write them to the file using the `writeExp()` method.

In this way, we create a new comma-separated value file with the list of ledger accounts.

There's more...

You probably already noticed that the `main()` method has the `client` modifier, which forces its code to run on the client. When dealing with large amounts of data, it is more effective to run the code on the server. In order to do that, we need to change the modifier to `server`. The following class generates exactly the same file as before, except that this file is created in the folder on the server's file system:

```
class CreateCommaFileServer
{
}

public static server void main(Args _args)
{
    CommaTextIo        file;
    container          line;
    MainAccount        mainAccount;
    FileIoPermission   perm;
    #define.filename('C:\\Temp\\accounts.csv')
    #File
```

```
        perm = new FileIoPermission(#filename, #io_write);
        perm.assert();

        file = new CommaTextIo(#filename, #io_write);

        if (!file || file.status() != IO_Status::Ok)
        {
            throw error("File cannot be opened.");
        }

        while select mainAccount
        {
            line = [
                mainAccount.MainAccountId,
                mainAccount.Name];
            file.writeExp(line);
        }

        CodeAccessPermission::revertAssert();

        info(strFmt("File %1 created.", #filename));

    }
```

File manipulation on the server is protected by Dynamics AX code access security and we must use the `FileIoPermission` class to make sure we match the requirements.

Finally, we call `CodeAccessPermission::revertAssert()` to revert the previous assertion.

Reading a comma-separated value file

Besides data import/export, CSV files can be used for integration between systems. It is probably the most simple integration approach, when one system generates CSV files in some network folder and another one reads those files at specified intervals. Although this is not very sophisticated real-time integration, in most cases it does the job and does not require any additional components, such as Dynamics AX Application Integration Framework or something similar.

Another well-known example is when external companies are hired to manage the payroll. On a periodic basis, they send CSV files to the finance department, which are then loaded into the **General journal** in Dynamics AX and processed as usual.

In this recipe, we will learn how to read CSV file from code. As an example, we will process the file created in a previous recipe.

How to do it...

Carry out the following steps in order to complete this recipe:

1. In the AOT, create a new class named `ReadCommaFile` with the following code:

```
class ReadCommaFile
{
}

public static client void main(Args _args)
{
    CommaTextIo         file;
    container           line;
    #define.filename(@'C:\Temp\accounts.csv')
    #File

    file = new CommaTextIo(#filename, #io_read);

    if (!file || file.status() != IO_Status::Ok)
    {
        throw error("File cannot be opened.");
    }

    line = file.read();

    while (file.status() == IO_Status::Ok)
    {
        info(con2Str(line, ' - '));
        line = file.read();
    }
}
```

2. Run the class to view the file's content, as shown in the following screenshot:

```
Message (03:13:56 pm)
   110100 - Cash and Cash Equivalents
   110110 - 110110
   119000 - TOTAL CASH & CASH EQUIVALENTS
   120100 - Bonds and marketable securities
   120300 - Bill of Exchange (BOE)
   120400 - Misc. Securities
   129900 - TOTAL SECURITIES
   130100 - Accounts Receivable
   130300 - Accounts Receivable - Clearing
   130350 - Accounts Receivable - Intercompany
```

How it works...

As in the previous recipe, we first create a new `file` object using the `CommaTextIo` class. This time we use `#io_read` as the mode to make sure that the existing file is read only. We also perform the same validations to make sure that the file object is correctly created, otherwise we show an error message.

Finally, we read the file line by line until we reach the end of the file. Here we use the `while` loop until the file status becomes not `IO_Status::OK`, meaning we have reached the file end. Inside the loop, we call the `read()` method on the `file` object, which returns the current line as a container and moves the internal file cursor to the next line. File data is then simply output to the screen using the standard global `info()` function in conjunction with the `con2Str()` function, which converts a container to a string for displaying.

The last element of code, where the data is output, should normally be replaced by proper code that processes the incoming data.

There's more...

File reading, could also be executed in a similar way as file writing on a server to improve performance. The modifier `client` has to be changed to `server`, and code with the `FileIoPermission` class has to be added to fulfil the code access security requirements. The modified class should look similar to the following code:

```
class ReadCommaFileServer
{
}
public static server void main(Args _args)
{
    CommaTextIo        file;
    container          line;
    FileIoPermission   perm;
    #define.filename('C:\\Temp\\accounts.csv')
    #File

    perm = new FileIoPermission(#filename, #io_read);
    perm.assert();

    file = new CommaTextIo(#filename, #io_read);
    if (!file || file.status() != IO_Status::Ok)
    {
        throw error("File cannot be opened.");
    }
```

```
line = file.read();

while (file.status() == IO_Status::Ok)
{
    info(con2Str(line, ' - '));
    line = file.read();
}

CodeAccessPermission::revertAssert();
}
```

Using the date effectiveness feature

Date effectiveness is a new feature in Dynamics AX 2012 allowing developers to easily create date range fields. Date ranges are used for defining record validity between the specified dates, for example, defining employee contract dates.

This feature significantly reduces the amount of time that developers spend writing code and also provides a consistent approach to implement data range fields.

This recipe will demonstrate the basics of date effectiveness. We will implement date range validation on the standard **E-mail templates** form.

How to do it...

Carry out the following steps in order to complete this recipe:

1. In the AOT, find the **SysEmailTable** table and change its property as shown in the following table:

Property	Value
ValidTimeStateFieldType	Date

2. Notice the two new fields that are automatically added to the table:

3. Add the newly created **ValidFrom** and **ValidTo** fields to the existing **emailIdIdx** index and change the properties shown in the following table:

Property	Value
AlternateKey	Yes
ValidTimeStateKey	Yes
ValidTimeStateMode	NoGap

4. The index should look similar to the following screenshot:

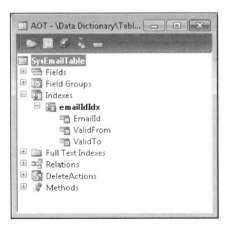

5. Next, add the **ValidFrom** and **ValidTo** fields to the table's **Identification** group:

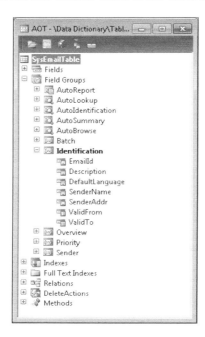

6. In the AOT, find the **SysEmailTable** form, refresh it using the **Restore** command which can be found in the form's right-click context menu. Then, locate its data source named **SysEmailTable** and change its properties as follows:

Property	Value
ValidTimeStateAutoQuery	DateRange
ValidTimeStateUpdate	Correction

7. In order to test the results, navigate to **Organization administration | Setup | E-mail templates** and notice the newly created fields: **Effective** and **Expiration** columns. Try creating records with the same **E-mail ID** and overlapping date ranges—you will notice how the system is proposing to maintain valid date ranges:

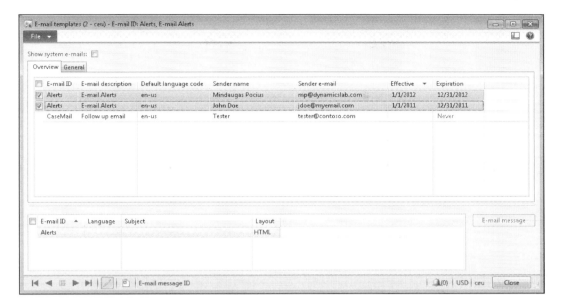

How it works...

We start the recipe by setting the **ValidTimeStateFieldType** property to **Date** on the **SysEmailTable** table. This automatically creates two new fields: **ValidFrom** and **ValidTo** that are used to define a date range.

Next, we add the created fields to the primary index where the **EmailId** field is used and adjust the following index's properties:

- ▸ We set the **AlternateKey** property to **Yes** to ensure that this index is a part of an alternate key.

- ▸ We set the **ValidTimeStateKey** property to **Yes** to specify that the index is used to determine the valid date ranges.

- ▸ We also set the **ValidTimeStateMode** property to **NoGap** to ensure that e-mail templates with the same identification number can be created within continuous periods. The property can also be set to **Gap** allowing non-continuous date ranges.

Finally, we adjust the **SysEmailTable** form to reflect the changes. We add the newly created **ValidFrom** and **ValidTo** fields to the **SysEmailTable** table's **Identification** group so that they automatically appear on the form's **Overview** grid. We also change a few properties of the **SysEmailTable** data source:

Set the **ValidTimeStateAutoQuery** property to **DateRange** to ensure that all records are visible. The default **AsOfDate** value could be used if we want to display only the records for the current period.

Set the **ValidTimeStateUpdate** property to **Correction**, allowing the user to modify the dates.

There's more...

Forms with date effective records can be enhanced with an automatically-generated toolbar for filtering the records. This can be done with the help of the DateEffectivenessPaneController application class.

In order to demonstrate that, let's modify the previously used **SysEmailTable** form and add the following code to the bottom of the form's init() method:

```
DateEffectivenessPaneController::constructWithForm(
    this,
    SysEmailTable_ds);
```

Now when you open the form, it contains an automatically-generated date effectiveness filter at the top:

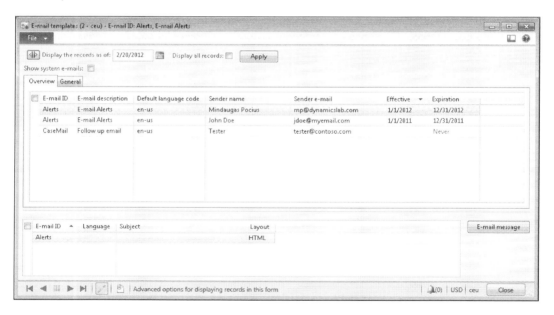

2
Working with Forms

In this chapter, we will cover:

- ▶ Creating a dialog
- ▶ Handling a dialog event
- ▶ Building a dynamic form
- ▶ Adding a form splitter
- ▶ Creating a modal form
- ▶ Modifying multiple forms dynamically
- ▶ Storing last form values
- ▶ Using a tree control
- ▶ Building a checklist
- ▶ Adding the View details link

Introduction

Forms in Dynamics AX represent the user interface and are mainly used for entering or modifying data. They are also used for running reports, executing user commands, validating data, and so on.

Normally, forms are created using the AOT by creating a form object and adding form controls such as tabs, tab pages, grids, groups, data fields, images, and others. Form behavior is controlled by its properties or the code in its member methods. The behavior and layout of form controls are also controlled by their properties and the code in their member methods. Although it is very rare, forms can also be created dynamically from the code.

In this chapter, we will cover various aspects of using Dynamics AX forms. We start with building Dynamics AX dialog, and explaining how to handle its events. The chapter will also show how to build a dynamic form, how to add a dynamic control to existing forms, and how to make a modal form.

This chapter also discusses the usage of a splitter and a tree control, how to create a checklist, save last user selections, and other things.

Creating a dialog

Dialogs are a way to present users with a simple input form. They are commonly used for small user tasks, such as filling in report values, running batch jobs, presenting only the most important fields to the user when creating a new record, and so on. Dialogs are normally created from X++ code without storing actual layout in the AOT.

The application class `Dialog` is used to build dialogs. Other application classes, such as `DialogField`, `DialogGroup`, `DialogTabPage`, and others, are used to create dialog controls. A common way of using dialogs is within the `RunBase` framework classes, where user input is required.

In this example, we will demonstrate how to build a dialog from the code using the `RunBase` framework class. The dialog will contain customer table fields shown in different groups and tabs for creating a new record. There will be two tab pages, **General** and **Details**. The first page will have **Customer account** and **Name** input controls. The second page will be divided into two groups, **Setup** and **Payment**, with relevant fields inside each group. The actual record will not be created, as it is out of scope of this example. However, for demonstration purposes, the information specified by the user will be displayed in the Infolog.

How to do it...

Carry out the following steps in order to complete this recipe:

1. Open the AOT, and create a new class `CustCreate` with the following code:

```
class CustCreate extends RunBase
{
    DialogField    fieldAccount;
    DialogField    fieldName;
    DialogField    fieldGroup;
    DialogField    fieldCurrency;
    DialogField    fieldPaymTermId;
    DialogField    fieldPaymMode;
    CustAccount    custAccount;
    CustName       custName;
    CustGroupId    custGroupId;
    CurrencyCode   currencyCode;
```

```
        CustPaymTermId paymTermId;
        CustPaymMode    paymMode;
    }

    public container pack()
    {
        return conNull();
    }

    public boolean unpack(container _packedClass)
    {
        return true;
    }

    protected Object dialog()
    {
        Dialog          dialog;
        DialogGroup     groupCustomer;
        DialogGroup     groupPayment;

        dialog = super();

        dialog.caption("Customer information");

        fieldAccount    = dialog.addField(
            extendedTypeStr(CustVendAC),
            "Customer account");

        fieldName       =
          dialog.addField(extendedTypeStr(CustName));

        dialog.addTabPage("Details");

        groupCustomer   = dialog.addGroup("Setup");
        fieldGroup      = dialog.addField(
            extendedTypeStr(CustGroupId));
        fieldCurrency   = dialog.addField(
            extendedTypeStr(CurrencyCode));

        groupPayment    = dialog.addGroup("Payment");
        fieldPaymTermId = dialog.addField(
            extendedTypeStr(CustPaymTermId));
        fieldPaymMode   = dialog.addField(
            extendedTypeStr(CustPaymMode));

        return dialog;
    }

    public boolean getFromDialog()
    {
        custAccount  = fieldAccount.value();
        custName     = fieldName.value();
```

```
        custGroupId   = fieldGroup.value();
        currencyCode  = fieldCurrency.value();
        paymTermId    = fieldPaymTermId.value();
        paymMode      = fieldPaymMode.value();
        return super();
    }

    public void run()
    {
        info("You have entered customer information:");
        info(strFmt("Account: %1", custAccount));
        info(strFmt("Name: %1", custName));
        info(strFmt("Group: %1", custGroupId));
        info(strFmt("Currency: %1", currencyCode));
        info(strFmt("Terms of payment: %1", paymTermId));
        info(strFmt("Method of payment: %1", paymMode));
    }

    public static void main(Args _args)
    {
        CustCreate custCreate = new CustCreate();

        if (custCreate.prompt())
        {
            custCreate.run();
        }
    }
}
```

2. In order to test the dialog, run the class. The following form should appear with the **General** tab page open initially:

3. Click on the **Details** tab page to see the following screen:

4. Enter some information into the fields and click **OK**. The results are displayed in the Infolog:

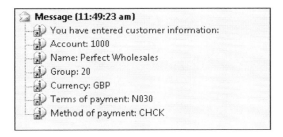

How it works...

First, we create a new class `CustCreate`. By extending it from `RunBase`, we utilize a standard approach of developing data manipulation functions in Dynamics AX. The `RunBase` class defines a common structure and automatically adds additional controls, such as **OK** and **Cancel** buttons to the dialog.

Then we declare class member variables, which will be used later. Variables of the `DialogField` type represent user input fields. Other variables are used to store the actual user input.

The `pack()` and `unpack()` methods are normally used to convert an object to a container, which is a format to store an object in the user cache (`SysLastValue`) or to transfer it between Server and Client tiers. `RunBase` requires those two methods to be implemented in all its subclasses. In this example, we are not using any of the `pack()`/`unpack()` features, but because those methods are mandatory, we return an empty container from `pack()` and `true` from `unpack()`.

The layout of the actual dialog is constructed in the `dialog()` member method. Here, we define local variables for the dialog itself—tab pages and groups. Those variables, as opposed to the dialog fields, do not store any value for further processing.

The `super()` of the `RunBase` framework creates the initial `dialog` object for us. The object is created using the `Dialog` application class. The class actually uses an AOT form named `Dialog` as a base, automatically adds the relevant controls, including **OK** and **Cancel** buttons, and presents it to the user as a dialog.

Additional controls are added to the dialog by using the `addField()`, `addGroup()`, and `addTabPage()` methods. There are more methods to add different types of controls, such as `addText()`, `addImage()`, `addMenuItemButton()`, and others. All controls have to be added to the dialog object directly. Adding an input control to groups or tabs is done by calling `addField()` right after `addGroup()` or `addTabPage()`. In the previous example, we added tab pages, groups, and fields in logical sequence top down. Notice that it is enough only to add a second tab page, the first one labeled **General** is added automatically by the `RunBase` framework.

Values from the dialog controls are assigned to variables by calling the `value()` member method of the `DialogField` class. If a dialog is used within the `RunBase` framework, as in this example, the best place to assign dialog control values to variables is the `getFormDialog()` member method. `RunBase` calls this method right after the user clicks **OK**.

The main processing is done in the `run()` method. For demonstration purposes, this class only shows the user input the Infolog.

In order to make this class runnable, the static method `main()` has to be created. Here, we create a new `CustCreate` object, invoke user dialog by calling the `prompt()` method, and once the user finishes entering customer details by clicking **OK**, we call the `run()` method to process the data.

See also

In this chapter:

> ▸ *Handling a dialog event*

Handling a dialog event

Sometimes in the user interface, it is required to change the status of one field, depending on the status of another field. For example, if the user marks the **Show filter** checkbox, then another field, **Filter**, appears or becomes enabled. In AOT forms, this can be done by using the input control `modified()` event. However, if this feature is required on runtime dialogs, handling events are not that straightforward.

Very often, existing dialogs have to be modified to support eventing. The easiest way of doing that is of course to convert a dialog into an AOT form. However, in cases when the existing dialog is complex enough, probably a more cost effective solution would be to implement dialog event handling instead of converting it into an AOT form. Event handling in dialogs is not as flexible as in AOT forms, but in most cases it does the job.

In this recipe, we will create a dialog very similar to the previous one, but instead of entering the customer number, we will be able to select it from the list. Once the customer is selected, the rest of the fields will be completed automatically by the system from the customer record.

How to do it...

Carry out the following steps in order to complete this recipe:

1. In the AOT, create a new class named `CustSelect` with the following code:

```
class CustSelect extends RunBase
{
    DialogField fieldAccount;
    DialogField fieldName;
    DialogField fieldGroup;
    DialogField fieldCurrency;
    DialogField fieldPaymTermId;
    DialogField fieldPaymMode;
}

public container pack()
{
    return conNull();
}

public boolean unpack(container _packedClass)
{
    return true;
}

protected Object dialog()
{
```

```
        Dialog          dialog;
        DialogGroup     groupCustomer;
        DialogGroup     groupPayment;

        dialog = super();

        dialog.caption("Customer information");
        dialog.allowUpdateOnSelectCtrl(true);

        fieldAccount    = dialog.addField(
            extendedTypeStr(CustAccount),
            "Customer account");

        fieldName       = dialog.addField(extendedTypeStr(CustName));
        fieldName.enabled(false);

        dialog.addTabPage("Details");

        groupCustomer   = dialog.addGroup("Setup");
        fieldGroup      = dialog.addField(
            extendedTypeStr(CustGroupId));
        fieldCurrency   = dialog.addField(
            extendedTypeStr(CurrencyCode));
        fieldGroup.enabled(false);
        fieldCurrency.enabled(false);

        groupPayment    = dialog.addGroup("Payment");
        fieldPaymTermId = dialog.addField(
            extendedTypeStr(CustPaymTermId));
        fieldPaymMode   = dialog.addField(
            extendedTypeStr(CustPaymMode));
        fieldPaymTermId.enabled(false);
        fieldPaymMode.enabled(false);

        return dialog;
    }

    public void dialogSelectCtrl()
    {
        CustTable custTable;

        custTable = CustTable::find(fieldAccount.value());
        fieldName.value(custTable.name());
        fieldGroup.value(custTable.CustGroup);
        fieldCurrency.value(custTable.Currency);
        fieldPaymTermId.value(custTable.PaymTermId);
        fieldPaymMode.value(custTable.PaymMode);
    }

    public static void main(Args _args)
    {
```

```
CustSelect custSelect = new CustSelect();

if (CustSelect.prompt())
{
    CustSelect.run();
}
}
```

2. Run the class, select any customer from the list, and move the cursor to the next control. Notice how the rest of the fields were populated automatically with the customer information:

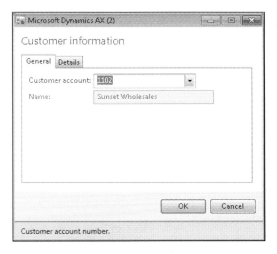

3. When you click on the **Details** tab page, you will see the details as shown in the following screenshot:

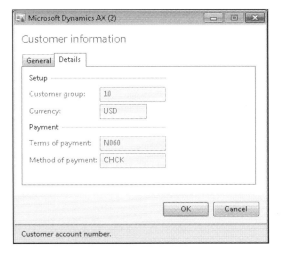

How it works...

The new class `CustSelect` is actually a copy of the `CustCreate` class from the previous recipe with a few changes. In its class declaration, we leave all `DialogField` declarations and remove the rest of the variables.

The methods `pack()`/`unpack()` remain the same as we are not using any of their features.

In the `dialog()` member method, we call the `allowUpdateOnSelectCtrl()` method with the argument `true` to enable input control event handling. We also disable all controls apart from the **Customer account** by calling `enable()` with parameter `false` for each control.

The member method `dialogSelectCtrl()` of the `RunBase` class is called every time the user modifies any input control in the dialog. It is the place where we have to add all the required code to ensure that, in our case, all controls are populated with the correct data from the customer record, once the **Customer account** is chosen.

The static `main()` method ensures that we can run this class.

There's more...

Usage of the `dialogSelectCtrl()` method sometimes might appear a bit limited as this method is only invoked when the dialog control loses its focus. Also, no other events can be controlled, and it can become messy if events on multiple controls need to be processed.

The `Dialog` class does not provide direct access to the underlying form's event handling functions, but we can easily access the form object within the dialog. Although we cannot create the usual event handling methods on runtime form controls, we can still control this in a slightly different way. Let us modify the previous example to include more events. We will add an event on the second tab page, which is triggered once the page is activated.

First, we have to override the `dialogPostRun()` method on the `CustSelect` class:

```
public void dialogPostRun(DialogRunbase dialog)
{
    dialog.formRun().controlMethodOverload(true);
    dialog.formRun().controlMethodOverloadObject(this);
    super(dialog);
}
```

Here, we enable event overloading on the runtime form after it is fully created and is ready for displaying on the screen. We also pass the `CustSelect` object as an argument to the `controlMethodOverloadObject()` method to make sure that the form knows where the overloaded events are located.

Next, we have to create a method that will be executed once the tab page is opened:

```
public void TabPg_1_pageActivated()
{
    info('Tab page activated');
}
```

The method name consists of the control name and event name joined with an underscore. Now run the class again, and select the **Details** tab page. The message should be displayed in the Infolog.

Before creating such methods, we first have to get the name of the runtime control. This is because the dialog form is created dynamically, and the system defines control names automatically without allowing the user to choose them. In this example, we have to temporarily add the following code to the bottom of the `dialog()`, which displays the name of the **Details** tab page control. Just replace the following code:

```
dialog.addTabPage("Details");
```

With the following code:

```
info(dialog.addTabPage("Details").name());
```

Running the class would display the name of the control in the Infolog.

Note that this approach may not work properly if the dialog contains an automatically-generated query. In such cases, control names will change if the user adds or removes query ranges.

See also

In this chapter:

- ▸ *Creating a dialog*

Building a dynamic form

A standard approach for creating forms in Dynamics AX is to create and store form objects in the AOT. Using this approach, it is possible to achieve a high level of complexity. However, in a number of cases, it is required to have forms created dynamically. In the standard Dynamics AX application we can see that application objects, such as the **Table browser** form, various lookups, or dialogs, are built dynamically.

In this recipe, we will create a dynamic form. In order to show how flexible it can be, we will replicate the layout of the existing **Customer groups** form located in the **Accounts receivable** module. It can be opened from **Accounts receivable | Setup | Customers**.

How to do it...

Carry out the following steps in order to complete this recipe:

1. In the AOT, create a new class called `CustGroupDynamic` with the following code:

```
class CustGroupDynamic
{
}

public static void main(Args _args)
{
    DictTable                           dictTable;
    Form                                form;
    FormBuildDesign                     design;
    FormBuildDataSource                 ds;
    FormBuildActionPaneControl          actionPane;
    FormBuildActionPaneTabControl       actionPaneTab;
    FormBuildButtonGroupControl         btngrp1;
    FormBuildButtonGroupControl         btngrp2;
    FormBuildCommandButtonControl       cmdNew;
    FormBuildCommandButtonControl       cmdDel;
    FormBuildMenuButtonControl          mbPosting;
    FormBuildFunctionButtonControl      mibPosting;
    FormBuildFunctionButtonControl      mibForecast;
    FormBuildGridControl                grid;
    FormBuildGroupControl               grpBody;
    Args                                args;
    FormRun                             formRun;
    #Task

    dictTable = new DictTable(tableNum(CustGroup));

    form = new Form();
    form.name("CustGroupDynamic");

    ds = form.addDataSource(dictTable.name());
    ds.table(dictTable.id());

    design = form.addDesign('Design');
    design.caption("Customer groups");
    design.style(FormStyle::SimpleList);
    design.titleDatasource(ds.id());

    actionPane = design.addControl(
        FormControlType::ActionPane, 'ActionPane');
    actionPane.style(ActionPaneStyle::Strip);
    actionPaneTab = actionPane.addControl(
        FormControlType::ActionPaneTab, 'ActionPaneTab');
```

```
btngrp1 = actionPaneTab.addControl(
    FormControlType::ButtonGroup, 'NewDeleteGroup');
btngrp2 = actionPaneTab.addControl(
    FormControlType::ButtonGroup, 'ButtonGroup');

cmdNew = btngrp1.addControl(
    FormControlType::CommandButton, 'NewButton');
cmdNew.buttonDisplay(FormButtonDisplay::TextAndImageLeft);
cmdNew.normalImage('11045');
cmdNew.imageLocation(SysImageLocation::EmbeddedResource);
cmdNew.primary(NoYes::Yes);
cmdNew.command(#taskNew);

cmdDel = btngrp1.addControl(
    FormControlType::CommandButton, 'NewButton');
cmdDel.text("Delete");
cmdDel.buttonDisplay(FormButtonDisplay::TextAndImageLeft);
cmdDel.normalImage('10121');
cmdDel.imageLocation(SysImageLocation::EmbeddedResource);
cmdDel.saveRecord(NoYes::Yes);
cmdDel.primary(NoYes::Yes);
cmdDel.command(#taskDeleteRecord);

mbPosting = btngrp2.addControl(
    FormControlType::MenuButton, 'MenuButtonPosting');
mbPosting.helpText("Set up related data for the group.");
mbPosting.text("Setup");

mibPosting = mbPosting.addControl(
    FormControlType::MenuFunctionButton, 'Posting');
mibPosting.text('Item posting');
mibPosting.saveRecord(NoYes::No);
mibPosting.dataSource(ds.id());
mibPosting.menuItemName(menuitemDisplayStr(InventPosting));

mibForecast = btngrp2.addControl(
    FormControlType::MenuFunctionButton, 'SalesForecast');
mibForecast.text('Forecast');
mibForecast.saveRecord(NoYes::No);
mibForecast.menuItemName(
    menuitemDisplayStr(ForecastSalesGroup));

grpBody = design.addControl(FormControlType::Group, 'Body');
grpBody.heightMode(FormHeight::ColumnHeight);
grpBody.columnspace(0);
grpBody.style(GroupStyle::BorderlessGridContainer);

grid = grpBody.addControl(FormControlType::Grid, "Grid");
grid.dataSource(ds.name());
grid.widthMode(FormWidth::ColumnWidth);
```

```
grid.heightMode(FormHeight::ColumnHeight);

grid.addDataField(
    ds.id(), fieldNum(CustGroup,CustGroup));

grid.addDataField(
    ds.id(), fieldNum(CustGroup,Name));

grid.addDataField(
    ds.id(), fieldNum(CustGroup,PaymTermId));

grid.addDataField(
    ds.id(), fieldnum(CustGroup,ClearingPeriod));

grid.addDataField(
    ds.id(), fieldNum(CustGroup,BankCustPaymIdTable));

grid.addDataField(
    ds.id(), fieldNum(CustGroup,TaxGroupId));

args = new Args();
args.object(form);

formRun = classFactory.formRunClass(args);
formRun.init();
formRun.run();

formRun.detach();
}
```

2. In order to test the form, run the class. Notice that the form is similar to the one in **Accounts receivable | Setup | Customers | Customer groups**:

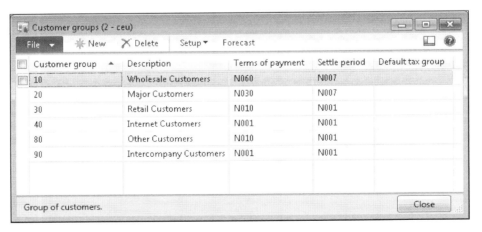

How it works...

We start the code by declaring some variables. Note that most of them begin with `FormBuild`, which is part of a set of the application classes used for building dynamic forms. Each of these types correspond to the control types manually used when building forms in the AOT.

Right after the variable declaration, we create a `dictTable` object based on the **CustGroup** table. We will use this object several times later in the code.

Then we create a new form object and set its AOT name by calling the following code:

```
form = new Form();
form.name("CustGroupDynamic");
```

The name is not important as this is a dynamic form, unless we are planning to save it in the AOT.

The form should have a data source, so we add one by calling the `addDataSource()` method on the `form` object and providing the previously created `dictTable` object.

```
ds = form.addDataSource(dictTable.name());
ds.table(dictTable.id());
```

Every form has a design, so we add a new design, define its style as a simple list, and set its title data source:

```
design = form.addDesign('Design');
design.caption("Customer groups");
design.style(FormStyle::SimpleList);
design.titleDatasource(ds.id());
```

Once the design is ready, we can start adding controls from the code as if we were doing this from the AOT. The first thing to do is to add a strip action pane with its buttons:

```
actionPane = design.addControl(
    FormControlType::ActionPane, 'ActionPane');
actionPane.style(ActionPaneStyle::Strip);
actionPaneTab = actionPane.addControl(
    FormControlType::ActionPaneTab, 'ActionPaneTab');
btngrp1 = actionPaneTab.addControl(
```

Right after the action pane, we add an automatically expanding `Grid` control pointing to the previously mentioned data source. Just to follow best practice, we place the grid inside of a `Group` control:

```
grpBody = design.addControl(FormControlType::Group, 'Body');
grpBody.heightMode(FormHeight::ColumnHeight);
grpBody.columnspace(0);
grpBody.style(GroupStyle::BorderlessGridContainer);

grid = grpBody.addControl(FormControlType::Grid, "Grid");
grid.dataSource(ds.name());
grid.widthMode(FormWidth::ColumnWidth);
grid.heightMode(FormHeight::ColumnHeight);
```

Next, we add a number of grid controls pointing to the relevant data source fields by calling `addDataField()` on the `grid` object.

The last thing is to initialize and run the form. Here we use a recommended approach to create and run forms using the globally available `classFactory` object.

Adding a form splitter

In Dynamics AX, more complex forms consist of one or more sections. Each section may contain grids, groups or any other element. In order to maintain section sizes while resizing the form, the sections are normally separated by so-called splitters. Splitters are not special Dynamics AX controls; they are group controls with the properties modified so they look like splitters. Most of the multisection forms in Dynamics AX already contain splitters.

In this recipe, to demonstrate the usage of splitters, we will modify one of the existing forms that does not have a splitter. We will modify the **Account reconciliation** form in the **Cash and bank management** module, which can be opened from **Cash and bank management | Bank accounts list** page, by clicking on the **Reconcile | Account reconciliation** button in the action pane, and then selecting any of the existing records and hitting the **Transactions** button. In the following screenshot, you can see that it is not possible to control the sizes of each grid individually, and they are resized automatically using a fixed ratio when resizing the form:

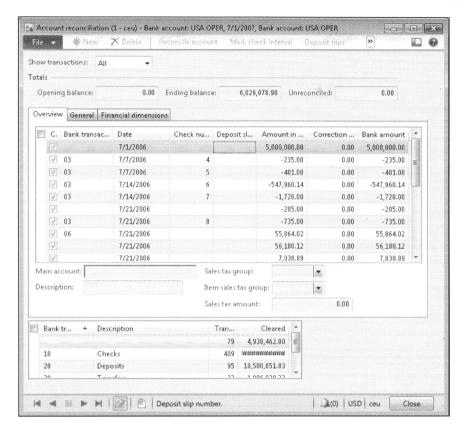

In this recipe, we will demonstrate the usage of splitters by resolving this situation. We will add a form splitter in the middle of the two grids in the mentioned form. It will allow users to define the size of both grids to make sure the data is optimally displayed.

How to do it...

Carry out the following steps in order to complete this recipe:

1. Open the **BankReconciliation** form in the AOT, and in the form's design add a new `Group` control right after the **ActionPage** control with the following properties:

Property	Value
Name	Top
AutoDeclaration	Yes
Width	Column width
FrameType	None

2. Move the **AllReconciled**, **Balances**, and **Tab** controls into the newly created group.

3. Add a new `Group` control right below the **Top** group with the following properties:

Property	Value
Name	Splitter
AutoDeclaration	Yes
Width	Column width
Height	5
FrameType	Raised 3D
BackgroundColor	Window background
HideIfEmpty	No

4. Add the following line of code to the bottom of the form's class declaration:

```
SysFormSplitter_Y fs;
```

5. Add the following line of code to the bottom of the form's `init()` method:

```
fs = new SysFormSplitter_Y(Splitter, Top, element);
```

6. Override three methods in the **Splitter** group with the following code:

```
public int mouseDown(
    int      _x,
    int      _y,
    int      _button,

    boolean _ctrl,
    boolean _shift)
{
    return fs.mouseDown(_x, _y, _button, _ctrl, _shift);
}

public int mouseMove(
    int      _x,
    int      _y,
    int      _button,
    boolean _ctrl,
    boolean _shift)
{
    return fs.mouseMove(_x, _y, _button, _ctrl, _shift);
}

public int mouseUp(
    int      _x,
```

```
        int     _y,
        int     _button,
        boolean _ctrl,
        boolean _shift)
    {
        return fs.mouseUp(_x, _y, _button, _ctrl, _shift);
    }
```

7. Change the following properties of the existing **BankTransTypeGroup** group:

Property	Value
Top	Auto
Width	Column width
Height	Column height

8. Change the following property of the exiting **TypeSums** grid located inside the **BankTransTypeGroup** group:

Property	Value
Height	Column height

9. In the AOT, the modified **BankReconciliation** form should look similar to the following screenshot:

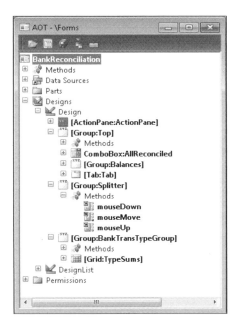

10. Now, to test the results, open **Cash and bank management | Bank accounts**, select any bank account, click **Reconcile | Account reconciliation**, choose an existing one or create a new bank statement, and click on the **Transactions** button. Notice that the form now has a nice splitter in the middle, which makes the form look better and allows resizing of both grids:

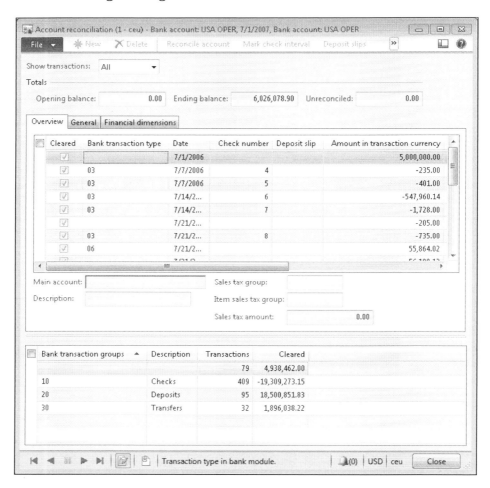

How it works...

Normally, a splitter has to be placed between two form groups. In this recipe, to follow that rule, we need to adjust the **BankReconciliation** form's design. The **AllReconciled**, **Balances** and **Tab** controls are moved to a new group called **Top**. We do not want this new group to be visible to the user, so we set **FrameType** to **None**. Setting **AutoDeclaration** to **Yes** allows us to access this object from the code. Finally, we make this group automatically expanding in the horizontal direction by setting its **Width** to **Column width**. At this stage, visual form layout does not change, but now we have the upper group ready.

The **BankTransTypeGroup** group could be used as a bottom group with slight changes. We change its **Top** behavior to **Auto** and make it fully expandable in the horizontal and vertical directions. The **Height** of the grid inside this group also has to be changed to **Column height** in order to fill all the vertical space.

In the middle of those two groups, we add a splitter. The splitter is nothing but another group, which looks like a splitter. In order to achieve that, we set the **Height** to **5**, **FrameType** to **Raised 3D**, and **BackgroundColor** to **Windows background**. This group does not hold any other controls inside, therefore, in order to make it visible we have to set the **HideIfEmpty** property to **No**. The **Column width** value of the property **Width** forces the splitter to automatically fill the form's width.

Mouse events are handled by the `SysFormSplitter_Y` application class. After it has been declared in the form's class declaration, we instantiate it in the form's `init()` method. We pass the name of the splitter control, the name of the top group, and the form itself as arguments when creating it.

A fully working splitter requires three mouse event handlers. It is implemented by overriding the `mouseMove()`, `mouseDown()`, and `mouseUp()` event methods in the splitter group control. All arguments are passed to the respective member methods of the `SysFormSplitter_Y` class, which does all the work.

In this way, horizontal splitters can easily be added to any form. The Dynamics AX application also contains nice examples about splitters, which can be found in the AOT in the `Tutorial_Form_Split` form. Vertical splitters can also be added to forms using a very similar approach. For this, we need to use another application class called `SysFormSplitter_X`.

Creating a modal form

Quite often people who are not familiar with computers and software tend to get lost among open application windows. The same could be applied to Dynamics AX. Often a user opens one form, clicks a button to open another one, and then goes back to the first one without closing the second one. Sometimes this happens intentionally, sometimes not, but the result is that the second form is hidden behind the first one and the user starts wondering why it is not possible to close or edit the first form.

Such issues can be easily solved by making the child form a modal window. In other words, the second form always stays on top of the first one until closed. In this recipe, we will do exactly that. As an example, we will make the **Create sales order** form a modal window.

How to do it...

Carry out the following steps in order to complete this recipe:

1. Open the **SalesCreateOrder** form in the AOT, and set its **Design** property:

Property	Value
WindowType	Popup

2. In order to test, open **Sales and marketing | Sales orders | All sales orders**, and start creating a new order. Notice that now the sales order creation form always stays on top:

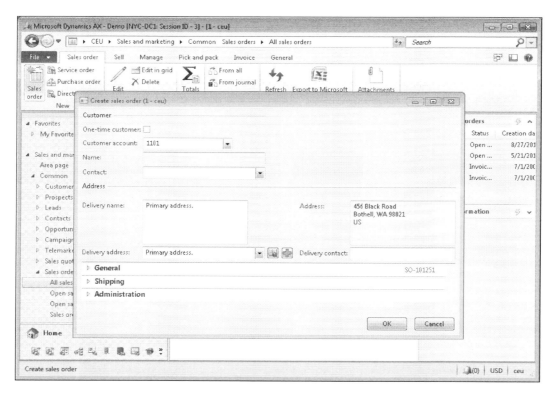

How it works...

The design of the form has a **WindowType** property, which is set to **Standard** by default. In order to make a form behave as a modal window, we have to change it to **Popup**. Such forms will always stay on top of the parent form.

There's more...

We already know that some of the Dynamics AX forms are created dynamically using the `Dialog` class. If we look deeper into the code, we could find that the `Dialog` class actually creates a runtime form. This means that we can apply the same principle—change the relevant form's design property. The following code could be added to the `Dialog` object and would do the job. The format is given as follows:

```
dialog.dialogForm().buildDesign().windowType(
    FormWindowType::Popup);
```

Here we get a reference to the form's design, by first using the `dialogForm()` method of the `dialog` object to get a reference to the `DialogForm` object, and then we call `buildDesign()` on the latter object. Finally, we set the design property by calling its `windowType()` with an argument `FormWindowType::Popup`.

See also

In this chapter:

▸   *Creating a dialog*

Modifying multiple forms dynamically

In the standard Dynamics AX application, there is a class called `SysSetupFormRun`. Every runtime form inherits that class; therefore the class could be used to override some of the common behavior for all Dynamics AX forms.

For example, form background color could be changed depending on some parameters, some controls could be hidden or added depending on specific circumstances, and so on.

In this recipe, we will modify the `SysSetupFormRun` class to automatically add an **About Microsoft Dynamics AX** button to every form in Dynamics AX.

How to do it...

Carry out the following steps in order to complete this recipe:

1. In the AOT, open `SysSetupFormRun` class, and create a new method with the following code:

```
private void addAboutButton()
{
    FormActionPaneControl    actionPane;
    FormActionPaneTabControl actionPaneTab;
    FormCommandButtonControl cmdAbout;
    FormButtonGroupControl    btngrp;
    #define.taskAbout(259)

    actionPane = this.design().controlNum(1);
    if (!actionPane ||
        !(actionPane is FormActionPaneControl) ||
        actionPane.style() == ActionPaneStyle::Strip)
    {
        return;
    }

    actionPaneTab = actionPane.controlNum(1);
    if (!actionPaneTab ||
        !(actionPaneTab is FormActionPaneTabControl))
    {
        return;
    }

    btngrp = actionPaneTab.addControl(
        FormControlType::ButtonGroup, 'ButtonGroup');
    btngrp.caption("About");

    cmdAbout = btngrp.addControl(
        FormControlType::CommandButton, 'About');
    cmdAbout.command(#taskAbout);
    cmdAbout.imageLocation(SysImageLocation::EmbeddedResource);
    cmdAbout.normalImage('412');
    cmdAbout.big(NoYes::Yes);
    cmdAbout.saveRecord(NoYes::No);
}
```

2. In the same class, override the `run()` method with the following code:

```
public void run()
{
    this.addAboutButton();
    super();
}
```

3. In order to test the results, open any list page, for example, **Accounts receivable | Customers | All customers** and look for the new button **About Microsoft Dynamics AX** in the action pane:

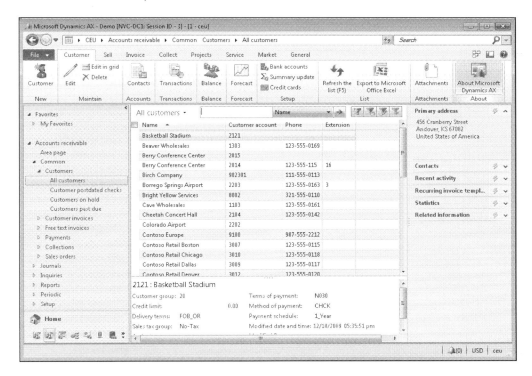

How it works...

`SysSetupFormRun` is the application class that is called by the system every time a user runs a form. The best place to add our custom control is to override the `run()` method.

We use the `this.design()` method to obtain a reference to the form's design, then we check if the first control in the design is an action pane, but not an action pane strip, and the first control in the action pane is an action pane tab. If one of those conditions is not met, we stop the code, otherwise we continue by adding a new separate button group and the **About Microsoft Dynamics AX** command button. Now every form in Dynamics AX with an action pane will have one more button.

Storing last form values

Dynamics AX has a very useful feature that allows saving of the latest user choices per user per form, report or any other object. This feature is implemented across a number of standard forms, reports, periodic jobs, and other objects, which requires a user input. When developing a new functionality for Dynamics AX, it is recommended to keep it that way.

In this recipe, we will demonstrate how to save the latest user selections. In order to make it as simple as possible, we will use existing filters on the **General journal** form, which can be opened from **General ledger | Journals | General journal**. This form contains two filters—**Show** and **Show user-created only**. The **Show** filter allows journals to be displayed by their posting status and the **Show user-created only** toggles between all journals and the currently logged in user's journals.

How to do it...

Carry out the following steps in order to complete this recipe:

1. In the AOT, find the **LedgerJournalTable** form, and add the following code to the bottom of its class declaration:

   ```
   AllOpenPosted    showStatus;
   NoYes            showCurrentUser;
   #define.CurrentVersion(1)
   #localmacro.CurrentList
       showStatus,
       showCurrentUser
   #endmacro
   ```

2. Create the following additional form methods:

   ```
   public void initParmDefault()
   {
       showStatus       = AllOpenPosted::Open;
       showCurrentUser = true;
   }

   public container pack()
   {
       return [#CurrentVersion, #CurrentList];
   }

   public boolean unpack(container _packedClass)
   {
       int version = RunBase::getVersion(_packedClass);
   ```

```
        switch (version)
        {
            case #CurrentVersion:
                [version, #CurrentList] = _packedClass;
                return true;
            default:
                return false;
        }
        return false;
    }

    public IdentifierName lastValueDesignName()
    {
        return element.args().menuItemName();
    }

    public IdentifierName lastValueElementName()
    {
        return this.name();
    }

    public UtilElementType lastValueType()
    {
        return UtilElementType::Form;
    }

    public UserId lastValueUserId()
    {
        return curUserId();
    }

    public DataAreaId lastValueDataAreaId()
    {
        return curext();
    }
```

3. Add the following code to the form's `run()` method right before its `super()`:

```
xSysLastValue::getLast(this);
AllOpenPostedField.selection(showStatus);
ShowUserCreatedOnly.value(showCurrentUser);
```

4. Add the following code to the bottom of the form's `close()` method:

```
showStatus      = AllOpenPostedField.selection();
showCurrentUser = ShowUserCreatedOnly.value();
xSysLastValue::saveLast(this);
```

5. Now to test the form, open **General ledger | Journals | General journal**, change the filter's values, close the form, and open it again. The latest filter selections should stay:

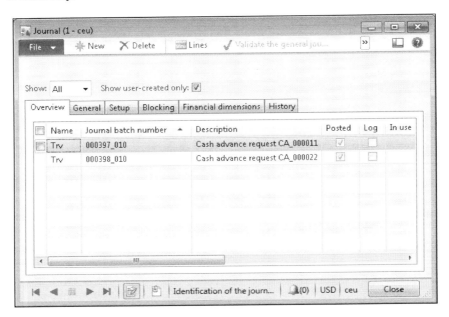

How it works...

First of all, we define two variables, one for each filter control. We will store the journal posting status filter value in `showStatus`, and the current user filter value in `showCurrentUser`.

The macro `#CurrentList` is used to define a list of variables that we are going to save in the usage data. Currently, we have both variables inside it.

The macro `#CurrentVersion` defines a version of the saved values. In other words, it says that the variables defined by the `#CurrentList`, which will be stored in system usage data, can be addressed using the number 1.

Normally, when implementing the last value saving for the first time for a particular object, `#CurrentVersion` is set to 1. Later on, if we decide to add new values or change existing ones, we have to change the value of `#CurrentVersion`, normally increasing it by 1. This ensures that the system addresses the correct list of variables in the usage data and does not break existing functionality.

The `initParmDefault()` method specifies default values if nothing is found in the usage data. Normally, this happens if we run a form for the first time, we change `#CurrentVersion` or clean the usage data. This method is automatically called by the `xSysLastValue` class.

The methods `pack()` and `unpack()` are responsible for formatting a storage container from variables and extracting variables from a storage container, respectively. In our case, `pack()` returns a container consisting of three values: version number, posting status, and current user toggle. These values will be sent to the system usage data storage after the form is closed. During an opening of the form, the `xSysLastValue` class uses `unpack()` to extract values from the stored container. It checks whether the container version in the usage data matches the current version number, and only then the values are considered correct and are assigned to the form variables.

A combination of the `lastValueDesignName()`, `lastValueElementName()`, `lastValueType()`, `lastValueUserId()`, and `lastValueDataAreaId()` method return values forms a unique string representing the saved values. This ensures that different users can store last values for different objects without overriding each other's values in the usage data.

The `lastValueDesignName()` method is meant to return the name of the object's current design in cases where the object can have several designs. In this recipe, there is only one design, so instead of leaving it empty, we used it for a slightly different purpose. The same `LedgerJournalTable` form can be opened from various menu places. For example, the form could be presented to the user as **General journal**, **Periodic journals** or **Payment journal** forms. In order to ensure that the user's latest choices are saved correctly, we include the caller menu item name as part of the unique string.

The last two pieces of code need to be added to the form's `run()` and `close()` methods. In the `run()` method, `xSysLastValue::getLast(this)` retrieves the saved user values from the usage data and assigns them to the form's variables. The next two lines assign the values to the respective form controls.

Finally, code lines in the `close()` method are responsible for assigning user selections to the variables and saving them to the usage data by calling `xSysLastValue::saveLast(this)`.

Using a tree control

Frequent users should notice that some of the Dynamics AX forms use tree controls instead of commonly used grids. In some cases, it is extremely useful, especially when there are parent-child relationships among records. It is a much clearer way to show the whole hierarchy compared to a flat list. For example, projects and their subprojects are displayed in the **Projects** form of the **Project management and accounting** module and give a much better overview when displayed in a tree layout.

This recipe will discuss the principles of how to build tree-based forms. As an example, we will use the **Budget model** form, which can be found in **Budgeting | Setup | Budget models**. This form contains a list of budget models and their submodels, and although the data is organized using a parent-child structure it is still displayed as a grid. In this recipe, to demonstrate the usage of tree controls, we will replace the grid with a new tree control.

How to do it...

Carry out the following steps in order to complete this recipe:

1. In the AOT, create a new class named `BudgetModelTree` with the following code:

```
class BudgetModelTree
{
    FormTreeControl tree;
    BudgetModelId   modelId;
}

public void new(
    FormTreeControl _formTreeControl,
    BudgetModelId   _budgetModelId)
{
    tree    = _formTreeControl;
    modelId = _budgetModelId;
}

public static BudgetModelTree construct(
    FormTreeControl _formTreeControl,
    BudgetModelId   _budgetModelId = '')
{
    return new BudgetModelTree(
        _formTreeControl,
        _budgetModelId);
}

private TreeItemIdx createNode(
    TreeItemIdx   _parentIdx,
    BudgetModelId _modelId,
    RecId         _recId)
{
    TreeItemIdx itemIdx;
    BudgetModel model;
    BudgetModel submodel;

    model = BudgetModel::find(HeadingSub::Heading, _modelId);

    itemIdx = SysFormTreeControl::addTreeItem(
        tree,
        _modelId + ' : ' + model.Txt,
        _parentIdx,
        _recId,
```

```
            0,
            true);
        if (modelId == _modelId)
        {
            tree.select(itemIdx);
        }
        while select submodel
            where submodel.ModelId == _modelId &&
                  submodel.Type    == HeadingSub::SubModel
        {
            this.createNode(
                itemIdx,
                submodel.SubModelId,
                submodel.RecId);
        }
        return itemIdx;
    }

    public void buildTree()
    {
        BudgetModel model;
        BudgetModel submodel;
        TreeItemIdx itemIdx;

        tree.deleteAll();
        tree.lock();
        while select RecId, ModelId from model
            where model.Type == HeadingSub::Heading
            notExists join submodel
                where submodel.SubModelId == model.ModelId &&
                      submodel.Type       == HeadingSub::SubModel
        {
            itemIdx = this.createNode(
                FormTreeAdd::Root,
                model.ModelId,
                model.RecId);
            SysFormTreeControl::expandTree(tree, itemIdx);
        }
        tree.unLock(true);
    }
```

2. In the AOT, open the **BudgetModel** form's design, expand the **Body** group, then expand the **GridContainer** group, and change the following property of the **BudgetModel** grid control:

Property	Value
Visible	No

3. Create a new `Tree` control right below the **BudgetModel** grid with the following properties:

Property	Value
Name	Tree
Width	Column width
Height	Column height
Border	Single line
RowSelect	Yes

4. Add the following code to the bottom of the form's class declaration:

```
BudgetModelTree modelTree;
```

5. Add the following code to the bottom of form's `init()`:

```
modelTree = BudgetModelTree::construct(Tree);
modelTree.buildTree();
```

6. Override `selectionChanged()` on the `Tree` control with the following code:

```
public void selectionChanged(
    FormTreeItem    _oldItem,
    FormTreeItem    _newItem,
    FormTreeSelect  _how)
{
    BudgetModel    model;
    BudgetModelId modelId;

    super(_oldItem, _newItem, _how);

    if (_newItem.data())
    {
        select firstOnly model
            where model.RecId == _newItem.data();
        if (model.Type == HeadingSub::SubModel)
        {
            modelId = model.SubModelId;
```

```
            select firstOnly model
                where model.ModelId == modelId
                   && model.Type    == HeadingSub::Heading;
        }
        BudgetModel_ds.findRecord(model);
        BudgetModel_ds.refresh();
    }

}
```

7. Override the `delete()` method on the **BudgetModel** data source with the following code:

```
public void delete()
{
    super();

    if (BudgetModel.RecId)
    {
        modelTree.buildTree();
    }
}
```

8. Override the `delete()` method on the **SubModel** data source with the following code:

```
public void delete()
{
    super();

    if (SubModel.RecId)
    {
        modelTree.buildTree();
    }
}
```

9. Add the following code to the bottom of the `write()` method on the **BudgetModel** data source:

```
modelTree.buildTree();
```

10. Override the `write()` method on the **SubModel** data source and add the following code to its bottom:

```
modelTree.buildTree();
```

11. In the AOT, the **BudgetModel** form should look like the following screenshot:

12. To test the tree control, open **Budgeting | Setup | Budget models**. Notice how the ledger budget models are presented as a hierarchy:

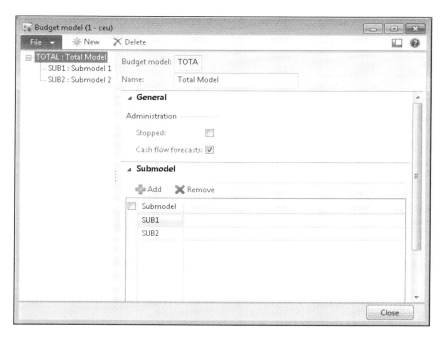

How it works...

This recipe contains a lot of code, so according to best practice we create a class to hold most of it. This allows us to reuse the code and keep the form less cluttered.

The new class contains a few common methods like `new()` and `construct()` for initializing the class and two methods, which actually generate the tree.

The first method is `createNode()` and is used for creating a single budget model node with its children, if any. It is a recursive method, and it calls itself to generate the children of the current node. It accepts a parent node and a budget model as arguments. In this method, we create the node by calling the `addTreeItem()` method of the `SysFormTreeControl` class. The rest of the code loops through all submodels and creates subnodes (if there are any) for each of them.

Secondly, we create the `buildTree()` method where the whole tree is created. Before we start building the tree, we delete all nodes and lock the tree control. Then, we add nodes by looping through all parent budget models and calling the previously mentioned `createNode()`. We call the `expandTree()` of the `SysFormTreeControl` class to display every parent budget model initially expanded. Once the hierarchy is ready, we unlock the tree control.

Next, we modify the **BudgetModel** form by hiding the existing grid section and adding a new tree control. Tree nodes are always generated from the code, and the class mentioned above will do exactly that. On the form, we declare and initialize the `modelTree` object and build the tree in the form's `init()`.

In order to ensure that the currently selected tree node is displayed on the form on the right, we override the tree control's `selectionChanged()` event which is triggered every time a tree node is selected. Here we locate a corresponding record and place a cursor on that record.

The rest of the code on the form is to ensure that the tree is rebuilt whenever the data is modified.

There's more...

In this section we will discuss how to improve tree control's performance and how to enable its drag-and-drop functionality.

Performance

Tree hierarchy generation might be time consuming, so for bigger trees it is not beneficial to build the whole tree initially. Instead, it is better to generate only a visible part of the tree, which most of the time is a first level of nodes, and generate the rest of the branches only when/if the user expands them. This could be achieved by placing the relevant code into the `expanding()` method of the tree control which represents an event when a tree node is being expanded. Such an approach ensures that no system resources are used on generating unused tree nodes.

Drag-and-drop

Besides hierarchical layout, tree controls also allow users to use drag-and-drop functionality. This makes daily operations much quicker and more effective. Let's modify the previous example to support drag-and-drop. We are going to allow the users to move ledger budget submodels to different parents within the tree. In order to do that, we need to make some changes to the BudgetModelTree class and the **BudgetModel** form. Add the following code to the BudgetModelTree class declaration:

```
TreeItemIdx dragItemIdx;
TreeItemIdx lastItemIdx;
```

Create the following additional methods in this class:

```
private boolean canMove()
{
    BudgetModel model;
    RecId        recId;

    recId = tree.getItem(dragItemIdx).data();

    select firstOnly recId from model
        where model.RecId == recId
            && model.Type  == HeadingSub::SubModel;

    return model.RecId ? true : false;
}

private void move(RecId _from, RecId _to)
{
    BudgetModel modelFrom;
    BudgetModel modelTo;

    select firstOnly ModelId from modelTo
        where modelTo.RecId == _to;

    ttsBegin;

    select firstOnly forupdate modelFrom
        where modelFrom.RecId == _from;

    modelFrom.ModelId = modelTo.ModelId;

    if (modelFrom.validateWrite())
    {
```

```
            modelFrom.update();
        }

        ttsCommit;
    }

    public void stateDropHilite(TreeItemIdx _idx)
    {
        FormTreeItem item;

        if (lastItemIdx)
        {
            item = tree.getItem(lastItemIdx);
            item.stateDropHilited(false);
            tree.setItem(item);
            lastItemIdx = 0;
        }

        if (_idx)
        {
            item = tree.getItem(_idx);
            item.stateDropHilited(true);
            tree.setItem(item);
            lastItemIdx = _idx;
        }
    }

    public int beginDrag(int _x, int _y)
    {
        [dragItemIdx] = tree.hitTest(_x, _y);
        return 1;
    }

    public FormDrag dragOver(
        FormControl _dragSource,
        FormDrag    _dragMode,
        int         _x,
        int         _y)
    {
        TreeItemIdx currItemIdx;

        if (!this.canMove())
        {
            return FormDrag::None;
```

```
        }

        [currItemIdx] = tree.hitTest(_x, _y);

        this.stateDropHilite(currItemIdx);

        return FormDrag::Move;
    }

    public void drop(
        FormControl  _dragSource,
        FormDrag     _dragMode,
        int          _x,
        int          _y)
    {
        TreeItemIdx currItemIdx;

        if (!this.canMove())
        {
            return;
        }

        this.stateDropHilite(0);

        [currItemIdx] = tree.hitTest(_x,_y);

        if (!currItemIdx)
        {
            return;
        }

        this.move(
            tree.getItem(dragItemIdx).data(),
            tree.getItem(currItemIdx).data());

        tree.moveItem(dragItemIdx, currItemIdx);

    }
```

In the AOT, locate the **BudgetModel** form, find its **Tree** control, and change the following property:

Property	Value
DragDrop	Manual

Also, override the following methods of the **Tree** control:

```
public int beginDrag(int _x, int _y)
{
    return modelTree.beginDrag(_x, _y);
}

public FormDrag dragOver(
    FormControl _dragSource,
    FormDrag    _dragMode,
    int         _x,
    int         _y)
{
    return modelTree.dragOver(
        _dragSource,
        _dragMode,
        _x,
        _y);
}

public void drop(
    FormControl _dragSource,
    FormDrag    _dragMode,
    int         _x,
    int         _y)
{
    modelTree.drop(_dragSource, _dragMode, _x, _y);
}
```

Now, when you open **Budgeting | Setup | Budget models**, you should be able to move budget models within the tree with a mouse.

The main element in the latter modification is the **DragDrop** property of the tree control. It enables the drag-and-drop functionality in the tree, once we set its value to **Manual**. The next step is to override the drag-and-drop events on the tree control. Trees can have a number of methods covering various drag-and-drop events. A good place to start investigating them is the **Tutorial_Form_TreeControl** form in the standard application. In this example, we will cover only three of them:

- ▶ `beginDrag()` is executed when dragging begins. Here, we normally store the number of the item that is being dragged for later processing.

- ▶ `dragOver()` is executed once the dragged item is over another node. This method is responsible for highlighting nodes when the dragged item is over them. Its return value defines the mouse cursor icon once the item is being dragged.

- ▶ `drop()` is executed when the mouse button is released that is, the dragged item is dropped over a node. Here, we normally place the code that does actual data modifications.

In this example, all logic is stored in the `BudgetModelTree` class. Each of the mentioned form methods call the corresponding method in the class. This is to reduce the amount of code placed on the form and allow the code to be reused on multiple forms. We added the following methods to the class:

- ▶ `canMove()` checks whether the currently selected node can be dragged. Although there might be more conditions, for this demonstration we only disallow dragging of top nodes.

- ▶ `move()` is where the actual movement of the budget model is performed that is, the submodel is assigned with another parent.

- ▶ `stateDropHilite()` is responsible for highlighting and removing highlighting from relevant items. Using `stateDropHilited()`, we highlight the current item and we remove highlighting from the previously highlighted one. This ensures that as we move the dragged item over the tree, items are highlighted once the dragged item is over them and the highlight is removed once the dragged item leaves them. This method is called later from several places to make sure node highlighting works correctly.

- ▶ `beginDrag()` saves the item currently being dragged into a variable.

- ▶ `dragOver()` first checks if the currently selected item can be moved. If not, then it returns `FormDrag::None`, which changes the mouse cursor to the forbidden sign. Otherwise, the cursor is changed to an icon representing node movement. This method also calls `stateDropHilite()` to ensure correct node highlighting.

- ▶ `drop()` also checks if the item being dropped can be moved. If yes, then it uses `move()` to update the data and `moveItem()` to visually change the node's place in the tree. It also calls `stateDropHilite()` to update tree node highlighting.

Chapter 3, Working with Data in Forms:

▶   *Preloading images*

Chapter 4, Building Lookups:

▶   *Building a tree lookup*

Building a checklist

Anyone who has performed a Dynamics AX application installation or upgrade has to be familiar with standard checklists. Normally, a checklist is a list of menu items displayed in a logical sequence. Each item represents either mandatory or optional action to be executed by the user in order to complete the whole procedure. In custom Dynamics AX implementations, checklists can be used as a convenient way to configure non-standard settings. Checklists can also be implemented as a part of third-party modules for their initial setup.

In this recipe, we will create a checklist for user-friendly ledger budget setup. The checklist will consist of two mandatory items and one optional item.

How to do it...

Carry out the following steps in order to complete this recipe:

1. Open the AOT, and create a new interface named `SysCheckListInterfaceBudget`:

```
interface SysCheckListInterfaceBudget
extends    SysCheckListInterface
{
}
```

2. Create three classes, one for each checklist item, with the following code:

```
class       SysCheckListItem_BudgetModel
extends     SysCheckListItem
implements SysCheckListInterfaceBudget
{
}

public str getCheckListGroup()
{
    return "Setup";
}
```

```
public str getHelpLink()
{
    #define.TopicId('Dynamics://DynamicsHelp/Topic?Id=' +
        '84030522-0057-412c-bfc7-dbeb4d40e5a1')
    return #TopicId;
}

public MenuItemName getMenuItemName()
{
    return menuitemDisplayStr(BudgetModel);
}

public MenuItemType getMenuItemType()
{
    return MenuItemType::Display;
}

public str label()
{
    return "Models";
}


class       SysCheckListItem_BudgetCode
extends     SysCheckListItem
implements SysCheckListInterfaceBudget
{
}

public void new()
{
    super();
    this.placeAfter(classNum(SysCheckListItem_BudgetModel));
}

public str getCheckListGroup()
{
    return "Setup";
}

public str getHelpLink()
{
    #define.TopicId('Dynamics://DynamicsHelp/Topic?Id=' +
        'd42c3c30-d3b3-4d71-aa86-396516a3c8ee')
```

```
        return #TopicId;
}

public MenuItemName getMenuItemName()
{
        return menuitemDisplayStr(BudgetTransactionCode);
}

public MenuItemType getMenuItemType()
{
        return MenuItemType::Display;
}

public str label()
{
        return "Codes";
}


class      SysCheckListItem_Budget
extends    SysCheckListItem
implements SysCheckListInterfaceBudget
{
}

public void new()
{
        super();

        this.addDependency(classNum(SysCheckListItem_BudgetModel));
        this.addDependency(classNum(SysCheckListItem_BudgetCode));
        this.placeAfter(classNum(SysCheckListItem_BudgetCode));
        this.indeterminate(true);
}

public str getCheckListGroup()
{
        return "Create budgets";
}

public str getHelpLink()
{
        #define.TopicId('Dynamics://DynamicsHelp/Topic?Id=' +
            '846e3e47-acc3-4a86-bbd3-678a62d2953f')
```

```
        return #TopicId;
    }

    public MenuItemName getMenuItemName()
    {
        return menuitemDisplayStr(BudgetTransactionListPage);
    }

    public MenuItemType getMenuItemType()
    {
        return MenuItemType::Display;
    }

    public str label()
    {
        return "Budget register entries";
    }
```

3. Create another class for the checklist itself, with the following code:

```
class SysCheckList_Budget extends SysCheckList
{
    container log;
}

protected str getCheckListCaption()
{
    return "Budget checklist";
}

protected str getHtmlHeader()
{
    return "Budget checklist";
}

protected ClassId getInterfaceId()
{
    return classNum(SysCheckListInterfaceBudget);
}

public void save(
    IdentifierName    _name,
    ClassDescription _description = "")
{
    if (!conFind(log, _name))
    {
        log = conIns(log, conLen(log)+1, _name);
```

```
        }
    }

    public boolean find(
        IdentifierName    _name,
        ClassDescription _description = "")
    {
        return conFind(log, _name) ? true : false;
    }

    protected boolean isRunnable()
    {
        return true;
    }

    public static void main(Args _args)
    {
        SysCheckList::runCheckListSpecific(
            classNum(SysCheckList_Budget),
            true);
    }
```

4. Find the `SysCheckList` class in the AOT, and replace its `checkListItemsHook()` and `checkListsHook()` methods with the following code:

```
    protected static container checkListItemsHook()
    {
        return [classNum(SysCheckListItem_Budget),
                classNum(SysCheckListItem_BudgetCode),
                classNum(SysCheckListItem_BudgetModel)];
    }

    protected static container checkListsHook()
    {
        return [classNum(SysCheckList_Budget)];
    }
```

5. Open the **BudgetModel** form in the AOT, and override its `close()` method with the following code:

```
    public void close()
    {
        super();

        SysCheckList::finished(
            classNum(SysCheckListItem_BudgetModel));
    }
```

6. Open the **BudgetTransactionCode** form in the AOT, and override its `close()` with the following code:

```
public void close()
{
    super();

    SysCheckList::finished(
        classNum(SysCheckListItem_BudgetCode));
}
```

7. In the AOT, create a new action menu item with the following properties:

Property	Value
Name	SysCheckList_Budget
Label	Budget checklist
ObjectType	Class
Object	SysCheckList_Budget

8. To test the checklist, run the **SysCheckList_Budget** menu item from the AOT. The following should appear on the right-hand side of the Dynamics AX window:

9. Click on the listed items to start and complete the relevant actions. Notice how the status icons change upon completion of each task.

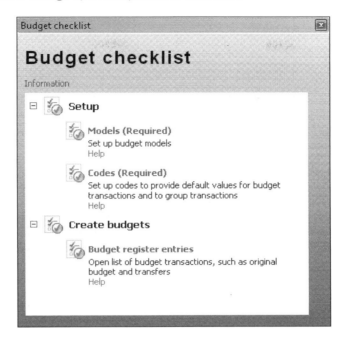

How it works...

The main principle when creating the checklist is that we have to create a main class, which represents the checklist itself, and a number of checklist item classes representing each item in the checklist. The main class has to extend the `SysCheckList` class, and the items must extend the `SysCheckListItem` class. The relation between the main class and the items is made by the use of an interface, that is, each list item implements it, and the main class holds the reference to it.

In this example, we create a new interface `SysCheckListInterfaceBudget` and specify it in the `getInterfaceId()` of the main checklist class `SysCheckList_Budget`. Next, we implement the interface in three `SysCheckListItem` classes, which correspond to **Models**, **Codes**, and **Budget register entries** items in the checklist.

Each `SysCheckListItem` class contains a set of inherited methods, which allows us to define a number of different parameters for individual items:

- ► All initialization code can be added to the `new()` methods. In this example, we use `placeAfter()` to determine the position of the item in the list relative to other items, `indeterminate()` to make an item optional and `addDependency()` to make an item inactive until another specified item is completed.

- ▶ `getCheckListGroup()` defines a group name of the current item. The budget checklist has two groups, **Setup** and **Create budgets**.

- ▶ `getHelpLink()` is responsible for placing the relevant help link.

- ▶ `getMenuItemName()` and `getMenuItemType()` contain a name and a type of a menu item, which is executed upon user request. Here, we have **Budget models**, **Budget codes**, and **Budget register entries** menu items, respectively, in each class.

- ▶ And, finally, custom labels can be set in the `label()` method.

Once the items are ready, we create the main checklist class `SysCheckList_Budget`, which extends the standard `SysCheckList` class. Next we override some of the methods to add custom functionality to the checklist:

- ▶ `getCheckListCaption()` sets the title of the checklist.

- ▶ `getHtmlHeader()` could be used to add some descriptive text.

- ▶ As mentioned earlier, `getInterfaceId()` is the place where we specify the name of the checklist item interface.

- ▶ The methods `save()` and `find()` are used to store and retrieve, respectively, the status of each item in the list. In this example, we store each status in the local variable `log` to make sure that each status is reset every time we run the checklist.

- ▶ The static method `main()` runs the class. Here, we use `runCheckListSpecific()` of the `SysCheckList` class to start the checklist.

The display menu item we have created points to the checklist class and may be used to add the checklist to a user menu.

When building checklists, it is necessary to add them and their items to the global checklist and checklist item list. The `SysCheckList` class contains two methods: `checkLists()` and `checkListItems()`, where all system checklists and their items are registered. The same class provides two more methods—`checkListsHook()` and `checkListItemsHook`—where custom checklists should be added. As a part of this example, we also add our budget checklist and its items to the `SysCheckList` class.

Final modifications have to be done on each form called by the checklist. We call the `finished()` method of the `SysCheckList` class, within the `close()` method of each form, to update the status of the corresponding checklist item. This means that the checklist item status will be set as completed when the user closes the form. Obviously, this will not ensure that each checklist item was completed successfully, but still gives some level of control. This code does not affect the normal use of the form when it is opened from the regular menu. Normally, more logic is added here if the completion of a specific item is not that straightforward.

There's more...

The checklist in this example stores each item status per single run. This means that every time you close the checklist, each status is lost and is set to their initial states upon checklist start. By replacing `save()` and `find()` in the `SysCheckList_Budget` with the following code, we can permanently store the status in the `SysSetupLog` table:

```
public boolean find(
    IdentifierName    _name,
    ClassDescription  _description = "")
{
    return (SysSetupLog::find(_name, _description).RecId != 0);
}

public void save(
    IdentifierName    _name,
    ClassDescription  _description = "")
{
    SysSetupLog::save(_name, _description);
}
```

In this case, every time the checklist starts, the system will pick up its last status from the `SysSetupLog` table and allow the user to continue the checklist.

Adding the View details link

Dynamics AX has a very useful feature, which allows the user to open the main record form with just a few mouse clicks on the current form. The feature is called **View details** and is available in the right-click context menu on some controls. It is based on table relationships and is available for those controls whose data fields have foreign key relationships with other tables.

Because of the data structure integrity, the **View details** feature works most of the time. However, when it comes to complex table relations, it does not work correctly or does not work at all. Another example of when this feature does not work automatically is when display or edit methods are used on a form. In those and many other cases, the **View details** feature has to be implemented manually.

In this recipe, to demonstrate how it works, we will modify the **General journal** form in the **General ledger** module and will add the **View details** feature to the **Description** control, allowing users to jump from the right-click context menu to the **Journal names** form.

How to do it...

Carry out the following steps in order to complete this recipe:

1. Open the **LedgerJournalTable** form in the AOT, expand its data sources, and override jumpRef() of the **Name** field on the **LedgerJournalTable** data source with the following code:

```
public void jumpRef()
{
    LedgerJournalName    name;
    Args                 args;
    MenuFunction         mf;

    name = LedgerJournalName::find(
        LedgerJournalTable.JournalName);

    if (!name)
    {
        return;
    }

    args = new Args();
    args.caller(element);
    args.record(name);

    mf = new MenuFunction(
        menuitemDisplayStr(LedgerJournalSetup),
        MenuItemType::Display);
    mf.run(args);
}
```

2. Go to **General ledger | Journals | General journal**, select any of the existing records, and right-click on the **Description** column. Notice that the **View details** option, which will open the **Journal names** form, is now available:

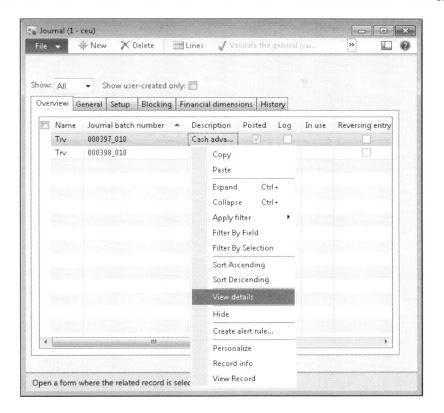

How it works...

Normally, the **View details** feature is controlled by the relationships between the underlying tables. If there are no relations or the form control is not bound to a table field, then this option is not available. We can force this option to appear by overriding the control's or data source field's `jumpRef()` method.

In this method, we add code that opens the relevant form. This can be done by declaring, instantiating, and running a `FormRun` object, but the easier way is to simply run the relevant menu item from code. In this recipe, the code in `jumpRef()` does exactly that.

In the code, first we check if a valid journal name record is found. If yes, we run the **LedgerJournalSetup** menu item with the `Args` object holding the journal name record and the current form object as a caller. The rest is done automatically by the system, that is, the **Journal names** form is opened with the currently selected journal name.

3
Working with Data in Forms

In this chapter, we will cover:

- ► Using a number sequence handler
- ► Creating a custom filter
- ► Creating a custom instant search filter
- ► Building a selected/available list
- ► Preloading images
- ► Creating a wizard
- ► Processing multiple records
- ► Coloring records
- ► Adding an image to records

Introduction

This chapter basically supplements the previous one and explains data organization in the forms. It shows how to add custom filters to forms in order to allow users to filter data and how to create record lists for quick data manipulation.

This chapter also discusses how displaying data could be enhanced by adding icons to record lists and trees, and how normal images could be stored along with the data, reusing existing Dynamics AX application objects.

A couple of recipes will show how to create wizards to guide users through complex tasks. This chapter will also show how to create a wizard to guide users through complex tasks. It will demonstrate several approaches for capturing user-selected records on forms, and how to distinguish specific records by coloring them.

Using a number sequence handler

As already discussed in the *Creating a new number sequence* recipe in *Chapter 1, Processing Data*, number sequences are widely used throughout the system as part of the standard application. Dynamics AX also provides a special number sequence handler class to be used on forms. It is called `NumberSeqFormHandler` and its purpose is to simplify the usage of record numbering on the user interface. Some of the standard Dynamics AX forms, such as **Customers** or **Vendors**, already have this feature implemented.

This recipe will show how to use the number sequence handler class. Although in this demonstration we will use an existing form, the same approach should be applied when creating brand new forms.

For demonstration purposes we will use an existing **Customer groups** form located in **Accounts receivable | Setup | Customers** and we will change the **Customer group** field from manual to automatic numbering. We will use the number sequence created earlier in the *Creating a new number sequence* recipe in *Chapter 1, Processing Data*.

How to do it...

Carry out the following steps in order to complete this recipe:

1. In the AOT, open the **CustGroup** form and add the following code to its class declaration:

    ```
    NumberSeqFormHandler numberSeqFormHandler;
    ```

2. Also, create a new method called `numberSeqFormHandler()` in the same form:

    ```
    public NumberSeqFormHandler numberSeqFormHandler()
    {
        if (!numberSeqFormHandler)
        {
            numberSeqFormHandler = NumberSeqFormHandler::newForm(
                CustParameters::numRefCustGroupId().NumberSequenceId,
                element,
                CustGroup_ds,
                fieldNum(CustGroup,CustGroup));
        }
        return numberSeqFormHandler;
    }
    ```

3. In the same form, override the **CustGroup** data source's `create()` method with the following code:

```
public void create(boolean _append = false)
{
    element.numberSeqFormHandler(
        ).formMethodData sourceCreatePre();

    super(_append);

    element.numberSeqFormHandler(
        ).formMethodData sourceCreate();
}
```

4. In the same data source, override its `delete()` method with the following code:

```
public void delete()
{
    ttsBegin;

    element.numberSeqFormHandler().formMethodData sourceDelete();

    super();

    ttsCommit;
}
```

5. In the same data source, override its `write()` method with the following code:

```
public void write()
{
    ttsBegin;

    super();

    element.numberSeqFormHandler().formMethodData sourceWrite();

    ttsCommit;
}
```

6. In the same data source, override its `validateWrite()` method with the following code:

```
public boolean validateWrite()
{
    boolean ret;
```

```
    ret = super();

    ret = element.numberSeqFormHandler(
        ).formMethodData sourceValidateWrite(ret) && ret;

    return ret;
}
```

7. In the same data source, override its `linkActive()` method with the following code:

```
public void linkActive()
{
    element.numberSeqFormHandler(
        ).formMethodData sourceLinkActive();

    super();
}
```

8. Finally, override the form's `close()` method with the following code:

```
public void close()
{
    if (numberSeqFormHandler)
    {
        numberSeqFormHandler.formMethodClose();
    }

    super();
}
```

9. In order to test the numbering, open **Accounts receivable | Setup | Customers | Customer groups** and try to create several new records—the **Customer group** value should be generated automatically:

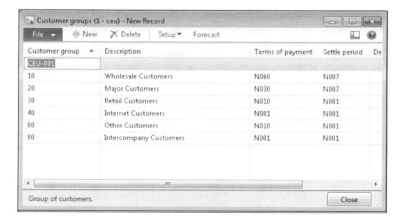

How it works...

First, we declare an object of type `NumberSeqFormHandler` in the form's class declaration. Then, we create a new corresponding form method `numberSeqFormHandler()`, which instantiates the object if it is not yet instantiated and returns it. This method allows us to hold the handler creation code in one place and reuse it many times within the form.

In the method, we use the `newForm()` constructor of the `NumberSeqFormHandler` class to create the `numberSeqFormHandler` object. It accepts the following arguments:

- ▸ The number sequence code, which was created in the prerequisite recipe, and which ensures a proper format of the customer group numbering. Here, we call the `numRefCustGroupId()` helper method from the `CustParameters` table to find which number sequence code should be used when creating new customer group record.
- ▸ The form object itself.
- ▸ The form data source where we need to apply the number sequence handler.
- ▸ The field number of the field into which the number sequence will be populated.

Finally, we add various `NumberSeqFormHandler` methods to the corresponding methods on the form's data source to ensure a proper handling of the numbering when various events are triggered.

See also

Chapter 1, Processing Data:

- ▸ *Creating a new number sequence*

Creating a custom filter

Filtering on forms in Dynamics AX is implemented in a variety of ways. As a part of the standard application, Dynamics AX provides various filtering options, such as **Filter By Selection**, **Filter By Grid**, or **Advanced Filter/Sort**, located in the toolbar to allow you to modify the underlying query of the currently displayed form. In addition to the standard filters, the Dynamics AX list pages normally allow quick filtering on most commonly used fields. Besides that, some of the existing forms have even more advanced filtering options, allowing users to quickly define complex search criteria. Although the latter option needs additional programming, it is more user-friendly than standard filtering and is a very common request in most Dynamics AX implementations.

In this recipe, we will learn how to add custom filters to a form. We will use the **Main accounts** form as a basis and will add a custom filter, allowing users to list only accounts of a certain type. We will also implement an option allowing you to quickly disable the filter.

How to do it...

Carry out the following steps in order to complete this recipe:

1. In the AOT, locate the **MainAccountListPage** form and change the following property for its **Filter** group:

Property	Value
Columns	2

2. In the same group, add a new CheckBox control with the following properties:

Property	Value
Name	FilterShowAll
AutoDeclaration	Yes
Label	Show all

3. Add a new ComboBox control to the same group with the following properties:

Property	Value
Name	FilterType
AutoDeclaration	Yes
EnumType	DimensionLedgerAccountType

4. Override the modified() methods for both the newly created controls with the following code:

```
public boolean modified()
{
    boolean ret;

    ret = super();

    if (ret)
    {
        MainAccount_ds.executeQuery();
    }
```

```
        return ret;
}
```

5. After all of these modifications in the AOT, the **MainAccountListPage** form should look similar to the following screenshot:

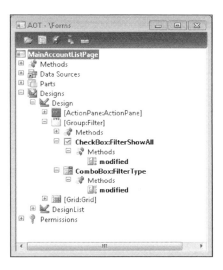

6. In the same form, override the `executeQuery()` method of the **MainAccount** data source with the following code:

```
public void executeQuery()
{
    QueryBuildRange qbrType;

    qbrType = SysQuery::findOrCreateRange(
        MainAccount_q.data sourceTable(tableNum(MainAccount)),
        fieldNum(MainAccount,Type));

    if (filterShowAll.value())
    {
        qbrType.value(SysQuery::valueUnlimited());
    }
    else
    {
        qbrType.value(queryValue(filterType.selection()));
    }

    super();
}
```

7. In order to test the filter, open **General ledger | Common | Main accounts** and change the values in the newly created filters—the account list should change reflecting the selected criteria:

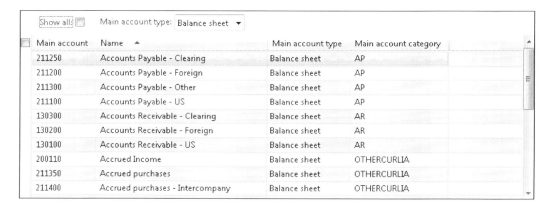

8. Click on the **Advanced Filter/Sort** button in the toolbar to inspect how the criteria was applied in the underlying query:

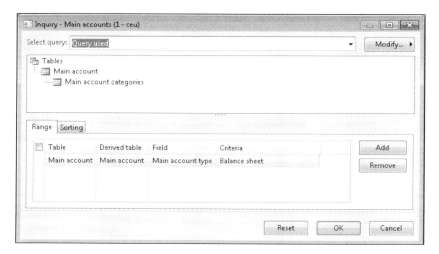

How it works...

We start by changing the **Columns** property of the existing empty **Filter** group control to make sure all our controls are placed from left to right in one line. It is good practice to have the **Filter** group on the list page forms even if it is empty; in some cases, it is added automatically by the system.

Next, we add two controls representing the **Show all** and **Main account type** filters and enable them to be automatically declared for later usage in the code. We also override the `modified()` event methods to ensure that the `MainAccount` data source's query is re-executed whenever the control values change.

Finally, we place all the code in the `executeQuery()` method, which is responsible for data fetching. The code has to be placed before `super()` to make sure the query is modified before fetching the data.

Here we declare and create a new `QueryBuildRange` object representing the type range on the query. We use the `findOrCreateRange()` method of the `SysQuery` application class to get the range object. The method is very useful as if the range already exists, it will return it, and if not then it will create a new one.

Once the range is ready, we set its value. If the **Show all** filter is selected, we use `valueUnlimited()` of the `SysQuery` application class to clear the range, to show all records. Otherwise, we pass the user selected account type to the range. The global `queryValue()` function—which is actually a shortcut to `SysQuery::value()`—ensures that only safe characters are passed to the range. It is recommended to use this function whenever the user is allowed to change query range values directly.

Note that the `SysQuery` helper class is very useful when working with queries, it does all kinds of input data conversions to make sure they can be safely used. Here is a brief summary of some of the `SysQuery` methods:

- `valueUnlimited()` returns a string representing an unlimited query range value, therefore no range at all.
- `value()` converts an argument to a safe string. Global `queryValue()` is a shortcut for this.
- `valueNot()` converts an argument to a safe string and adds an inversion sign before it.

See also

In *Chapter 1, Processing Data*:

- *Building a query object*

Creating a custom instant search filter

The standard form filters and the majority of customized form filters in Dynamics AX are only applied once the user presses a button or a key. It is acceptable in most cases, especially if multiple criteria are used. However, when the result retrieval speed and usage simplicity has priority over system performance, it is possible to set up the search function so the record list is updated instantly while the user is typing.

In this recipe, to demonstrate the instant search we will modify the **Main accounts** form. We will add a custom filter **Account name**, which will update the account list automatically while the user is typing.

How to do it...

Carry out the following steps in order to complete this recipe:

1. In the AOT, open the **MainAccountListPage** form and add a new `StringEdit` control with the following properties to the existing **Filter** group:

Property	Value
Name	FilterName
AutoDeclaration	Yes
ExtendedDataType	AccountName

2. Override its `textChange()` method with the following code:

   ```
   public void textChange()
   {
       super();

       MainAccount_ds.executeQuery();
   }
   ```

3. Override the control's `enter()` method with the following code:

   ```
   public void enter()
   {
       super();
       this.setSelection(
           strLen(this.text()),
           strLen(this.text()));
   }
   ```

4. Override the `executeQuery()` method of the **MainAccount** data source with the following code:

   ```
   public void executeQuery()
   {
       QueryBuildRange qbrName;

       qbrName = SysQuery::findOrCreateRange(
           this.queryBuildData source(),
           fieldNum(MainAccount, Name));
   ```

```
qbrName.value(
    FilterName.text() ?
    '*'+queryValue(FilterName.text())+'*' :
    SysQuery::valueUnlimited());

    super();
}
```

5. In order to test the search, open **General ledger | Common | Main accounts** and start typing in the **Account name** filter. Notice how the account list is being filtered automatically:

Account name:	cash			
Main account	Name ▲	Main account type	Main account category	
110155	All Other Cash Advanc...	Balance sheet	CASH	
110153	CAD Cash Advances A...	Balance sheet	CASH	
110101	Cash Advance returns	Balance sheet	CASH	
520201	Cash Discounts Received	Profit and loss		
520200	Cash discounts taken	Profit and loss	SALERETDIS	
618150	Cash discrepancies	Profit and loss	OTHEREXP	
110170	Cash in bank - US (Fixe...	Balance sheet	CASH	
110152	EUR Cash Advances Ac...	Balance sheet	CASH	
110180	Petty cash account	Balance sheet	CASH	

How it works...

First, we add a new control which represents the **Account name** filter. Normally the user typing triggers the `textChange()` event method on the active control every time a character is entered. So we override this method and add code to re-execute the form's query whenever a new character is typed in.

Next, we have to correct the cursor's behavior. Currently, once the user types in the first character, the search is executed and the system moves the focus out of this control and then moves back to the control, selecting all the typed text. If the user continues typing, the existing text will be overwritten with the new character and the loop will continue.

In order to fix this behavior, we have to override the control's `enter()` event method. This method is called every time the control receives a focus, whether it was done by the user's mouse, key, or by the system. Here, we call the `setSelection()` method. Normally, the purpose of this method is to mark a control's text or a part of it as selected. Its first argument specifies the beginning of the selection and the second one specifies the end. In this recipe, we are using this method in a slightly different way. We pass the length of the typed text as a first argument, which means the selection starts at the end of the text. We pass the same value as a second argument, which means that selection ends at the end of the text. It does not make any sense from the selection point of view, but it ensures that the cursor always stays at the end of the typed text, allowing the user to continue typing.

The last thing to do is to add some code to the `executeQuery()` method to change the query before it is executed. Modifying the query was discussed in detail in the *Creating a custom filter* recipe in this chapter. The only thing to note here is that we add asterisks to the beginning and the end of the search string to make the search by a partial string.

Notice that system performance might be affected as the data search is executed every time the user types in a character. It is not recommended to use this approach for large tables.

See also

In this chapter:

> ▶ *Creating a custom filter*

Building a selected/available list

Frequent users might notice that some of the Dynamics AX forms contain two sections placed next to each other and allow moving items from one side to the other. Normally, the right section contains a list of possible values and the left one contains a list of the already selected values. Buttons in the middle allow data to be moved from one side to another. Double-click and drag-and-drop mouse events are also supported. Such a design improves the user experience as data manipulation becomes more user-friendly. Some of the examples in the standard application are **General ledger** | **Setup** | **Financial dimensions** | **Financial dimension sets** or **System administration** | **Common** | **Users** | **User groups**.

This functionality is based on the `SysListPanelRelationTable` application class. Developers only need to create its instance with the required parameters on the form where the list is required, and the rest is done automatically.

This recipe will show the basic principle of how to create selected/available lists. We will add an option for assigning customers to buyer groups in the **Buyer groups** form in the **Inventory management** module.

How to do it...

Carry out the following steps in order to complete this recipe:

1. In the AOT, create a new table named **InventBuyerGroupList**. Do not change any of the properties as this table is for demonstration only.

2. Add a new field to the table with the following properties (click on **Yes** if asked to add a new relation to the table):

Property	Value
Type	String
Name	GroupId
ExtendedDataType	ItemBuyerGroupId

3. Add another field to the table with the following properties:

Property	Value
Type	String
Name	CustAccount
ExtendedDataType	CustAccount

4. In the AOT, open the **InventBuyerGroup** form and change the design properties as follows:

Property	Value
Style	Auto

5. Add a new Tab control with the following properties, to the bottom of the design:

Property	Value
Width	Column width
Height	Column height

6. Add a new TabPage control with the following properties to the newly created tab:

Property	Value
Name	BuyerGroups
Caption	Buyer groups

7. Add another TabPage control with the following properties to the newly created tab:

Property	Value
Name	Customers
Caption	Customers

8. Move the existing **Grid** control to the first tab page and hide the existing **Body** group by setting the property:

Property	Value
Visible	No

9. The form should look similar to the following screenshot:

10. Add the following line to the form's class declaration:

```
SysListPanelRelationTable sysListPanel;
```

11. Override the form's `init()` method with the following code:

```
public void init()
{
    container columns;
    #ResAppl

    columns = [fieldNum(CustTable, AccountNum)];


    sysListPanel = SysListPanelRelationTable::newForm(
        element,
        element.controlId(
            formControlStr(InventBuyerGroup,Customers)),
        "Selected",
        "Available",
```

```
                #ImageCustomer,
                tableNum(InventBuyerGroupList),
                fieldNum(InventBuyerGroupList,CustAccount),
                fieldNum(InventBuyerGroupList,GroupId),
                tableNum(CustTable),
                fieldNum(CustTable,AccountNum),
                columns);

        super();

        sysListPanel.init();

    }
```

12. Override the `pageActivated()` method on the newly created **Customers** tab page with the following code:

```
public void pageActivated()
{
    sysListPanel.parmRelationRangeValue(
        InventBuyerGroup.Group);

    sysListPanel.parmRelationRangeRecId(
        InventBuyerGroup.RecId);

    sysListPanel.fill();

    super();
}
```

13. In order to test the list, open **Inventory and warehouse management | Setup | Inventory | Buyer groups**, select any group, go to the **Customers** tab page and use the buttons provided to move records from one side to the other. You could also do a double-click or drag-and-drop with your mouse:

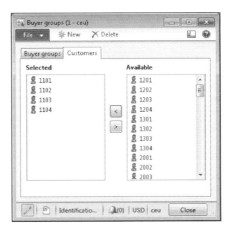

How it works...

In this recipe, the **InventBuyerGroupList** table is used as a many-to-many relationship table between buyer groups and customers.

In terms of form design, the only thing that needs to be added is a new tab page. The rest is created dynamically by the `SysListPanelRelationTable` application class.

In the form's class declaration, we declare a new variable based on the `SysListPanelRelationTable` class and instantiate it in the form's `init()` method using the `newForm()` constructor. The method accepts the following parameters:

- ▸ The form object.
- ▸ The name of the tab page.
- ▸ The label of the left section.
- ▸ The label of the right section.
- ▸ The number of the image that is shown next to each record in the list.
- ▸ The relationship table number.
- ▸ The field number in the relationship table representing the child record. In our case it is the customer account number—**CustAccount**.
- ▸ The field number in the relationship table representing the parent table. In this case, it is the buyer group number—**GroupId**.
- ▸ The number of the table that is displayed in the list.
- ▸ A container of the field numbers displayed in each column.

We also have to initialize the list by calling the member method `init()` in the form's `init()` method right after its `super()`.

The list controls are created dynamically when the **Customers** tab page is opened. In order to accommodate that we add the list's creation code to the `pageActivated()` event method of the newly created tab page. In this way, we ensure that the list is populated whenever a new buyer group is selected.

There's more...

The `SysListPanelRelationTable` class can only display fields from one table. In the previous example, we only used the customer account number, but it would have been impossible for the customer name to be stored in a different table as it can only be retrieved by using the `name()` method on the **CustTable** table.

For this purpose, we can use another application class named
`SysListPanelRelationTableCallback`, which allows you to create customized lists.
In order to demonstrate its capabilities, we will expand the previous example to display the
customer name along with its account number.

First, in the form's class declaration, we have to change the list declaration to the following
code line:

```
SysListPanelRelationTableCallback sysListPanel;
```

Next, we create two new methods—one for the left list, the other for the right – which
generates and returns data containers to be displayed in each section:

```
private container selectedCustomers()
{
    container             ret;
    container             data;
    CustTable             custTable;
    InventBuyerGroupList groupList;

    while select custTable
        exists join groupList
            where groupList.CustAccount == custTable.AccountNum
                && groupList.GroupId     == InventBuyerGroup.Group

    {
        data = [custTable.AccountNum,
                custTable.AccountNum,
                custTable.name()];

        ret = conIns(ret, conLen(ret)+1, data);
    }

    return ret;
}

private container availableCustomers()
{
    container             ret;
    container             data;
    CustTable             custTable;
    InventBuyerGroupList groupList;

    while select custTable
        notExists join firstOnly groupList
            where groupList.CustAccount == custTable.AccountNum
```

```
                    && groupList.GroupId      == InventBuyerGroup.Group
        {
            data = [custTable.AccountNum,
                    custTable.AccountNum,
                    custTable.name()];

            ret = conIns(ret, conLen(ret)+1, data);
        }


        return ret;
    }
```

Each method returns a container of containers. The inner container represents one line in the section and it contains three items—the first is an identification number of the line and the next two are displayed on the screen.

Finally, we replace the form's init() method with the following code:

```
    public void init()
    {
        container columns;
        #ResAppl

        columns = [0, 0];

        sysListPanel = SysListPanelRelationTableCallback::newForm(
            element,
            element.controlId(
                formControlStr(InventBuyerGroup,Customers)),
            "Selected",
            "Available",
            #ImageCustomer,
            tableNum(InventBuyerGroupList),
            fieldNum(InventBuyerGroupList,CustAccount),
            fieldNum(InventBuyerGroupList,GroupId),
            tableNum(CustTable),
            fieldNum(CustTable,AccountNum),
            columns,
            0,
            '',
            '',
            identifierStr(selectedCustomers),
            identifierStr(availableCustomers));

        super();

        sysListPanel.init();

    }
```

This time we used the `newForm()` constructor of the `SysListPanelRelationTableCallback` class, which is very similar to the previous one but accepts the names of methods as arguments, which will be used to populate the data in the right and left sections.

Notice, that the `columns` container that previously held a list of fields now contains two zeros. By doing this, we simply define that there will be two columns in each list and because the lists actually are generated outside the `SysListPanelRelationTableCallback` class, we do not need to specify the field numbers of the columns anymore.

Now, when you run the **Buyer groups** form, both sections contain a customer name column:

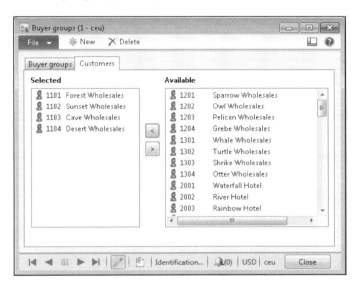

Preloading images

Some of the Dynamics AX controls, such as trees or lists, in most cases have small icon images in front of the text. The icons make the user interface look better and could represent a type, status, availability, or any other property of the current item in the control.

Images are binary data and processing them might be resource-demanding. The Dynamics AX application provides a way of handling images to increase application performance. Normally, for the forms with lists or trees, all required images are preloaded during the form initialization. This reduces the image loading time when the image is actually displayed to the user.

For this purpose, Dynamics AX contains a set of `ImageListAppl` derivative classes, which hold a specific set of image data required in specific circumstances. For example, the `ImageListAppl_Proj` class in the **Project management and accounting** module preloads project-related images representing project types during the project tree initialization. So, virtually no time is consumed for displaying the images later, when the user starts browsing the project tree control.

In this recipe, we will create a new image list class for image preloading. As a base, we will use the list created in the *Building a selected/available list* recipe in this chapter. We will enhance that list by showing different icons for customers on hold.

How to do it...

Carry out the following steps in order to complete this recipe:

1. In the AOT, create a new class named `ImageListAppl_Cust` with the following code:

   ```
   class ImageListAppl_Cust extends ImageListAppl
   {
   }

   protected void build()
   {
       super();
       this.add(#ImageCustomer);
       this.add(#ImageWarning);
   }
   ```

2. In the AOT, find the `SysListPanelRelationTableCallback` class and modify the `newForm()` method by adding one more argument to the end of the argument list:

   ```
   ImageListAppl _imageListAppl = null
   ```

3. In the same method, add the following code right before `sysListPanel.build()`:

   ```
   sysListPanel.parmImageList(_imageListAppl);
   ```

4. In the AOT, find the **InventBuyerGroup** form and add the following code to its class declaration:

   ```
   #ResAppl
   ```

5. On the same form, replace the existing methods with the following code:

   ```
   public void init()
   {
       container columns;
       ImageListAppl_Cust imageListAppl;
   ```

```
        columns = [0, 0];

        imageListAppl = new ImageListAppl_Cust(
            Imagelist::smallIconWidth(),
            Imagelist::smallIconHeight());

        sysListPanel = SysListPanelRelationTableCallback::newForm(
            element,
            element.controlId(
                formControlStr(InventBuyerGroup,Customers)),
            "Selected",
            "Available",
            0,
            tableNum(InventBuyerGroupList),
            fieldNum(InventBuyerGroupList,CustAccount),
            fieldNum(InventBuyerGroupList,GroupId),
            tableNum(CustTable),
            fieldNum(CustTable,AccountNum),
            columns,
            0,
            '',
            '',
            identifierStr(selectedCustomers),
            identifierStr(availableCustomers),
            0,
            imageListAppl);

        super();

        sysListPanel.init();

    }

    private container selectedCustomers()
    {
        container             ret;
        container             data;
        CustTable             custTable;
        InventBuyerGroupList groupList;

        while select custTable
            exists join groupList
                where groupList.CustAccount == custTable.AccountNum
                    && groupList.GroupId     == InventBuyerGroup.Group
```

```
    {
        data = [custTable.AccountNum,
                (custTable.Blocked==CustVendorBlocked::No ?
                    #ImageCustomer :
                    #ImageWarning),
                custTable.AccountNum,
                custTable.name()];

        ret = conIns(ret, conLen(ret)+1, data);
    }

    return ret;
}


private container availableCustomers()
{
    container           ret;
    container           data;
    CustTable           custTable;
    InventBuyerGroupList groupList;

    while select custTable
        notExists join firstOnly groupList
            where groupList.CustAccount == custTable.AccountNum
                && groupList.GroupId    == InventBuyerGroup.Group
    {
        data = [custTable.AccountNum,
                (custTable.Blocked==CustVendorBlocked::No ?
                    #ImageCustomer :
                    #ImageWarning),
                custTable.AccountNum,
                custTable.name()];

        ret = conIns(ret, conLen(ret)+1, data);
    }

    return ret;
}
```

6. In order to test the results, open **Inventory and warehouse management | Setup | Inventory | Buyer groups**, go to the **Customers** tab page and notice that customers on hold are now marked with a different icon:

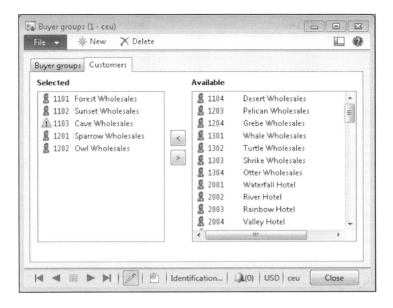

How it works...

The first task in this recipe is to create a class that handles the required set of images. We only need two different images—one for normal customers and one for customers on hold.

Standard Dynamics AX has lots of image resources, which we can select from for any given scenario. Most of these are listed in the `#ResAppl` macro library. We use the `add()` method to include relevant resources within the `build()` method of the new `ImageListAppl_Cust` class.

The second step is to modify the `SysListPanelRelationTableCallback` class to make sure the `newForm()` method accepts `ImageListAppl` as an argument and passes it to the class using the `parmImageList()` method. A new method could have been created here but it is not a good idea to copy so much code, especially when our changes are very small and do not affect the standard method's behavior as the parameter is set to `null` by default.

The final step is to modify the form. First, we instantiate a new `imageListAppl` object based on our class and pass it to the modified `newForm()` method as a last argument. At this stage, `sysListPanel` holds the images that we are going to use when displaying the lists and is going to reuse them from cache instead of loading every time from the original source. Then, we modify the form's `selectedItems()` and `availableItems()` methods to include image resource numbers in the returned data. We use the `#ImageCustomer` macro for normal customers and `#ImageWarning` for customers on hold. Notice that the inner container structure when using the `SysListPanelRelationTableCallback` class is different—the second element is an image resource number.

There's more...

As mentioned earlier, images can be used on tree controls too. In this section, we will enhance the tree created in the *Using a tree control* recipe in *Chapter 2, Working with Forms*. We will add small icons in front of each node.

First, in the AOT we create a new class called `ImageListAppl_LedgerBudget` with the following code:

```
class ImageListAppl_LedgerBudget extends ImageListAppl
{
}

protected void build()
{
    super();
    this.add(#ImageFolder);
    this.add(#ImageLedgerBudget);
}
```

As in the previous example, the class extends `ImageListAppl` and is responsible for preloading the images to be used on the tree. We will use only two different images—a folder icon for parent ledger budget models and a budget icon for submodels.

Next, we need to modify the `BudgetModelTree` class created in the earlier chapter. Let us add the following line to the bottom of the class declaration:

```
ImageListAppl imageListAppl;
```

Add the following code to the `buildTree()` method, right after the variable declaration section:

```
imageListAppl = new ImageListAppl_LedgerBudget();
tree.setImagelist(imageListAppl.imageList());
```

This creates an instance of the `ImageListAppl_LedgerBudget` class and passes it to the tree control.

Replace the `createNode()` method with the following code:

```
private TreeItemIdx createNode(
    TreeItemIdx    _parentIdx,
    BudgetModelId  _modelId,
    RecId          _recId)
{
    TreeItemIdx itemIdx;
    BudgetModel model;
    BudgetModel submodel;
    ImageRes    imageRes;
```

```
#ResAppl

if (_parentIdx == FormTreeAdd::Root)
{
    imageRes = imageListAppl.image(#ImageFolder);
}
else
{
    imageRes = imageListAppl.image(#ImageLedgerBudget);
}

model = BudgetModel::find(HeadingSub::Heading, _modelId);

itemIdx = SysFormTreeControl::addTreeItem(
    tree,
    _modelId + ' : ' + model.Txt,
    _parentIdx,
    _recId,
    imageRes,
    true);

if (modelId == _modelId)
{
    tree.select(itemIdx);
}

while select submodel
    where submodel.ModelId == _modelId &&
          submodel.Type     == HeadingSub::SubModel
{
    this.createNode(
        itemIdx,
        submodel.SubModelId,
        submodel.RecId);
}

return itemIdx;
}
```

At the top of this method, we check whether the current node is a parent node. If yes, then we set the image as the folder icon, otherwise—the budget model icon. Then, we pass the image to the addTreeItem() method.

In order to test the tree icons, open **Budgeting | Setup | Budget models** and notice how the tree has changed:

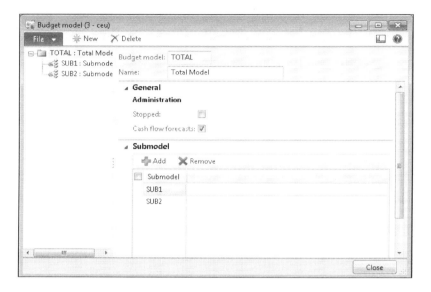

Chapter 2, Working with Forms:

▶ *Using a tree control*

Creating a wizard

Wizards in Dynamics AX are used to help a user to perform a specific task. Some examples of standard Dynamics AX wizards are **Report Wizard**, **Project Wizard**, **Number Sequence Wizard**, and so on.

Normally, a wizard is presented to a user as a form with a series of steps. While running the wizard, all user inputs are stored in temporary memory until the user presses the **Finish** button on the last wizard page.

In this recipe, we will create a new wizard for creating main accounts. First, we will use the standard Dynamics AX Wizard to create a framework and then we will manually add some additional controls.

How to do it...

Carry out the following steps in order to complete this recipe:

1. Open **Tools | Wizards | Wizard**.

2. Click on **Next** on the first page:

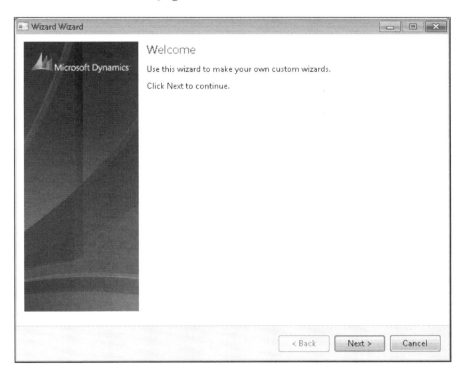

3. Select **Standard Wizard** and click on **Next**:

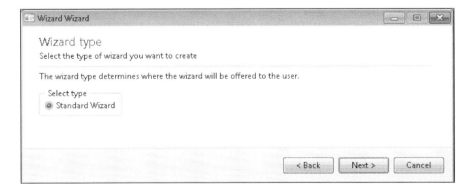

4. Specify **MainAccount** in the name field and click on **Next**:

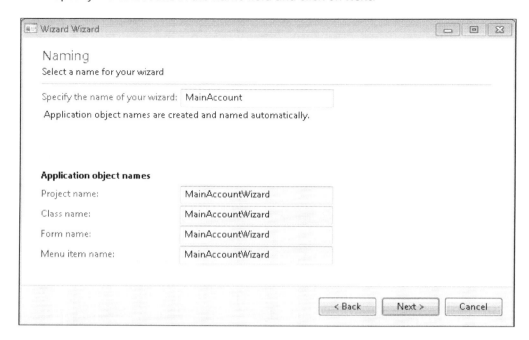

5. Accept the default number of steps and click on **Next**:

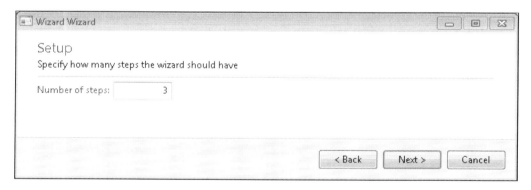

6. Click on **Finish** to complete the wizard:

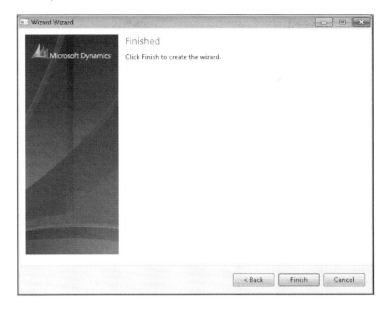

7. The wizard creates an AOT development project, with three new objects in it: a form, a class, and a menu item, as shown in the following screenshot:

8. Create a new macro library named `MainAccountWizard` with the following code:

```
#define.tabStep2(2)
```

9. Modify the `MainAccountWizard` class by adding the following code to its class declaration:

```
MainAccount mainAccount;
#MainAccountWizard
```

10. Add the following line to the existing `setupNavigation()` method in the same class:

```
nextEnabled[#tabStep2] = false;
```

11. Override the `finish()` method of the class with the following code:

```
protected void finish()
{
    mainAccount.initValue();
    mainAccount.LedgerChartOfAccounts =
        LedgerChartOfAccounts::current();
    mainAccount.MainAccountId = formRun.accountNum();
    mainAccount.Name = formRun.accountName();
    mainAccount.Type = formRun.accountType();

    super();
}
```

12. Replace the `validate()` method of the same class with the following code:

```
boolean validate()
{
    return mainAccount.validateWrite();
}
```

13. Replace the `run()` method of the same class with the following code:

```
void run()
{
    mainAccount.insert();

    info(strFmt(
        "Ledger account '%1' was successfully created",
        mainAccount.MainAccountId));
}
```

14. In the **MainAccountWizard** form, add the following code to the class declaration:

    ```
    #MainAccountWizard
    ```

15. Change the form's design property:

Property	Value
Caption	Main account wizard

16. Modify the properties of the **Step1** tab page as follows:

Property	Value
Caption	Welcome

17. Add a new StaticText control in this tab page with the following properties:

Property	Value
Name	WelcomeTxt
Text	This wizard helps you to create a new main account.

18. Modify the properties of the **Step2** tab page:

Property	Value
HelpText	Specify account number, name, and type.
Caption	Account setup

19. Add a new StringEdit control in this tab page with the following properties:

Property	Value
Name	AccountNum
AutoDeclaration	Yes
Label	Main account
ExtendedDataType	AccountNum

20. Add one more `StringEdit` control in this tab page with the following properties:

Property	Value
Name	AccountName
AutoDeclaration	Yes
ExtendedDataType	AccountName

21. Add a new `ComboBox` control in this tab page with the following properties:

Property	Value
Name	AccountType
AutoDeclaration	Yes
EnumType	DimensionLedgerAccountType

22. Modify the properties of the **Step3** tab page as follows:

Property	Value
Caption	Finish

23. Add a new `StaticText` control in this tab page with the following properties:

Property	Value
Name	FinishTxt
Text	This wizard is now ready to create new main account.

24. Create the following four methods at the top level of the form:

```
public MainAccountNum accountNum()
{
    return AccountNum.text();
}

public AccountName accountName()
{
    return AccountName.text();
}

public DimensionLedgerAccountType accountType()
{
    return AccountType.selection();
}
```

```
public void setNext()
{
    sysWizard.nextEnabled(
        this.accountNum() && this.accountName(),
        #tabStep2,
        false);
}
```

25. Now override the `textChange()` method on the **AccountNum** and **AccountName** controls with the following code:

```
public void textChange()
{
    super();
    element.setNext();
}
```

26. After all of the modifications, the form should look as follows:

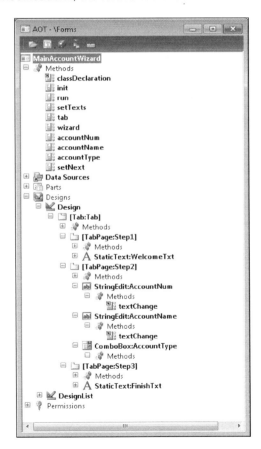

27. In order to test the newly created wizard, run the **MainAccountWizard** menu item. The wizard should appear. On the first page click **Next**:

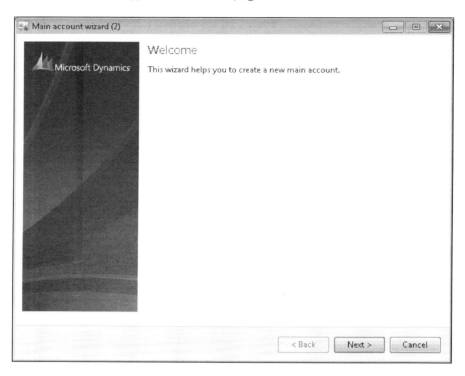

28. On the second page, specify **Main account**, **Account name**, and **Main account type**:

29. On the last page, click on **Finish** to complete the wizard:

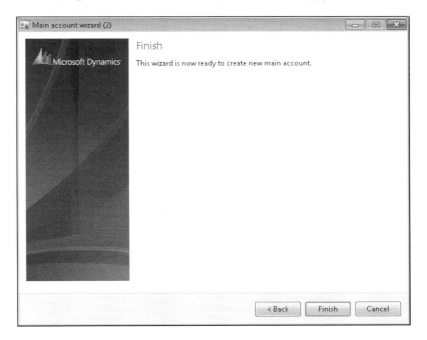

30. The Infolog should display a message to show that a new account was created successfully:

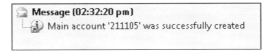

How it works...

The wizard creates three AOT objects for us:

► The `MainAccountWizard` class, which contains all the logic required to run the wizard.

► The **MainAccountWizard** form, which is the wizard layout.

► Finally, the **MainAccountWizard** display menu item, which is used to start the wizard and could be added to a menu.

We start by defining a macro #tabStep2, which holds the number of the second tab page. We are going to refer to this page several times, so it is good practice to define its number in one place.

In the `MainAccountWizard` class, we override the `setupNavigation()` method, which is used for defining initial button states. We use this method to disable the **Next** button on the second page by default. The variable `nextEnabled` is an array holding the initial enabled or disabled state for each tab page.

The overridden `finish()` method is called when the user clicks on the **Finish** button. Here, we initialize the record and assign user input to the corresponding field values.

In the `validate()` method, we check the account that will be created. This method is called right after the user clicks on the **Finish** button at the end of the wizard and before the main code is executed in the `run()` method. Here, we simply call the `validateWrite()` method for the record, from the main account table.

The last thing to do in the class is to place the main wizard code—insert the record and display a message—in the `run()` method.

In the **MainAccountWizard** form's design, we modify properties of each tab page and add text to explain to the user the purpose of each step. Notice that the **HelpText** property value on the second tab page appears as a step description right below the step title during runtime. This is done automatically by the `SysWizard` class.

Finally, on the second tab page, we place three controls for user input. Then we create three methods, which return the control values: account number, name, and type values, respectively. We also override the `textChange()` event methods on the controls to determine and update the runtime state of the **Next** button. The methods call the `setNext()` method, which actually controls the behavior of the **Next** button. In our case, we enable the **Next** button as soon as all input controls have values.

Processing multiple records

In Dynamics AX, by default most of the functions available on forms are related to a currently selected single record. It is also possible to process several selected records at once, although some modifications are required.

In this recipe, we will explore how a selection of multiple records can be processed on a form. For this demonstration, we will add a button to the action pane on the **Main account** list page to show multiple selected accounts in the Infolog.

How to do it...

Carry out the following steps in order to complete this recipe:

1. In the AOT, open the **MainAccountListPage** form and create a new method with the following code:

```
public void processSelected()
```

```
{
    MainAccount tmpMainAccount;

    tmpMainAccount = MainAccount_ds.getFirst(1) ?
        MainAccount_ds.getFirst(1) :
        MainAccount_ds.cursor();

    while (tmpMainAccount)
    {
        info(strFmt(
            "You've selected '%1'",
            tmpMainAccount.MainAccountId));
        tmpMainAccount = MainAccount_ds.getNext();
    }
}
```

2. Add a new `Button` control anywhere in the form's action pane with the following properties:

Property	Value
Name	ProcessSelected
Text	Process
MultiSelect	Yes

3. Override the button's `clicked()` event method with the following code:

```
void clicked()
{
    super();
    element.processSelected();
}
```

4. In order to test the record selection, navigate to **General ledger | Common | Main accounts**, select several records and click on the new **Process** button. The selected items should be displayed in the Infolog:

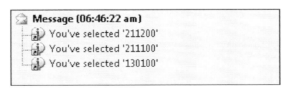

How it works...

The key element in this recipe is the `processSelected()` method. In this method we have to determine if multiple records were marked by the user. This can be done by calling `getFirst(1)` on the `MainAccount` form data source, which returns the first marked record. If nothing is marked, we use the current cursor. The latter normally happens if a single record is selected without explicitly marking it using the checkbox on the left.

Next, we go through all marked records and process them one by one. In this demonstration, we simply show them on the screen.

The last thing to do is to add the **ProcessSelected** button to the form and call the `processSelected()` method from the button's `clicked()` method. Notice that the button property **MultiSelect** is set to **Yes** to ensure it is enabled when multiple records are marked.

Coloring records

One of the exciting Dynamics AX features that can enhance the user experience is the ability to color individual records. User will find the system more intuitive and user-friendly through this modification.

For example, by emphasizing the importance of disabled records, such as terminated employees or stopped customers, marking them in red, allow users to identify relevant records at a glance. Another example is to show processed records, such as posted journals or invoiced sales orders in green.

In this recipe, we will learn how to change the color of a record. We will modify the existing **Users** form located in **System administration | Users** and show disabled users in red.

How to do it...

Carry out the following steps in order to complete this recipe:

1. In the AOT, open the **SysUserInfoPage** form and override the `displayOption()` method in the **UserInfo** data source with the following code:

```
public void displayOption(
    Common _record,
    FormRowDisplayOption _options)
{
    if (!_record.(fieldNum(UserInfo,Enable)))
    {
        _options.backColor(WinAPI::RGB2int(255,100,100));
    }

    super(_record, _options);
}
```

2. In order to test the record coloring, open **System administration | Users | Users** and notice how disabled users are now displayed in a different color:

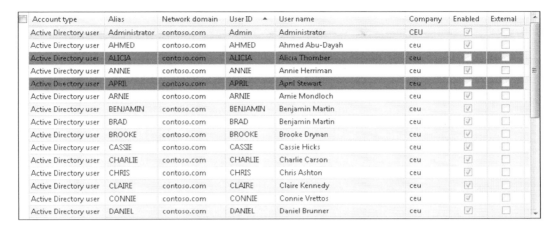

How it works...

The method `displayOption()` on the data source of any form can be used to change some of its visual options. Before displaying each record, this method is called by the system with two arguments—the first is the current record and the second is a `FormRowDisplayOption` object—whose properties can be used to change a record's visual settings. In this example, we check if the current user is disabled, and if yes we change the background property to light red by calling the `backColor()` method with the color code.

Note that for demonstration purposes, we specified the color directly in the code, but it is good practice if the color code comes from some configuration tables.

Adding an image to records

Company-specific images in Dynamics AX can be stored along with the data in the database tables. They could be used for different purposes, such as a company logo that is displayed in every printed document, employee photos, inventory pictures, and so on.

Images are binary objects and can be stored in `container` table fields. In order to enable the system to perform better, it is always recommended to store the images in a separate table so it does not affect the retrieval speed of the main data.

One of the most convenient ways to attach images to any record is to use the **Document handling** feature of Dynamics AX. It does not require any changes in the application. However, the **Document handling** feature is a very generic way of attaching files to any record and might not be suitable for specific circumstances.

Another way of attaching images to records could be to utilize the standard application objects, though minor application changes are required. For example, the company logo in the **Organization administration | Setup | Organization | Legal entities** form is one of the places where the images are stored that way.

In this recipe, we will explore the latter option. As an example, we will add the ability to store an image for each customer. We will add a new button, **Image**, on the **Customers** list page, allowing attaching or removing images for customers.

How to do it...

Carry out the following steps in order to complete this recipe:

1. Open the **CustTableListPage** form in the AOT. Add a new `MenuItemButton` control to the bottom of the **MaintainGroup** button group, which is located in the **HomeTab** tab of the form's action pane. Set the following button's properties:

Property	Value
Name	Image
Text	Image
ButtonDisplay	Text & Image above
NormalImage	10598
ImageLocation	EmbeddedResource
Data source	CustTable
MenuItemType	Display
MenuItemName	CompanyImage

2. Open **Accounts receivable | Common | Customers | All customers** and notice the new **Image** button in the action pane:

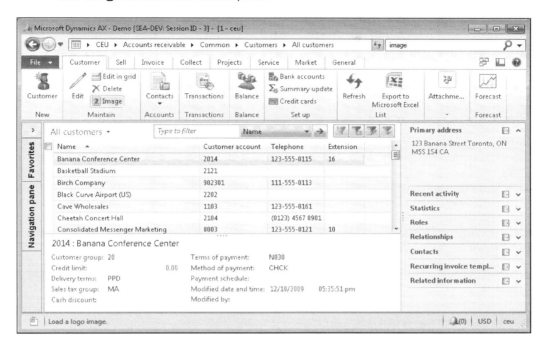

3. Click on the button and then use the **Change** button to upload a new image for the selected item:

4. The **Remove** button could be used to delete an existing image.

How it works...

In this demonstration there are only three standard Dynamics AX objects used:

▶ The **CompanyImage** table, which holds image data and the information about the record to which the image is attached. The separate table allows easy hooking image functionality to any other existing table without modifying it or decreasing its performance.

▶ The **CompanyImage** form, which shows an image and allows it to be modified.

▶ The display menu item **CompanyImage**, which opens the form.

We added the menu item to the **CustTableListPage** form and modified some of its visual properties. This ensures that it looks consistent with the rest of the action pane. We also changed its **Data source** property to the **CustTable** data source to make sure that the image is stored against that record.

There's more...

The following two topics will explain how a stored image could be displayed as a new tab page on the main form and how it could be saved back to a file.

Displaying an image as part of a form

In this section, we will extend the recipe by displaying the stored image on a new tab page on the **Customers** form.

First, we need to add a new tab page to the end of the **CustTable** form's **TabHeader** control, which is located inside another tab page called **TabPageDetails**. This is where our image will be displayed. Set the properties of the new tab page as shown in the following table:

Property	Value
Name	TabImage
AutoDeclaration	Yes
Height	Column height
Caption	Image

Add a new `Window` type control to the tab page. This control will be used to display the image. Set the properties as follows:

Property	Value
Name	CustImage
AutoDeclaration	Yes
Width	Column width
Height	Column height
AlignControl	No

Setting the **Height** and **Width** properties to **Column height** and **Column width**, respectively, will ensure that the image control occupies all available space. The image does not have a label, so we exclude it from the form's label alignment by setting the **AlignControl** property to **No**.

Next, let's create a new method at the top level of the **CustTable** form:

```
public void loadImage()
{
    Image        img;
    CompanyImage companyImage;

    companyImage = CompanyImage::find(
        CustTable.dataAreaId,
        CustTable.TableId,
        CustTable.RecId);

    if (companyImage.Image)
    {
        img = new Image();
        img.setData(companyImage.Image);
        CustImage.image(img);
    }
    else
    {
        CustImage.image(null);
    }

}
```

This method finds a **CompanyImage** record first, which is attached to the current record, and then displays the binary data using the **CustImage** control. If no image is attached, the Window control is cleared to display an empty space.

Next, we override the `selectionChanged()` method of the **CustTable** data source to ensure that the image is loaded for a currently selected record:

```
public void selectionChanged()
{
    super();
    element.loadImage();
}
```

In the AOT, the form should look similar to the following screenshot:

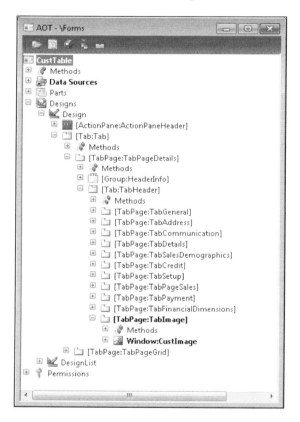

Now open **Account receivable | Common | Customers | All customers**, select previously used customers, and click on the **Edit** button in the action pane. On the **Customers** form, notice the new tab page with the image displayed:

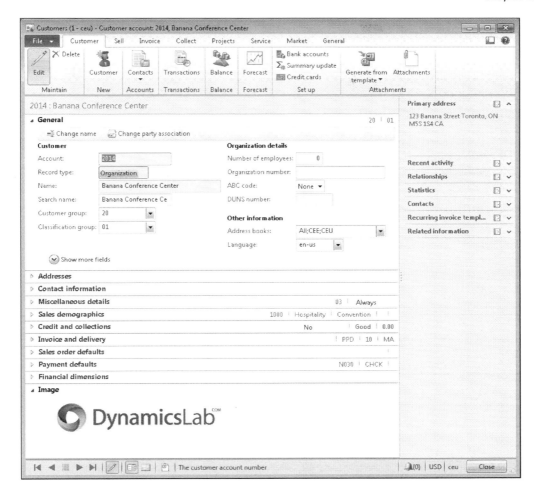

Saving a stored image as a file

This section will describe how the stored image could be restored back to a file. This is quite a common case when the original image file is lost. We will enhance the standard **Image** form by adding a new **Save as** button, which allows us to save the stored image to a file.

Let us find the **CompanyImage** form in the AOT and add a new `Button` control to the form's **ButtonGroup**, which is located in the first tab of the action pane. Set the button's properties as follows:

Property	Value
Name	SaveAs
Text	Save as

Create a new method on the form:

```
public void saveImage()
{
    Image     img;
    Filename name;
    str       type;
    #File

    if (!imageContainer)
    {
        return;
    }

    img = new Image();
    img.setData(imageContainer);

    type = '.'+strLwr(enum2value(img.saveType()));
    name = WinAPI::getSaveFileName(
        element.hWnd(),
        [WinAPI::fileType(type),#AllFilesName+type],
        '',
        '');

    if (name)
    {
        img.saveImage(name);
    }
}
```

This method will present the users with the **Save as** dialog, allowing them to choose the desired file name for saving the current image. Notice that the imageContainer variable holds image data. If it is empty, it means there is no image attached and we do not run any of the code. We also determine the loaded file type to make sure our **Save as** dialog shows only files of that particular type, for example JPG.

Override the button's clicked() method with the following code to make sure that the saveImage() method is executed once the user clicks on the button:

```
void clicked()
{
    super();
    element.saveImage();
}
```

In the AOT, the form should look similar to the following screenshot:

Now when you open the image form, a new button **Save as** is available:

Use this button to save the stored image to a file:

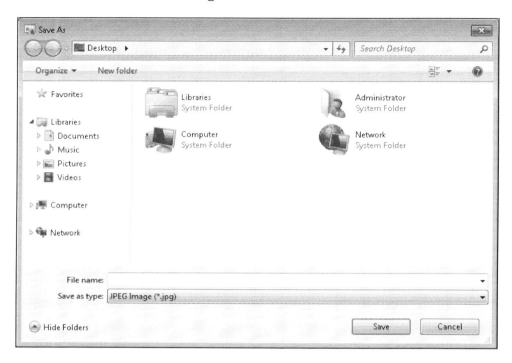

Note that the **CompanyImage** form is used system-wide and the new button is available across the whole system now.

4

Building Lookups

In this chapter, we will cover the following recipes:

- ► Creating an automatic lookup
- ► Creating a lookup dynamically
- ► Using a form for building a lookup
- ► Building a tree lookup
- ► Displaying a list of custom options
- ► Another way of displaying custom options
- ► Building a lookup based on record description
- ► Building the Browse for Folder lookup
- ► Building a lookup for selecting a file
- ► Creating a color picker lookup

Introduction

Lookups are the standard way to display a list of possible selection values to the user, while editing or creating database records. Normally, standard lookups are created automatically by the system, and are based on extended data types and table setup. It is also possible to override the standard functionality by creating your own lookups from the code or using the Dynamics AX forms.

In this chapter, we will cover various lookup types, such as file selector, color picker, or tree lookup, as well as the different approaches to create them.

Creating an automatic lookup

Simple lookups in Dynamics AX can be created in seconds without any programming knowledge. They are based on table relations, and appear automatically. No additional modifications are required.

This recipe will show how to create a very basic automatic lookup using table relations. To demonstrate this, we will add a new **Method of Payment** control to the existing **Customer group** form.

How to do it...

1. Open the **CustGroup** table in the AOT, and create a new field with the following properties:

Property	Value
Type	String
Name	PaymMode
ExtendedDataType	CustPaymMode

2. Add the newly created field to the end of the **Overview** field group of the table.

3. Open the **EDT relation migration tool** form located in **Tools | Code upgrade**. Find the **CustGroup** table on the left (refresh relation data before, if required). In the **EDT relations** section, change the value in the **Migration action** field to **Migrate**, where the **Field name** is set to **PaymMode**, as follows:

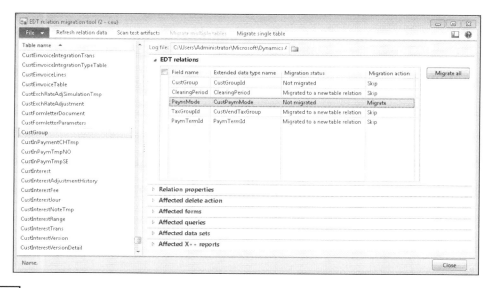

4. Click on the **Migrate single table** button to migrate the relation. The Infolog should prompt a message to inform that the migration is successful.

5. To check the results, open **Accounts receivable | Setup | Customers | Customer groups**, and notice the newly created **Method of payment** column with the lookup:

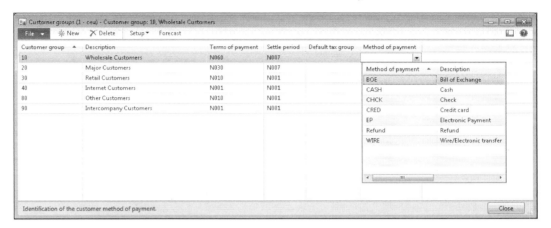

How it works...

The newly created **PaymMode** field is based on the **CustPaymMode** extended data type, and therefore it automatically inherits its relation. To follow best practices, we run the **EDT relation migration tool** to copy the relation from the extended data type to the table. We also add the newly created field to the table's **Overview** group to make sure that the field automatically appears on the **Customer group** form. The relation ensures that the field has an automatic lookup.

There's more...

The automatically generated lookup in the preceding example has only two columns—**Method of payment** and **Description**. Dynamics AX allows us to add more columns or change the existing columns with minimum effort by changing various properties. Lookup columns can be controlled in several different places:

▶ Relation fields, on either an extended data type or a table itself, are always shown on lookups as columns.

▶ Fields defined in the table's **TitleField1** and **TitleField2** properties are also displayed as lookup columns.

▶ The first field of every table's index is displayed as a column.

▶ The index fields and the **TitleField1** and **TitleField2** properties are in effect only when the **AutoLookup** field group of a table is empty. Otherwise, the fields defined in the **AutoLookup** group are displayed as lookup columns, along with the relation columns.

▶ Duplicate columns are shown only once.

Now, to demonstrate how the **AutoLookup** group can affect lookup columns, let's modify the previous example by adding an additional field to this group. Let's add the **PaymSumBy** field to the **AutoLookup** group on the **CustPaymModeTable** table in the middle between the **PaymMode** and **Name** fields. Now, the lookup has one more column as displayed in the following screenshot:

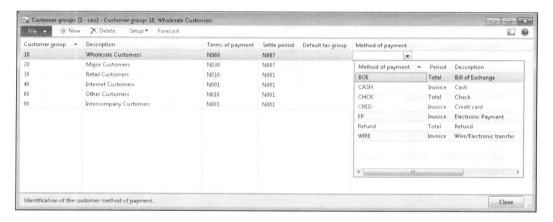

It is also possible to add display methods to the lookup's column list. We can extend our example by adding the `paymAccountName()` display method to the **AutoLookup** group on the **CustPaymModeTable** table right after the **PaymSumBy**. And here is the result:

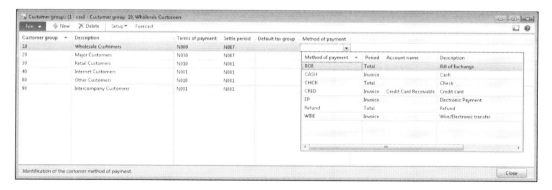

Creating a lookup dynamically

Automatic lookups, mentioned in the previous recipe, are widely used across the system, and are very useful in simple scenarios. When it comes to showing different fields from different data sources, applying various static or dynamic filters, or similar, some coding is required. Dynamics AX is flexible enough that the developer can create custom lookups, either using AOT forms, or by running them dynamically from the X++ code.

This recipe will show how to dynamically build a runtime lookup from the code. In this demonstration, we will modify the **Vendor account** lookup on the **Customers** form to allow users to select only those vendors that use the same currency as the currently selected customer.

How to do it...

1. Open the **VendTable** table in the AOT, and create a new method:

```
public static void lookupVendorByCurrency(
    FormControl   _callingControl,
    CurrencyCode  _currency)
{
    Query                  query;
    QueryBuildDataSource   qbds;
    QueryBuildRange        qbr;
    SysTableLookup         lookup;

    query = new Query();

    qbds = query.addDataSource(tableNum(VendTable));

    qbr = qbds.addRange(fieldNum(VendTable,Currency));

    qbr.value(queryvalue(_currency));

    lookup = SysTableLookup::newParameters(
        tableNum(VendTable),
        _callingControl,
        true);

    lookup.parmQuery(query);

    lookup.addLookupField(
        fieldNum(VendTable, AccountNum),
        true);

    lookup.addLookupField(fieldNum(VendTable,Party));

    lookup.addLookupField(fieldNum(VendTable,Currency));

    lookup.performFormLookup();
}
```

2. In the AOT, open the **CustTable** form, and override the lookup() method of the **VendAccount** field on the **CustTable** data source with the following code:

```
public void lookup(FormControl _formControl, str _filterStr)
{
    VendTable::lookupVendorByCurrency(
        _formControl,
        CustTable.Currency);
}
```

3. To test this, open **Accounts receivable | Customers | All customers**, select any of the customers, and click on the **Edit** button in the action pane. Once the **Customers** form is displayed, expand the **Vendor** account lookup located in the **Miscellaneous details** tab page, under the **Remittance** group. The modified lookup now has an additional column named **Currency**, and vendors in the list should match the customer's currency:

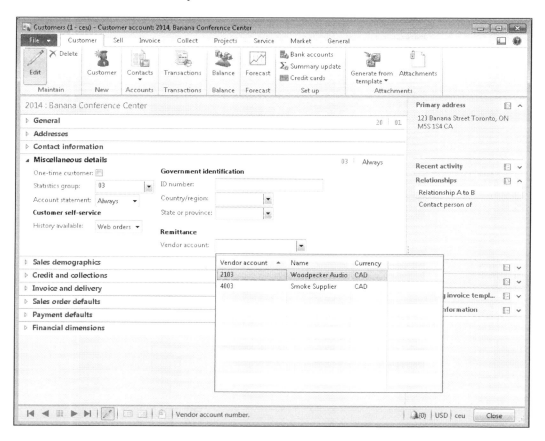

How it works...

First, on the **VendTable** table, we create a new method that generates the lookup. This is the most convenient place for such a method, taking into consideration that it may be reused in a number of other places.

In this method, we first create a new query which will be the base for lookup records. In the query, we add a new data source based on the **VendTable** table and define a new range based on the **Currency** field.

Next, we create the actual lookup object and pass the query object through the `parmQuery()` member method. The lookup object is created by using the `newParameters()` constructor of the `SysTableLookup` class. It accepts three parameters:

1. The table ID, which is going to be displayed.
2. A reference to the form calling the control.
3. An optional boolean value, which specifies that the current control value should be highlighted in the lookup. The default is `true`.

We use the `addLookupField()` method to add three columns—**Vendor account**, **Name**, and **Currency**. This method accepts the following parameters:

▶ The field ID of the field that will be displayed as a column.

▶ An optional boolean value that defines which column value is returned to the caller form upon user selection. The default is `false`.

Finally, we run the lookup by calling the `performFormLookup()` method.

The last thing to do is to add some code to the `lookup()` method of the **VendAccount** field of the **CustTable** data source in the **CustTable** form. By replacing its `super()` with our custom code, we override the standard automatically generated lookup with the custom one.

Using a form for building a lookup

For the most complex scenarios, Dynamics AX offers the possibility to create and use a form as a lookup. For example, it might be a lookup with tab pages or a search filter.

In this recipe, we will demonstrate how to create a lookup using a form. As an example, we will modify the standard customer account lookup to display only active customers.

How to do it...

1. In the AOT, create a new form named **CustLookup**. Add a new data source with the following properties:

Property	Value
Name	CustTable
Table	CustTable
Index	AccountIdx
AllowCheck	No
AllowEdit	No
AllowCreate	No
AllowDelete	No
OnlyFetchActive	Yes

2. Change the properties of the form's design as follows:

Property	Value
Frame	Border
WindowType	Popup

3. Add a new Grid control to the form's design, with the following properties:

Property	Value
Name	Customers
ShowRowLabels	No
DataSource	CustTable

4. Add a new StringEdit control to the grid, with the following properties:

Property	Value
Name	AccountNum
AutoDeclaration	Yes
DataSource	CustTable
DataField	AccountNum

5. Add a new `ReferenceGroup` control to the grid with the following properties, right after the **AccountNum**:

Property	Value
Name	Name
DataSource	CustTable
ReferenceField	Party

6. Add one more `StringEdit` control to the grid with the following properties, right after the **Name**:

Property	Value
Name	Phone
DataSource	CustTable
DataMethod	phone

7. Add a new `ComboBox` control with the following properties to the end of the **Customers** grid:

Property	Value
Name	Blocked
DataSource	CustTable
DataField	Blocked

8. Override the form's `init()` method with the following code:

```
public void init()
{
    super();
    element.selectMode(AccountNum);
}
```

9. Override the form's `run()` method with the following code:

```
public void run()
{
    FormStringControl callingControl;
    boolean          filterLookup;

    callingControl = SysTableLookup::getCallerStringControl(
        element.args());
```

```
filterLookup = SysTableLookup::filterLookupPreRun(
    callingControl,
    AccountNum,
    CustTable_ds);

super();

SysTableLookup::filterLookupPostRun(
    filterLookup,
    callingControl.text(),
    AccountNum,
    CustTable_ds);
}
```

10. Finally, override the init() method of the **CustTable** data source with the following code:

```
public void init()
{
    Query                query;
    QueryBuildDataSource qbds;
    QueryBuildRange      qbr;

    query = new Query();

    qbds  = query.addDataSource(tableNum(CustTable));

    qbr = qbds.addRange(fieldNum(CustTable,Blocked));

    qbr.value(queryvalue(CustVendorBlocked::No));

    this.query(query);
}
```

11. The form in the AOT should look similar to the following screenshot:

12. Locate the **CustAccount** extended data type in the AOT, and change its property as follows:

Property	Value
FormHelp	CustLookup

13. To test the results, open **Sales and marketing | Common | Sales orders | All sales orders**, and start creating a new sales order. Notice that now the **Customer account** lookup is different, and it includes only active customers:

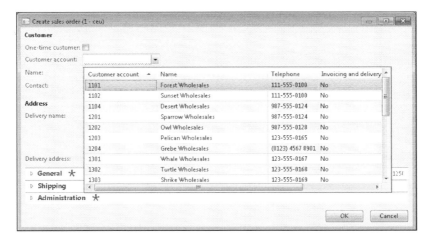

How it works...

The newly created **CustLookup** form will replace the standard automatically generated customer account lookup. It is recommended to append the text **Lookup** at the end of the form name, so that lookup forms can be easily distinguished from other AOT forms.

First, we add a new data source and change its properties. We do not allow any data updates by setting the **AllowEdit**, **AllowCreate**, and **AllowDelete** properties to **No**. Security checks should be disabled by setting **AllowCheck** to **No**. To increase performance, we set **OnlyFetchActive** to **Yes**, which will reduce the size of the database result set to only the fields that are visible on the form. We also set the data source index to define initial data sorting.

Next, in order to make our form lookup look exactly like a standard lookup, we have to adjust its layout. So, we set its form design **Frame** and **WindowType** properties, respectively, to **Border** and **Popup**. This removes form borders and makes the form very similar to a standard lookup. Then, we add a new `Grid` control with four controls inside, which are bound to the relevant **CustTable** table fields and methods. We set the **ShowRowLabels** property of the grid to **No**, to hide the grid's row labels.

After this, we have to define which form control will be used for returning a value from the lookup to the calling form. We need to specify it manually in the form's `init()` method, by calling `element.selectMode()`, with the name of the control as argument.

In the form's `run()`, we add some filtering, which allows the user to use the asterisk (*) symbol to search for records in the lookup. For example, if the user types **1*** into the **Customer account** control, the lookup will open automatically with all customer accounts starting with **1**. To achieve that, we use the `filterLookupPreRun()` and `filterLookupPostRun()` methods of the standard `SysTableLookup` class. Both the methods require a calling control, which we get by using the `getCallerStringControl()` method of the same `SysTableLookup` class. The first method reads the user input and returns `true` if a search is being performed, otherwise, `false`. It must be called before the `super()` in the form's `run()`, and accepts four arguments:

1. The calling control on the parent form.
2. The returning control on the lookup form.
3. The lookup data source.
4. An optional list of other lookup data sources.

The `filterLookupPostRun()` method must be called after the `super()` in the form's run() method, and also accepts four arguments:

1. A result value from the previously called `filterLookupPreRun()` method.
2. The user text specified in the calling control.
3. The returning control on the lookup form.
4. The lookup data source.

The code in the **CustTable** data source's `init()` method replaces the data source query created by its `super()` with the custom one. Basically, here we create a new `Query` object, and change its range to include only active customers.

The **FormHelp** property of the **CustAccount** extended data type will make sure that this form is opened every time the user opens the **Customer account** lookup.

See also

Chapter 1, Processing Data:

▶ *Building a query object*

Building a tree lookup

Form tree controls are a user-friendly way of displaying a hierarchy of related records, such as a company's organizational structure, inventory bill of materials, projects with their subprojects, and so on. Such hierarchies can also be displayed in the custom lookups, allowing users to browse and select the required value in a more convenient way.

In the *Using a tree control* recipe in *Chapter 2, Working with Forms*, it was explained how to present the budget model hierarchy as a tree in the **Budget model** form. In this recipe, we will reuse the previously created **BudgetModelTree** class, and will demonstrate how to build a budget model tree lookup.

How to do it...

1. In the AOT, create a new form named **BudgetModelLookup**. Set its design properties as follows:

Property	Value
Frame	Border
WindowType	Popup

2. Add a new `Tree` control to the design, with the following properties:

Property	Value
Name	ModelTree

3. Add the following line to the form's class declaration:

   ```
   BudgetModelTree budgetModelTree;
   ```

4. Override the form's `init()` method with the following code:

```
public void init()
{
    FormStringControl callingControl;

    callingControl = SysTableLookup::getCallerStringControl(
        this.args());

    super();

    budgetModelTree = BudgetModelTree::construct(
        ModelTree,
        callingControl.text());

    budgetModelTree.buildTree();
}
```

5. Override the `mouseDblClick()` and `mouseUp()` methods of the **ModelTree** control with the following code, respectively:

```
public int mouseDblClick(
    int _x,
    int _y,
    int _button,
    boolean _ctrl,
    boolean _shift)
{
    int          ret;
    FormTreeItem formTreeItem;
    BudgetModel  budgetModel;

    ret = super(_x, _y, _button, _ctrl, _shift);

    formTreeItem = this.getItem(this.getSelection());

    select firstOnly SubModelId from budgetModel
        where budgetModel.RecId == formTreeItem.data();

    element.closeSelect(budgetModel.SubModelId);

    return ret;
}

public int mouseUp(
    int _x,
    int _y,
    int _button,
    boolean _ctrl,
    boolean _shift)
{
    int ret;

    ret = super(_x, _y, _button, _ctrl, _shift);

    return 1;
}
```

6. The form should look similar to the following screenshot:

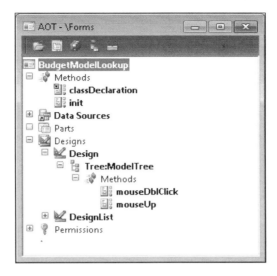

7. In the AOT, open the **BudgetModel** table, and change its `lookupBudgetModel()` method with the following code:

```
public static void lookupBudgetModel(
    FormStringControl _ctrl,
    boolean _showStopped = false)
{
    Args    args;
    Object  formRun;

    args = new Args();
    args.name(formStr(BudgetModelLookup));
    args.caller(_ctrl);

    formRun = classfactory.formRunClass(args);
    formRun.init();

    _ctrl.performFormLookup(formRun);
}
```

8. To see the results, open **Budgeting | Common | Budget register entries**. Start creating a new entry by clicking on the **Budget register entry** button in the action pane, and expand the **Budget model** lookup:

How it works...

First, we create a new form named **BudgetModelLookup**, which we will use as a custom lookup. We set the design **Frame** and **WindowType** to **Border** and **Popup**, respectively, to change the layout of the form, so that it looks like a lookup. We also add a new `Tree` control to the form's design.

In the form's class declaration, we define the `BudgetModelTree` class, which we have already created in the *Using a tree control* recipe in *Chapter 2, Working with Forms*.

The code in the form's `init()` builds the tree. Here, we create a new `BudgetModelTree` object, by calling the constructor `construct()`, which accepts two arguments:

1. Tree control which represents the actual tree.

2. Budget model, which is going to be preselected initially. Normally, it's a value of the calling control, which can be detected by using the `getCallerStringControl()` method of the `SysTableLookup` application class.

The code in the `mouseDblClick()` returns the user-selected value from the tree node back to the calling control, and closes the lookup.

Finally, the `mouseUp()` method has to be overridden to return `1`, to make sure that the lookup does not close while the user expands or collapses the tree nodes.

See also

Chapter 2, Working with Forms:

▶   *Using a tree control*

Displaying a list of custom options

Besides normal lookups, Dynamics AX provides a number of other ways to present the available data for user selection. It doesn't necessarily have to be a record from the database; it could be a list of "hardcoded" options, or some external data. Normally, such lists are much smaller as opposed to those of the data-driven lookups, and are used for very specific tasks.

In this recipe, we will create a lookup of several pre-defined options. We will use a job for this demonstration.

How to do it...

1.   In the AOT, create a new job named `PickList` with the following code:

```
static void PickList(Args _args)
{
    Map choices;
    str ret;

    choices = new Map(
        Types::Integer,
        Types::String);
    choices.insert(1, "Axapta 3.0");
    choices.insert(2, "Dynamics AX 4.0");
    choices.insert(3, "Dynamics AX 2009");
    choices.insert(4, "Dynamics AX 2012");

    ret = pickList(choices, "", "Choose version");

    if (ret)
    {
        info(strFmt("You've selected option No. %1", ret));
    }
}
```

2.   Run the job to view the results:

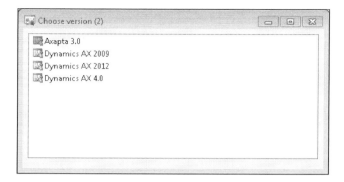

3.   Double-click on one of the options to show the selected option in the Infolog:

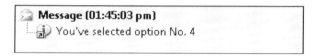

How it works...

The key element in this recipe is the global `pickList()` function. Lookups created using this function are based on values stored in a map. In our example, we define and initialize a new map. Then, we insert few key-value pairs and pass the map to the `pickList()`. This function accepts three parameters:

1.   A map, which contains lookup values.
2.   A column header, which is not used here.
3.   A lookup title.

The function that displays values from the map returns the corresponding keys, once the option is selected.

There's more...

The global `pickList()` function could basically display any list of values. Besides that, Dynamics AX also provides a number of other global lookup functions, which can be used in more specific scenarios. Here are a few of them:

▶   `pickDataArea()` shows a list of Dynamics AX companies.

▶   `pickUserGroups()` shows a list of user groups in the system.

▶   `pickUser()` shows a list of Dynamics AX users.

- ► `pickTable()` shows all Dynamics AX tables.
- ► `pickField()` shows table fields. Table number has to be specified as an argument for the function.
- ► `pickClass()` shows a list of Dynamics AX classes.

Another way of displaying custom options

The global system functions, such as `pickList()`, `pickUser()`, and so on, allow developers to build various lookups displaying a list of custom options. Besides that, the standard Dynamics AX application contains a few more quite useful functions, allowing us to build more complex lookups of custom options.

One of the functions is called `selectSingle()`, and it presents the user with a list of options. It also displays a checkbox next to each option, allowing users to select the option. To demonstrate this, we will create a new job that shows the usage of this function.

How to do it...

1. In the AOT, create a new job named `SysListSelectSingle`:

```
static void SysListSelectSingle(Args _args)
{
    container choices;
    container headers;
    container selection;
    container selected;
    boolean   ok;

    choices = [
        ["3.0\nAxapta 3.0", 1, false],
        ["4.0\nDynamics AX 4.0", 2, false],
        ["2009\nDynamics AX 2009", 3, false],
        ["2012\nDynamics AX 2012", 4, true]];

    headers = ["Version", "Description"];

    selection = selectSingle(
        "Choose version",
        "Please select Dynamics AX version",
        choices,
        headers);
```

```
        [ok, selected] = selection;

        if (ok && conLen(selected))
        {
            info(strFmt(
                "You've selected option No. %1",
                conPeek(selected,1)));
        }
    }
}
```

2. Run the job to display the options:

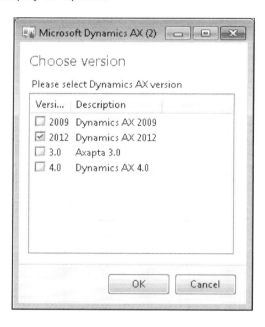

3. Select any of the options, click the **OK** button, and notice your choice displayed in the Infolog:

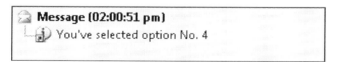

How it works...

We start with defining the choices variable and setting its values. The variable is a container of containers, where each container inside the parent container is made of three elements, and represents one selectable option in the list:

1. The first element is a text displayed on the lookup. By default, in the lookup, only one column is displayed, but it is possible to define more columns, simply by separating the text using the new line symbol.

2. The second element is a number of an item in the list. This value is returned from the lookup.

3. The third value specifies whether the option is marked by default.

Now, when the list values are ready, we call the `selectSingle()` function to build the actual lookup. This function accepts five arguments:

1. The window title.

2. The lookup description.

3. A container of list values.

4. A container representing column headings.

5. An optional reference to a caller object.

The `singleSelect()` function returns a container of two elements:

1. `true` or `false`, depending on if the lookup was closed using the **OK** button or not.

2. Numeric value of the selected option.

There's more...

You may have noticed that the lookup, which is created using the `singleSelect()`, allows only one option to be chosen from the list. There is another similar function named `selectMultiple()`, which is exactly the same except that the user can select multiple options from the list. The following code demonstrates its usage:

```
static void SysListSelectMultiple(Args _args)
{
    container choices;
    container headers;
    container selection;
    container selected;
    boolean   ok;
    int       i;
```

```
choices = [
    ["3.0\nAxapta 3.0", 1, false],
    ["4.0\nDynamics AX 4.0", 2, false],
    ["2009\nDynamics AX 2009", 3, true],
    ["2012\nDynamics AX 2012", 4, true]];

headers = ["Version", "Description"];

selection = selectMultiple(
    "Choose version",
    "Please select Dynamics AX version",
    choices,
    headers);

[ok, selected] = selection;

if (ok && conLen(selected) > 0)
{
    for (i = 1; i <= conLen(selected); i++)
    {
        info(strFmt(
            "You've selected option No. %1",
            conPeek(selected,i)));
    }
}
```

Now, in the lookup, it is possible to select multiple options:

Notice that in this case, the returned value is a container holding the selected options.

Building a lookup based on record description

Normally, data lookups in Dynamics AX display a list of records where the first column always contains a value, which is returned to a calling form. The first column in the lookup normally contains a unique record identification value, which is used to build relations between tables. For example, the customer lookup displays the customer account number, the customer name, and some other fields; the inventory item lookup displays the item number, the item name, and other fields.

In some cases, the record identifier may not be so informative. For example, it is much more convenient to display a person's name versus its number. In the standard application, you can find a number of places where the contact person is displayed as a person's name, even though the actual table relation is based on the contact person's ID.

In this recipe, we will create such a lookup. We will replace the vendor group selection lookup on the **Vendors** form to show group description, instead of group ID.

How to do it...

1. In the AOT, create a new `String` extended data type:

Property	Value
Name	VendGroupDescriptionExt
Label	Group
Extends	Description

2. Open the **VendTable** table and create a new method with the following code:

```
public edit VendGroupDescriptionExt editVendGroup(
    boolean                   _set,
    VendGroupDescriptionExt _group)
{
    VendGroup vendGroup;

    if (_set)
    {
        if (_group)
        {
            if (VendGroup::exist(_group))
            {
                this.VendGroup = _group;
            }
        }
```

```
            else
            {
                select firstOnly VendGroup from vendGroup
                    where vendGroup.Name == _group;
                this.VendGroup = vendGroup.VendGroup;
            }
        }
        else
        {
            this.VendGroup = '';
        }
    }

    return VendGroup::name(this.VendGroup);
}
```

3. In the AOT, find the **VendTable** form, locate the **Posting** group control inside **MainTab | TabPageDetails | Tab | TabGeneral | UpperGroup | Identification**, and modify its properties as follows:

Property	Value
DataGroup	

4. In the same form, in the **Posting** group, modify the **Posting_VendGroup** control as follows:

Property	Value
DataField	
DataMethod	editVendGroup

5. Override the `lookup()` method of the **Posting_VendGroup** control, with the following code:

```
public void lookup()
{
    this.performTypeLookup(extendedTypeNum(VendGroupId));
}
```

6. To check the results, open **Accounts payable | Common | Vendors | All vendors**, select any record, and click on the **Edit** button in the action pane. In the opened form, check the newly created lookup on the **Group** control, located in the **General** tab of the page:

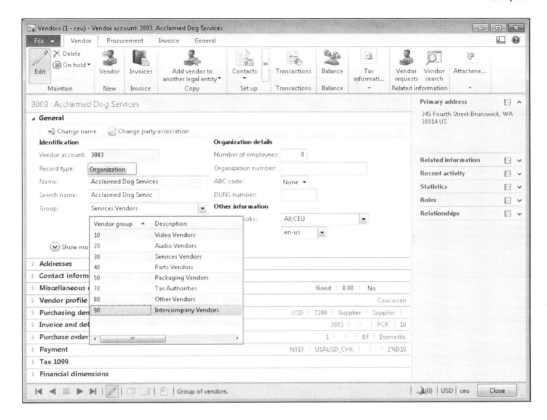

How it works...

First, we create a new extended data type, which we will use as basis for the vendor group selection control. The type extends the existing **Description** extended data type, as it has to be of the same size as the vendor group name. It should also have the same label as the **VendGroupId**, because it is going to replace the existing **Group** control on the form.

Next, we create a new edit method, which is used to show the group description instead of the group ID on the form. It also allows changing the control's value.

The edit method is created on the **VendTable** table—most convenient place for reuse—and it uses the newly created extended data type. This ensures that the label of the user control stays the same. The method accepts two arguments, as this is a mandatory requirement for the edit methods. The first argument defines whether the control was modified by the user, and if yes, the second argument holds the modified value. In this recipe, the second value can be either group ID—if the user selects a value from the lookup—or group description—if the user decides to manually type the value into the control. We use the extended data type, which is bigger in size, that is, the **VendGroupDescriptionExt**. The method returns a vendor group name, which is shown on the form.

Next, we need to modify the **VendTable** form. We change the existing vendor group ID control to use the newly created edit method. By doing so, we make the control unbound, and therefore we lose the standard lookup functionality. To correct this, we override the `lookup()` method on the control. Here, we use the `performTypeLookup()` method to restore the lookup's functionality.

There's more...

In the previous example, you may have noticed that the lookup does not find the currently selected group. This is because the system tries to search group ID by group description. This section will show how to solve this issue.

First, we have to create a new form named **VendGroupLookup**, which will act as a lookup. Add a new data source to the form, with the following properties:

Property	Value
Name	VendGroup
Table	VendGroup
Index	GroupIdx
AllowCheck	No
AllowEdit	No
AllowCreate	No
AllowDelete	No
OnlyFetchActive	Yes

Change the properties of the form's design as follows:

Property	Value
Frame	Border
WindowType	Popup

Add a new `Grid` control to the form's design, with the following properties:

Property	Value
Name	VendGroups
ShowRowLabels	No
DataSource	VendGroup
DataGroup	Overview

Five new controls should appear in the grid automatically. Change the properties of the
VendGroups_VendGroup control as follows:

Property	Value
AutoDeclaration	Yes

Override the form's `init()` and `run()` methods, with the following code, respectively:

```
public void init()
{
    super();
    element.selectMode(VendGroups_VendGroup);
}
public void run()
{
    VendGroupId groupId;

    groupId = element.args().lookupValue();

    super();

    VendGroup_ds.findValue(
        fieldNum(VendGroup,VendGroup), groupId);
}
```

The key element here is the `findValue()` method in the form's `run()` method. It places
the cursor on the currently selected vendor group record. The group ID is retrieved from the
arguments object by using the `lookupValue()` method.

In the AOT, the form should look similar to the following screenshot:

Next, we need to create a new static method on the **VendGroup** table, which opens the new lookup form:

```
public static void lookupVendorGroupForm(
    FormStringControl _callingControl,
    VendGroupId        _groupId)
{
    FormRun formRun;
    Args    args;

    args = new Args();
    args.name(formStr(VendGroupLookup));
    args.lookupValue(_groupId);

    formRun = classFactory.formRunClass(args);
    formRun.init();

    _callingControl.performFormLookup(formRun);
}
```

Here, we use the `formRunClass()` method of the global `classFactory` object. Notice that here we pass the group ID to the form through the `Args` object.

The final touch is to change the code in the `lookup()` method of the **VendGroups_VendGroup** control on the **VendTable** form:

```
public void lookup()
{
    VendGroup::lookupVendorGroupForm(this, VendTable.VendGroup);
}
```

Now, when you open the **Vendors** form, the current vendor group in the **Group** lookup is pre-selected correctly:

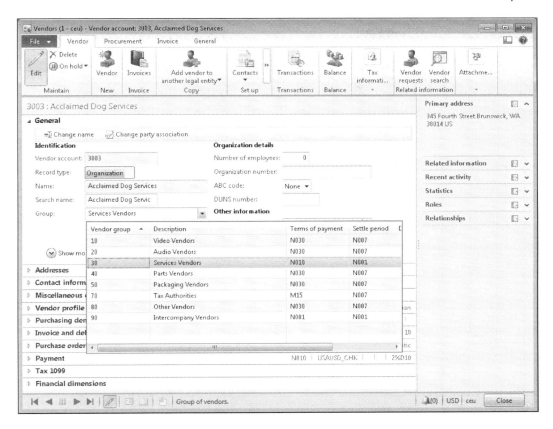

Building the Browse for Folder lookup

Folder browsing lookups can be used when the user is required to specify a local or network folder, for storing or retrieving external files. Such lookups are generated outside of Dynamics AX, by using Windows API.

In this recipe, we will learn how to create a lookup for folder browsing. As an example, we will create a new field and control named **Documents** in the **General ledger parameters** form, which will allow us to store a folder path.

How to do it...

1. In the AOT, open the **LedgerParameters** table, and create a new field with the following properties:

Property	Value
Type	String
Name	DocumentPath
Label	Documents
ExtendedDataType	FilePath

2. Add the newly created field to the bottom of the table's **General** field group.

3. In the AOT, open the **LedgerParameters** form, and create a new method with the following code:

    ```
    public str filePathLookupTitle()
    {
        return "Select document folder";
    }
    ```

4. To test the results, open **General ledger | Setup | General ledger parameters**, and notice the newly created **Documents** control, which allows you to select a folder:

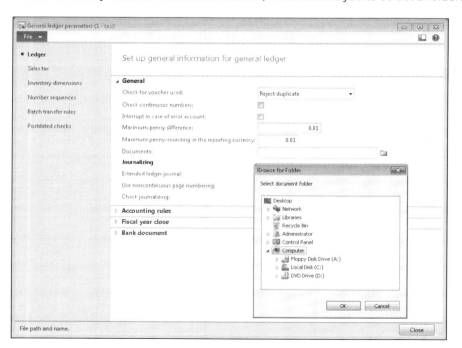

How it works...

The folder browsing lookup form is bound to the **FilePath** extended data type, and it appears automatically for every control that is based on that type. In this recipe, we create a new field, which extends the **FilePath**, and consequently inherits the lookup. We also add the newly created field to the field group, in order for it to appear on the form automatically.

We also create a new form method named `filePathLookupTitle()`, which is required by the browse for folder lookup. This method holds the description displayed on the lookup window. The system will show an error if this method is not present on a caller form.

There's more...

In this section, we will explore few more enhancements to the previous example. Firstly, we will build exactly the same lookup but use a slightly different technique, and secondly, we will enable the **Make New Folder** button on the lookup, allowing users to create new folders.

Manual folder browsing lookup

The lookup created in this recipe has a few programming limitations. First, the lookup requires the `filePathLookupTitle()` method to be present on a caller form. The name of this method has to be exactly like this, and cannot be prefixed with a three-letter code, as per best practice recommendations, and it might lead to confusion when performing system changes in the future.

Another reason is that a single form cannot have two or more folder browsing lookups unless they share the same description. Every lookup calls the same `filePathLookupTitle()` method, and will obviously have the same descriptions.

Internally, the browsing for folder lookup is generated with the help of the `browseForPath()` method of the `WinAPI` class. The method invokes the standard Windows folder browsing dialog, and we can call this method directly without using the extended data type.

Let's modify our previous example by deleting the `filePathLookupTitle()` method from the **LedgerParameters** form, and overriding the `lookup()` method of the **DocumentPath** field in the **LedgerParameters** form data source with the following code:

```
public void lookup(FormControl _formControl, str _filterStr)
{
    FilePath path;

    path = WinAPI::browseForPath(
        element.hWnd(),
        "Select document folder extended");

    LedgerParameters.DocumentPath = path;
    LedgerParameters_ds.refresh();
}
```

Now, if you open the lookup, you may notice that it looks exactly the same as before, apart from its description. The description is defined in the `lookup()` method, and is only used for this particular lookup. Using this technique, we can create more than one folder browsing lookup on the same form, without adding additional methods to the form itself.

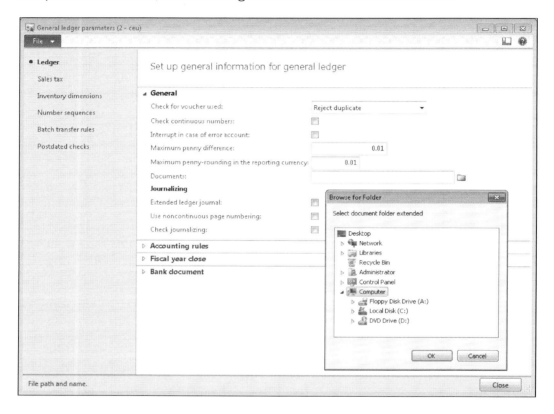

Adding a Make New Folder button

The mentioned `WinAPI` class has one more method named `browseForFolderDialog()`. Besides folder browsing, it also allows creating a new one. The method accepts three optional arguments:

1. The lookup description.
2. The folder path selected initially.
3. The boolean value, where `true` shows and `false` hides the **Make New Folder** button. The button is shown by default if this argument is omitted.

Let's replace the `lookup()` method of the **DocumentPath** field in the **LedgerParameters** form data source with the following code:

```
public void lookup(FormControl _formControl, str _filterStr)
{
    FilePath path;

    path = WinAPI::browseForFolderDialog(
        "Select document folder extended",
        LedgerParameters.DocumentPath,
        true);

    LedgerParameters.DocumentPath = path;
    LedgerParameters_ds.refresh();
}
```

Now, the folder browsing lookup has a new **Make New Folder** button, which allows the user to create a new folder straight away without leaving the lookup:

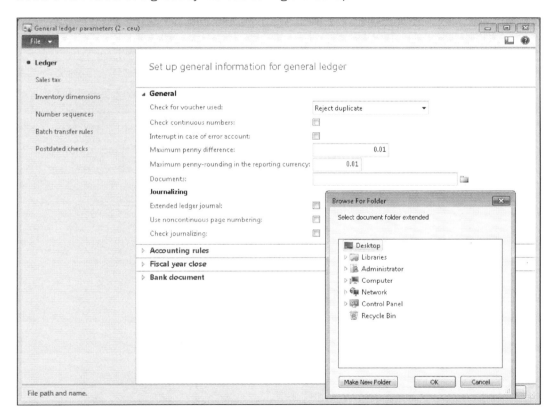

Building a lookup for selecting a file

In Dynamics AX, file reading or saving is a very common operation. Most of the non-automated file reading or writing operations prompts the user to specify the file name.

This recipe will demonstrate how the user could be presented with the file browse dialog, in order to choose a file in a convenient way. As an example, we will create a new control called **Terms & conditions** in the **Form setup** form in the **Procurement and sourcing** module, which allows storing of a path to the text document.

How to do it...

1. In the AOT, open the **VendFormLetterParameters** table and create a new field with the following properties:

Property	Value
Type	String
Name	TermsAndConditions
Label	Terms & conditions
ExtendedDataType	FilenameOpen

2. Then add the field to the bottom of the table's **PurchaseOrder** field group.

3. Next, open the **PurchFormLetterParameters** form, and create the following four methods:

```
public str fileNameLookupTitle()
{
    return "Select Terms & conditions document";
}

public str fileNameLookupInitialPath()
{
    container file;

    file = fileNameSplit(
        VendFormletterParameters.TermsAndConditions);

    return conPeek(file ,1);
}

public str fileNameLookupFilename()
{
    Filename     path;
```

```
Filename     name;
Filename     type;

[path, name, type] = fileNameSplit(
    VendFormletterParameters.TermsAndConditions);

return name + type;
}

public container fileNameLookupFilter()
{
    #File

    return [WinAPI::fileType(#txt), #AllFilesName+#txt];
}
```

4. As a result, we should be able to select and store a text file in the **Procurement and sourcing | Setup | Forms | Form setup** form in the **Terms & conditions** field under the **Purchase order** tab of the page:

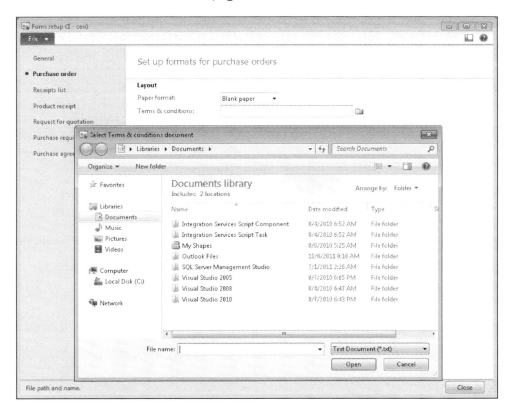

How it works...

In this recipe, we first create a new field where we will store the file location. We use the **FilenameOpen** extended data type, which is bound to the file selection dialog. The newly created field automatically inherits the dialog. We also add this field to the field group in the table to ensure that it is displayed on the form automatically.

The following four form methods are called by the lookup, and must be present on a caller form:

1. The `fileNameLookupTitle()` method contains a text to be displayed as the lookup title.

2. The `fileNameLookupInitialPath()` method defines the initial folder. In our example, if there is a value in the `Terms & conditions` field, then this method strips the filename part and returns the directory path to the lookup to be used as a starting point. Here, we use the global `fileNameSplit()` function to process the stored file path.

3. The `fileNameLookupFilename()` method detects the current value in the field, and extracts the filename to be displayed on the lookup. We use the global `fileNameSplit()` function again to separate the given directory path into three parts—directory path, filename, and file extension. For example, if the current **Terms & conditions** value is **\\LONDON\Documents\terms.txt**, then once the user clicks on the lookup button, the method returns only the filename **terms.txt** (file name + file extension) separated from the rest of the directory path.

4. The `fileNameLookupFilter()` method is responsible for displaying a list of allowed file extensions. It returns a container of allowed extensions in pairs of two. The first, third, fifth, and other odd values hold the name of the file extension, and the second, fourth, sixth, and other even values contain an extension filter. In this example, only the text files are allowed, and the method returns two values in the container. The first value is a string **Text Document**, and the second one is ***.txt**. In order to avoid literals in the X++ code, we use two definitions from the `#File` macro: `#txt` and `#AllFileName`, which contain the **.txt** and ***** strings, respectively, and which are concatenated by the lookup to present the user with the **Text Document (*.txt)** filter. The `fileType()` method of the `WinAPI` class converts file extensions to their textual representation.

There's more...

Although the file browsing dialog created in this recipe is technically correct, it still has some limitations. Firstly, it requires creating a number of methods on the caller form, and secondly, it will not work with multiple file lookups on the same form. A slightly different approach could be used to avoid those issues and keep the lookup's appearance unchanged.

Let's modify the previous example by removing all the four methods from the form itself and overriding the `lookup()` method on the **TermAndConditions** field, with the following code:

```
public void lookup(FormControl _formControl, str _filterStr)
{
    FilenameOpen file;
    Filename     path;
    Filename     name;
    Filename     type;
    #File

    [path, name, type] = fileNameSplit(
        VendFormLetterParameters.TermsAndConditions);

    file  = WinAPI::getOpenFileName(
        element.hWnd(),
        [WinAPI::fileType(#txt), #AllFilesName+#txt],
        path,
        "Select Terms & conditions document",
        "",
        name + type);

    if (file)
    {
        VendFormLetterParameters.TermsAndConditions = file;
        VendFormLetterParameters_ds.refresh();
    }
}
```

The file browsing dialog is in the `getOpenFileName()` method of the `WinAPI` class, which in turn opens the Windows file browsing dialog. The method accepts a number of arguments:

- A handler to the calling window.
- A container of allowed file extensions. This is exactly what the `fileNameLookupFilter()` method returns in the previous example.
- The file path selected initially.
- The lookup's title.
- The default file name.

In this way we can create multiple file browsing lookups on the same form.

Creating a color picker lookup

In Dynamics AX, the color selection dialog boxes are used in various places, allowing the user to select and store a color code in a table. The stored color code can be used in various scenarios, such as marking important records, changing the control's background, and so on.

In this recipe, we will create a color lookup. For demonstration purposes, we will add an option to set a color for each legal entity in the system.

How to do it...

1. In the AOT, open the **CompanyInfo** table and create a new field with the following properties:

Property	Value
Type	Integer
Name	CompanyColor
ExtendedDataType	CCColor

2. Open the **OMLegalEntity** form, locate the **TopPanel** group in **Body | Content | Tab | General**, and add a new `IntEdit` control with the following properties to the bottom of the group:

Property	Value
Name	CompanyColor
AutoDeclaration	Yes
LookupButton	Always
ShowZero	No
ColorScheme	RGB
Label	Company color

3. In the same form, create a new method with the following code in the **CompanyInfo** data source:

    ```
    public edit CCColor editCompanyColor(
        boolean     _set,
        CompanyInfo _companyInfo,
        CCColor     _color)
    {
        if (_companyInfo.CompanyColor)
        {
            CompanyColor.backgroundColor(
    ```

```
            _companyInfo.CompanyColor);
    }
    else
    {
        CompanyColor.backgroundColor(
            WinAPI::RGB2int(255,255,255));
    }

    return 0;
}
```

4. Update the properties of the newly created **CompanyColor** control as follows:

Property	Value
DataSource	CompanyInfo
DataMethod	editCompanyColor

5. In the same control, override its lookup() method with the following code:

```
public void lookup()
{
    int       red;
    int       green;
    int       blue;
    container color;

    [red, green, blue] = WinApi::RGBint2Con(
        CompanyColor.backgroundColor());

    color = WinAPI::chooseColor(
        element.hWnd(),
        red,
        green,
        blue,
        null,
        true);

    if (color)
    {
        [red, green, blue] = color;
        CompanyInfo.CompanyColor = WinAPI::RGB2int(
            red,
            green,
```

```
        blue);

    CompanyColor.backgroundColor(
        CompanyInfo.CompanyColor);
    }
}
```

6. To test the results, open **Organization administration | Setup | Organization | Legal entities** and click on the **Company color** lookup:

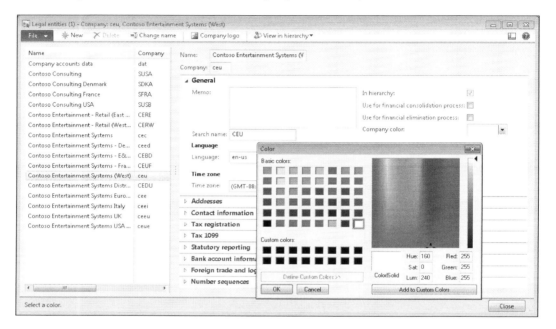

How it works...

Dynamics AX does not have a special control for selecting colors. So, we have to create a fake control, which is presented to the user as a color selection.

Colors in Dynamics AX are stored as integers, so we first create a new `Integer` field on the **CompanyInfo** table. On the form we create a new control, which will display the color. The created control does not have any automatic lookup, and, therefore, it does not have the lookup button next to it. We have to force the button to appear by setting the control's **LookupButton** property to **Always**. We also need to set the **ColorScheme** to **RGB** to make sure the control allows us to set its color using red-green-blue code.

Next, we create a new edit method, which is then set on the created control as a data method. The method is responsible for changing the control's background to match the stored color. This gives an impression to the user that the chosen color was saved. The background is set to white if no value is present. The method always returns 0, because we do not want to show the actual color code in it. The control's **ShowZero** property is set to **No** to ensure that even the returned 0 is not displayed. In this way, we create a control that looks like a real color selection control.

The last thing to do is to override the control's lookup() method with the code that invokes the color selection dialog. Here we use the RGBint2Con() method of the WinAPI class to convert the current control's background color into a red-green-blue component set. The set is then passed to the chooseColor() method of the same WinAPI class to make sure that currently set color is initially selected on the lookup. The chooseColor() method is the main method which invokes the lookup. It accepts the following arguments:

- The current window handle.
- The red color component.
- The green color component.
- The blue color component.
- A binary object representing up to 16 custom colors.
- A boolean value, which defines whether the full or short version of the lookup is displayed initially.

This method returns a container of red, green, and blue color components, which has to be converted back to a numeric value in order to store it in the table field.

There's more...

You probably must have noticed that the fifth argument in the preceding example is set to null. This is because we did not use custom colors. This feature is not that important, but may be used in some circumstances.

To demonstrate how it can be used, let's modify the lookup() method with the following code in order to implement the custom colors:

```
public void lookup()
{
    int       red;
    int       green;
    int       blue;
    container color;
    Binary    customColors;
```

```
customColors = new Binary(64);

customColors.byte(0,255);
customColors.byte(1,255);
customColors.byte(2,0);

customColors.byte(4,0);
customColors.byte(5,255);
customColors.byte(6,0);

customColors.byte(8,255);
customColors.byte(9,0);
customColors.byte(10,0);

[red, green, blue] = WinApi::RGBint2Con(
    CompanyColor.backgroundColor());

color = WinAPI::chooseColor(
    element.hWnd(),
    red,
    green,
    blue,
    customColors,
    true);

if (color)
{
    [red, green, blue] = color;
    CompanyInfo.CompanyColor = WinAPI::RGB2int(
        red,
        green,
        blue);

    CompanyColor.backgroundColor(
        CompanyInfo.CompanyColor);
}
}
```

Here, we define the customColors variable as a binary object, for storing the initial set of custom colors. The object structure contains 64 elements for storing the color codes. The set of red, green, and blue components for each color is stored in three subsequent elements in the object, followed by an empty element. In our code, we store yellow (red = 255, green = 255, and blue = 0) in the elements from 0 to 2, green (red = 0, green, = 255, blue = 0) in the elements from 4 to 6, and red (red = 255, green = 0, blue = 0) in the elements from 8 to 10. The system allows you to create up to 16 custom colors.

After implementing those changes, the color selection dialog now has three predefined custom colors, as shown in the following screenshot:

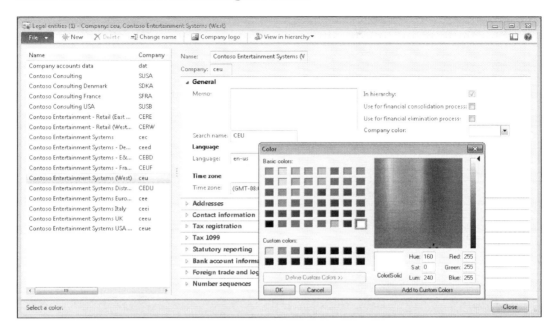

The custom colors can also be modified by the user, and can be saved in a table field or cache for later use by storing the whole binary `customColors` object.

5
Processing Business Tasks

In this chapter, we will cover the following recipes:

- ▶ Using a segmented entry control
- ▶ Creating a general journal
- ▶ Posting a general journal
- ▶ Processing a project journal
- ▶ Creating and posting a ledger voucher
- ▶ Changing an automatic transaction text
- ▶ Creating a purchase order
- ▶ Posting a purchase order
- ▶ Creating a sales order
- ▶ Posting a sales order
- ▶ Creating an electronic payment format

Introduction

This chapter explains how to process various business operations in Dynamics AX. We will discuss how to use the segmented entry control and how to create and post various journals. The chapter also explains how to work with the ledger voucher object and how to enhance the setup of the automatically-generated transaction texts. It also covers how to create and post purchase and sales orders, as well as creating electronic payment format.

Using a segmented entry control

In Dynamics AX, segmented entry control can simplify the task of entering complex main account and dimension combinations. The control consists of a dynamic number of elements named segments. The number of segments may vary, depending on the setup, and their lookup values may be dependent on the values specified in other segments in the same control. The segmented entry control always uses the controller class, which handles the entry and display in the control.

In this recipe, we will show how a segmented entry control can be added to a form. In this demonstration, we will add a new **Ledger account** control to the **General ledger parameters** form, assuming that the control could be used as a default ledger account for various functions. The example does not make much sense in practice, but it is perfectly suitable to demonstrate the usage of the segmented entry control.

How to do it...

1. In the AOT, locate the **LedgerParameters** table and create a new field with the following properties (click on **Yes** to automatically add a foreign key relation once asked):

Property	Value
Type	Int64
Name	LedgerDimension
ExtendedDataType	LedgerDimensionAccount

2. Add the newly created fields to the **General** group in the table.

3. Find the table's relation named **DimensionAttributeValueCombination**, and change its property as follows:

Property	Value
UseDefaultRoleNames	No

4. In the AOT, find the **LedgerParameters** form, and add the following code to its class declaration:

   ```
   LedgerDimensionAccountController ledgerDimensionAccountController;
   ```

5. Add the following code to the bottom of the form's `init()` method:

   ```
   ledgerDimensionAccountController =
       LedgerDimensionAccountController::construct(
           LedgerParameters_ds,
           fieldStr(LedgerParameters,LedgerDimension));
   ```

6. On the same form, locate the **General_LedgerDimension** segmented entry control located in **Tab | LedgerTab | LedgerTabBody | LedgerTabFastTab | GeneralTabPage | General**, and override three of its methods with the following code:

```
public void loadAutoCompleteData(LoadAutoCompleteDataEventArgs _e)
{
    super(_e);
    ledgerDimensionAccountController.loadAutoCompleteData(_e);
}

public void loadSegments()
{
    super();
    ledgerDimensionAccountController.parmControl(this);
    ledgerDimensionAccountController.loadSegments();
}

public void segmentValueChanged(SegmentValueChangedEventArgs _e)
{
    super(_e);
    ledgerDimensionAccountController.segmentValueChanged(_e);
}
```

7. On the same form, in its **LedgerParameters** data source, locate the **LedgerDimension** field, and override three of its methods with the following code:

```
public Common resolveReference(
    FormReferenceControl _formReferenceControl)
{
    return ledgerDimensionAccountController.resolveReference();
}

public void jumpRef()
{
    super();
    ledgerDimensionAccountController.jumpRef();
}

public boolean validate()
{
    boolean ret;

    ret = super();

    ret = ledgerDimensionAccountController.validate() && ret;

    return ret;
}
```

8. To test the results, open **General ledger | Setup | General ledger parameters**, and notice the newly created **Ledger account** control, allowing to select and save the main account, and a number of financial dimensions:

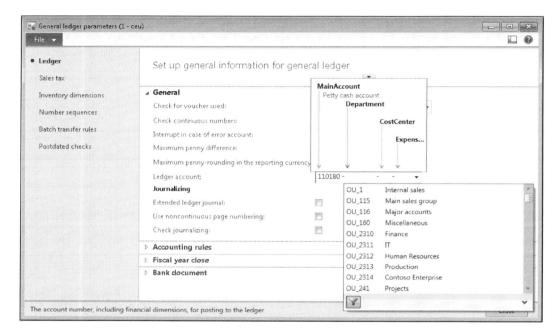

How it works...

We start the recipe by creating a new field in the **LedgerParameters** table. The field extends the **LedgerDimensionAccount** extended data type, to ensure that the segmented entry control appears automatically once this field is added to the user interface. We also add the newly created field to one of the table's groups to make sure that it appears on the form automatically.

Next, we have to modify the **LedgerParameters** form. In its class declaration and the init() method, we define and instantiate the LedgerDimensionAccountController class, which handles the events raised by the segmented entry control. The combination of the class and the control allows the user to see a dynamic number of segments, based on the system configuration.

Then we override the following methods on the control:

▶ loadAutoCompleteData() retrieves the autocomplete data.

▶ loadSegments() loads the stored value in the table field to the control.

▶ segmentedValueChanged() updates the controller class when the value of the control is changed by the user.

Lastly, we override the following methods on the data source field:

- ▸ resolveReference() finds the ledger account record specified by the user.
- ▸ jumpRef() enables the **View details** link in the control's right-click context menu.
- ▸ validate() performs user input validation.

There's more...

In this section, we will discuss how the input of the segmented entry control can be simulated from code. It is very useful when migrating or importing the data into the system. In the AOT, locate the **DimensionAttributeValueCombination** table and create a new method with the following code:

```
public static LedgerDimensionAccount getLedgerDimension(
    MainAccountNum _mainAccountId,
    container      _dimensions,
    container      _values)
{
    MainAccount                     mainAccount;
    DimensionHierarchy              dimHier;
    LedgerChartOfAccountsStructure  coaStruct;
    Map                             dimSpec;
    Name                            dimName;
    Name                            dimValue;
    DimensionAttribute              dimAttr;
    DimensionAttributeValue         dimAttrValue;
    List                            dimSources;
    DimensionDefaultingEngine       dimEng;
    int                             i;

    mainAccount = MainAccount::findByMainAccountId(
        _mainAccountId);

    if (!mainAccount.RecId)
    {
        return 0;
    }

    select firstOnly RecId from dimHier
        where dimHier.StructureType ==
          DimensionHierarchyType::AccountStructure
          && dimHier.IsDraft == NoYes::No
        exists join coaStruct
```

```
                where coaStruct.ChartOfAccounts ==
                    LedgerChartOfAccounts::current()
                    && coaStruct.DimensionHierarchy == dimHier.RecId;
        if (!dimHier.RecId)
        {
            return 0;
        }

        dimSpec =
            DimensionDefaultingEngine::createEmptyDimensionSpecifiers();

        for (i = 1; i <= conLen(_dimensions); i++)
        {
            dimName  = conPeek(_dimensions, i);
            dimValue = conPeek(_values, i);

            dimAttr = DimensionAttribute::findByName(dimName);
            if (!dimAttr.RecId)
            {
                continue;
            }

            dimAttrValue =
                DimensionAttributeValue::findByDimensionAttributeAndValue(
                    dimAttr, dimValue, false, true);
            if (dimAttrValue.IsDeleted)
            {
                continue;
            }

            DimensionDefaultingEngine::insertDimensionSpecifer(
                dimSpec,
                dimAttr.RecId,
                dimValue,
                dimAttrValue.RecId,
                dimAttrValue.HashKey);
        }

        dimSources = new List(Types::Class);
        dimSources.addEnd(dimSpec);

        dimEng = DimensionDefaultingEngine::constructForMainAccountId(
            mainAccount.RecId,
            dimHier.RecId);
```

```
        dimEng.applyDimensionSources(dimSources);

        return dimEng.getLedgerDimension();
    }
```

This method can be used to convert a combination of a main account and a number of financial dimension values into a ledger account. The method accepts three arguments:

1. The main account number.
2. A container of dimension names.
3. A container of dimension values.

We start this method by searching for the main account record. We also locate the record of the hierarchy of the current chart of accounts.

Next, we fill an empty map with the dimensions values. Before inserting each value, we try to locate if the dimension and its value is present in the system. Here we use the methods on the **DimensionAttribute** and the **DimensionAttributeValue** tables to do that.

We end the method by creating a new `DimensionDefaultingEngine` object and passing the list of dimensions and their values to it. Now, when everything is ready, the `getLedgerDimension()` method of `DimensionDefaultingEngine` returns the ledger account number.

See also

In this chapter:

▶ *Creating a general journal*
▶ *Creating and posting a ledger voucher*

Creating a general journal

Journals in Dynamics AX are manual worksheets that can be posted into the system. One of the frequently used journals for financial operations is the **General journal**. It allows processing virtually any type of operation: ledger account transfers, fixed asset operations, customer/vendor payments, bank operations, project expenses, and so on. Journals, such as the **Fixed assets** journal, or the **Payment journal** in the **Accounts receivable** or **Accounts payable** modules, and many others, are optimized for specific business tasks, but they basically do the same job.

In this recipe, we will demonstrate how to create a new general journal record from code. The journal will hold a single line for debiting one ledger account and crediting another one. For demonstration purposes, we will specify all the input values in the code.

How to do it...

1. In the AOT, create a new class named `LedgerJournalTransData` with the following code:

```
class LedgerJournalTransData extends JournalTransData
{
}


public void create(
    boolean _doInsert        = false,
    boolean _initVoucherList = true)
{
    lastLineNum++;

    journalTrans.LineNum = lastLineNum;

    if (journalTableData.journalVoucherNum())
    {
        this.initVoucher(
            lastVoucher,
            false,
            _initVoucherList);
    }

    this.addTotal(false, false);

    if (_doInsert)
    {
        journalTrans.doInsert();
    }
    else
    {
        journalTrans.insert();
    }

    if (journalTableData.journalVoucherNum())
    {
        lastVoucher = journalTrans.Voucher;
    }
}
```

2. Open the `LedgerJournalStatic` class, and replace its `newJournalTransData()` method with the following code:

```
JournalTransData newJournalTransData(
    JournalTransMap  _journalTrans,
    JournalTableData _journalTableData)
{
    return new LedgerJournalTransData(
        _journalTrans,
        _journalTableData);
}
```

3. Double check that the `getLedgerDimension()` method exists on the **DimensionAttributeValueCombination** table. If not, create it as described in the first recipe in this chapter.

4. Create a new job named `LedgerJournalCreate`, with the following code:

```
static void LedgerJournalCreate(Args _args)
{
    LedgerJournalTable       jourTable;
    LedgerJournalTrans       jourTrans;
    LedgerJournalTableData   jourTableData;
    LedgerJournalTransData   jourTransData;
    LedgerJournalStatic      jourStatic;
    DimensionDynamicAccount  ledgerDim;
    DimensionDynamicAccount  offsetLedgerDim;

    ttsBegin;

    ledgerDim =
        DimensionAttributeValueCombination::getLedgerDimension(
            '110180',
            ['Department', 'CostCenter', 'ExpensePurpose'],
            ['OU_2311', 'OU_3568', 'Training']);

    offsetLedgerDim =
        DimensionAttributeValueCombination::getLedgerDimension(
            '170150',
            ['Department', 'CostCenter', 'ExpensePurpose'],
            ['OU_2311', 'OU_3568', 'Training']);

    jourTableData = JournalTableData::newTable(jourTable);

    jourTable.JournalNum  = jourTableData.nextJournalId();
    jourTable.JournalType = LedgerJournalType::Daily;
    jourTable.JournalName = 'GenJrn';

    jourTableData.initFromJournalName(
```

```
                    LedgerJournalName::find(jourTable.JournalName));

        jourStatic     = jourTableData.journalStatic();

        jourTransData = jourStatic.newJournalTransData(
            jourTrans,
            jourTableData);

        jourTransData.initFromJournalTable();

        jourTrans.CurrencyCode            = 'USD';
        jourTrans.initValue();
        jourTrans.TransDate               = systemDateGet();
        jourTrans.LedgerDimension         = ledgerDim;
        jourTrans.Txt                     = 'General journal demo';
        jourTrans.OffsetLedgerDimension = offsetLedgerDim;
        jourTrans.AmountCurDebit           = 1000;

        jourTransData.create();

        jourTable.insert();

        ttsCommit;

        info(strFmt(
            "Journal '%1' has been created", jourTable.JournalNum));
    }
```

5. Run the job and check the results by opening **General ledger | Journals | General journal**:

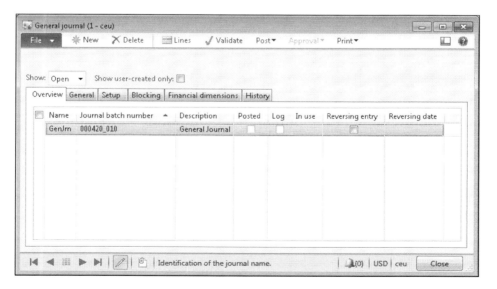

6. Click on the **Lines** button to open journal lines and notice the newly created line:

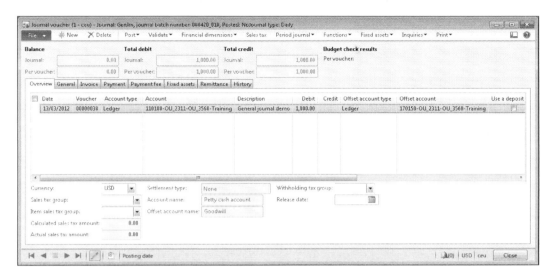

How it works...

We start the recipe by creating the `LedgerJournalTransData` class, which will handle the creation of journal lines. It inherits everything from the `JournalTransData` class, apart from its `create()` method. Actually, this method is also a copy of the same method from the `JournalTransData` class, with the exception that it does not check the **VoucherDraw** field on the **LedgerJournalTable** table, as this functionality is not relevant here. We also modify the `newJournalTransData()` constructor of the `LedgerJournalStatic` class to use our new class.

For demonstrating the journal creation, we create a new job. Here, we use the `getLedgerDimension()` method from the previous recipe to get ledger dimensions. We also create a new `jourTableData` object used for journal record handling. Then, we set the journal number, type, and name, and call the `initFromJournalName()` method to initialize some additional values from the journal name settings. At this stage, the journal header record is ready.

Next, we create a journal line. We create a new `jourTransData` object for handling the journal line, and call its `initFromJournalTable()` method to initialize additional values from the journal header. Then, we set some of the journal line values, such as currency, transaction date, and so on.

Finally, we call the `create()` method on the `jourTransData` object, and the `insert()` method on the `jourTable` object to create the journal line and the header records, respectively. The journal is ready now for reviewing.

There's more

The preceding example could easily be modified to create different journals, not just the **General journal**. For instance, the **Payment journal** in the **Accounts payable** module is based on the same data sources as the **General journal**, and some of its code is the same. So, let's create a new, very similar job named VendPaymJournalCreate with the following code:

```
static void VendPaymJournalCreate(Args _args)
{
    LedgerJournalTable        jourTable;
    LedgerJournalTrans        jourTrans;
    LedgerJournalTableData    jourTableData;
    LedgerJournalTransData    jourTransData;
    LedgerJournalStatic       jourStatic;
    DimensionDynamicAccount   ledgerDim;
    DimensionDynamicAccount   offsetLedgerDim;

    ttsBegin;

    ledgerDim = DimensionStorage::getDynamicAccount(
        '1001',
        LedgerJournalACType::Vend);

    offsetLedgerDim = DimensionStorage::getDynamicAccount(
        'USA OPER',
        LedgerJournalACType::Bank);

    jourTableData = JournalTableData::newTable(jourTable);

    jourTable.JournalNum  = jourTableData.nextJournalId();
    jourTable.JournalType = LedgerJournalType::Payment;
    jourTable.JournalName = 'APPay';

    jourTableData.initFromJournalName(
        LedgerJournalName::find(jourTable.JournalName));

    jourStatic    = jourTableData.journalStatic();

    jourTransData = jourStatic.newJournalTransData(
        jourTrans,
        jourTableData);

    jourTransData.initFromJournalTable();
```

```
    jourTrans.CurrencyCode             = 'USD';
    jourTrans.initValue();
    jourTrans.TransDate                = systemDateGet();
    jourTrans.AccountType              = LedgerJournalACType::Vend;
    jourTrans.LedgerDimension          = ledgerDim;
    jourTrans.Txt                      = 'Vendor payment journal demo';
    jourTrans.OffsetAccountType        = LedgerJournalACType::Bank;
    jourTrans.OffsetLedgerDimension    = offsetLedgerDim;
    jourTrans.AmountCurDebit           = 1000;

    jourTransData.create();

    jourTable.insert();

    ttsCommit;

    info(strFmt(
        "Journal '%1' has been created", jourTable.JournalNum));
}
```

Now, the newly created journal can be found in **Accounts payable | Journals | Payments | Payment journal**:

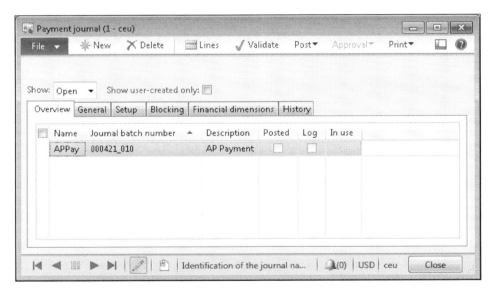

The journal lines should reflect what we've specified in the code:

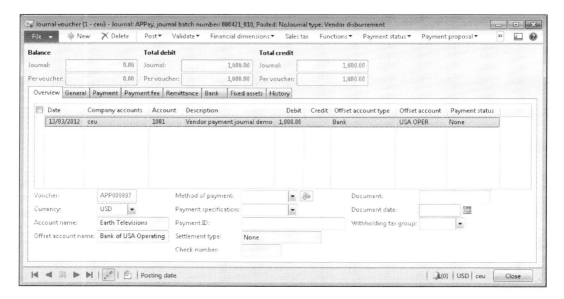

The code in this section has only slight differences compared to the previous example:

▶ The ledger dimension contains a reference to a vendor account, and offset ledger dimension refers to a bank account record.

▶ The journal type was changed to a vendor disbursement, that is, `LedgerJournalType::Payment`.

▶ The journal name is different to match the payment journal configuration.

▶ The journal line account type was set to vendor, and the offset account type was set to bank.

See also

In this chapter:

▶ *Using a segmented entry control*

▶ *Posting a general journal*

Posting a general journal

Journal posting is the next step to do once the journal has been created. Although most of the time journals are posted from the user interface, it is also possible to perform the same operation from the code.

In this recipe, we will explore how a general journal can be posted from code. We are going to process the journal created in the previous recipe.

How to do it...

1. Open **General ledger | Journals | General journal**, and find previously created journal or manually create a new one. Note the journal's number.

2. In the AOT, create a new job named LedgerJournalPost with the following code (replace the text 000420_010 with the journal's number from the previous step):

```
static void LedgerJournalPost(Args _args)
{
    LedgerJournalCheckPost    jourPost;
    LedgerJournalTable        jourTable;

    jourTable = LedgerJournalTable::find('000420_010');

    jourPost = LedgerJournalCheckPost::newLedgerJournalTable(
        jourTable,
        NoYes::Yes);

    jourPost.run();
}
```

3. Run the job, and notice the Infolog, confirming that the journal was successfully posted:

Message (09:30:44 am)
Number of vouchers posted to the journal: 1

4. Open **General ledger | Journals | General journal** and locate the journal to make sure that it was posted:

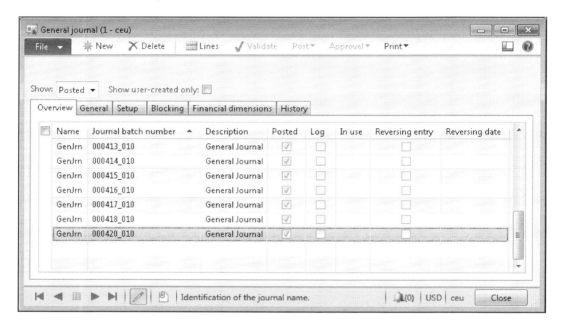

How it works...

In this recipe, we create a new job named `LedgerJournalPost`, which holds all of the code. Here, we use the `LedgerJournalCheckPost` class, which does all the work. This class ensures that all the necessary validations are performed. It also locks the journal so that no user can access it from the user interface.

In the job, we create the `jourPost` object by calling the `newLedgerJournalTable()` constructor on the `LedgerJournalCheckPost` class. This method accepts a journal header record to be processed, and a second argument defining whether the journal should be validated and posted, or only validated. In this recipe, we find the previously created journal record and pass it to the `LedgerJournalCheckPost` class along with the second argument, instructing it to perform both validation and posting.

See also

In this chapter:

▸ *Creating a general journal*

Processing a project journal

As with most of the modules in Dynamics AX, the **Project management and accounting** module contains serveral journals, such as **Hour**, **Expense**, **Fee**, or **Item** journals. Although they are similar to the **General journal**, they provide a more convenient user interface for working with projects, and contain some module-specific features.

In this recipe, we will create and post a project journal from code. We will process an **Hour** journal, holding a registered employee's time.

How to do it...

1. In the AOT, create a new job named `ProjJournalCreate` with the following code:

```
static void ProjJournalCreate(Args _args)
{

    ProjJournalTable        jourTable;
    ProjJournalTrans        jourTrans;
    ProjJournalTableData    jourTableData;
    ProjJournalTransData    jourTransData;
    ProjJournalStatic       jourStatic;

    ttsBegin;

    jourTableData = JournalTableData::newTable(jourTable);

    jourTable.JournalId     = jourTableData.nextJournalId();
    jourTable.JournalType   = ProjJournalType::Hour;
    jourTable.JournalNameId = 'Hours';

    jourTableData.initFromJournalName(
        ProjJournalName::find(jourTable.JournalNameId));

    jourStatic = jourTableData.journalStatic();

    jourTransData = jourStatic.newJournalTransData(
        jourTrans,
        jourTableData);

    jourTransData.initFromJournalTable();

    jourTrans.initValue();

    jourTrans.ProjId = '10001';
    jourTrans.initFromProjTable(
        ProjTable::find(jourTrans.ProjId));
```

```
        jourTrans.TransDate      = systemDateGet();
        jourTrans.ProjTransDate = jourTrans.TransDate;

        jourTrans.CategoryId = 'Design';
        jourTrans.setHourCostPrice();
        jourTrans.setHourSalesPrice();
        jourTrans.TaxItemGroupId =
            ProjCategory::find(jourTrans.CategoryId).TaxItemGroupId;

        jourTrans.Worker =
            HcmWorker::findByPersonnelNumber('000062').RecId;
        jourTrans.Txt = 'Design documentation';
        jourTrans.Qty = 8;

        jourTransData.create();

        jourTable.insert();

        ttsCommit;

        info(strFmt(
            "Journal '%1' has been created", jourTable.JournalId));
    }
```

2. Run the job and check the results by going to **Project management and accounting | Journals | Hour**:

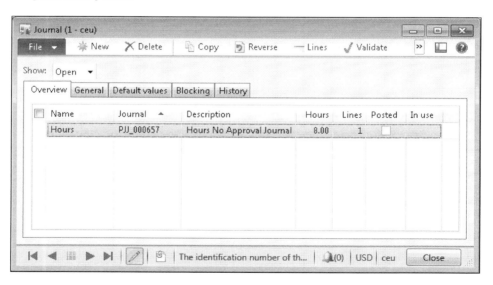

3. Click on the **Lines** button to open the journal lines, and notice the newly created record:

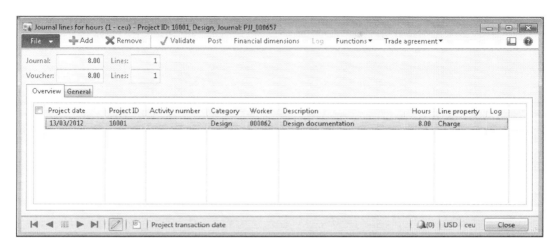

How it works...

In this recipe, we create a new job where we store all the code. In the job, we use the ProjJournalTableData and the ProjJournalTransData classes in a very similar way as we used the LedgerJournalTableData and the LedgerJournalTransData classes in the *Creating a general journal* recipe. Here, we create a new jourTableData object used for journal record handling. Then we initialize the journal number, the type, and the name of the actual journal record. For demonstration purposes, we set the journal name in the code, but it could be easily replaced with a value from some parameter. Next, we call initFromJournalName() on the jourTableData object to initialize some additional values from the journal name settings. At this stage, the journal header record is ready.

Next, we create a journal line. Here we first create a new jourTransData object for handling the journal line. Then, we call its initFromJournalTable() method to initialize the additional values from the journal header. Finally, we set some of the journal line values, such as transaction and project date, category, worker number, and so on. Normally, these values have to be taken from the user input, external data, or any other source, depending on the functionality being built. In this example, we simply specify the values in the code.

Lastly, we call create() on the jourTransData, and insert() on the jourTable, to create the journal line and the header records, respectively. The journal is now ready for reviewing.

There's more...

For further journal processing, we can use the class named `ProjJournalCheckPost` for posting project journals from code. In the AOT, let's create another job named `ProjJournalPost` with the following code (replace `PJJ_000657` with your journal number):

```
static void ProjJournalPost(Args _args)
{
    ProjJournalCheckPost jourPost;

    jourPost = ProjJournalCheckPost::newJournalCheckPost(
        true,
        true,
        JournalCheckPostType::Post,
        tableNum(ProjJournalTable),
        'PJJ_000657');

    jourPost.run();
}
```

Run the job to post the journal. The Infolog should display the confirmation:

In the newly created job, we use the `newJournalCheckPost()` constructor of the `ProjJournalCheckPost` class. The constructor accepts the following arguments:

- ▶ A boolean value that specifies whether to block the journal while it is being posted or not. It is good practice to set it to `true`, as this ensures that no one modifies this journal while it is being posted.

- ▶ A boolean value that specifies whether to display results in the Infolog.

- ▶ The type of action being performed. The possible values for this class are either `JournalCheckPostType::Post` or `JournalCheckPostType::Check`. The latter one only validates the journal, and the first one validates and posts the journal at once.

- ▶ The table ID of the journal being posted.

- ▶ The journal number to be posted.

And finally, we call the `run()` method which posts the journal.

Creating and posting a ledger voucher

In Dynamics AX, all financial transactions, regardless of where they are originated, end up in the **General ledger** module. When it comes to customized functionality, developers should use Dynamics AX APIs to create the required system entries. No transactions can be created directly in the tables as it may affect the accuracy of financial data.

In order to ensure data consistency, the system provides numerous APIs for developers to use. One of them is ledger voucher processing. It allows posting a financial voucher in the **General ledger**. Vouchers in Dynamics AX are balancing financial entries representing a single operation. They include two or more ledger transactions. The ledger voucher API ensures that all required criteria, such as voucher numbers, financial periods, ledger accounts, financial dimensions, balances, and others, are valid.

In this recipe, we will demonstrate how a ledger voucher can be created and posted from code. We will create a single voucher with two balancing transactions.

How to do it...

1. Double-check that the getLedgerDimension() method exists in the **DimensionAttributeValueCombination** table. If not, create it as described in the first recipe in this chapter.

2. In the AOT, create a new job named LedgerVoucherPost with the following code:

```
static void LedgerVoucherPost(Args _args)
{
    LedgerVoucher                voucher;
    LedgerVoucherObject          voucherObj;
    LedgerVoucherTransObject     voucherTrObj1;
    LedgerVoucherTransObject     voucherTrObj2;
    DimensionDynamicAccount      ledgerDim;
    DimensionDynamicAccount      offsetLedgerDim;
    CurrencyExchangeHelper       currencyExchHelper;
    CompanyInfo                  companyInfo;

    ledgerDim =
        DimensionAttributeValueCombination::getLedgerDimension(
            '110180',
            ['Department', 'CostCenter', 'ExpensePurpose'],
            ['OU_2311', 'OU_3568', 'Training']);

    offsetLedgerDim =
        DimensionAttributeValueCombination::getLedgerDimension(
            '170150',
```

```
                ['Department', 'CostCenter', 'ExpensePurpose'],
                ['OU_2311', 'OU_3568', 'Training']);

    voucher = LedgerVoucher::newLedgerPost(
        DetailSummary::Detail,
        SysModule::Ledger,
        '');

    voucherObj = LedgerVoucherObject::newVoucher('TEST00001');

    companyInfo = CompanyInfo::findDataArea(curext());

    currencyExchHelper = CurrencyExchangeHelper::newExchangeDate(
        Ledger::primaryLedger(companyInfo.RecId),
        voucherObj.parmAccountingDate());

    voucher.addVoucher(voucherObj);

    voucherTrObj1 =
        LedgerVoucherTransObject::newTransactionAmountDefault(
            voucherObj,
            LedgerPostingType::LedgerJournal,
            ledgerDim,
            'USD',
            1000,
            currencyExchHelper);

    voucherTrObj2 =
        LedgerVoucherTransObject::newTransactionAmountDefault(
            voucherObj,
            LedgerPostingType::LedgerJournal,
            offsetLedgerDim,
            'USD',
            -1000,
            currencyExchHelper);

    voucher.addTrans(voucherTrObj1);
    voucher.addTrans(voucherTrObj2);

    voucher.end();

    info(strFmt(
        "Voucher '%1' has been posted", voucher.lastVoucher()));
}
```

3. Run the class to create a new ledger voucher.

4. To check what has been posted, open **General Ledger | Inquiries | Voucher transactions** and type in the voucher number used in the code:

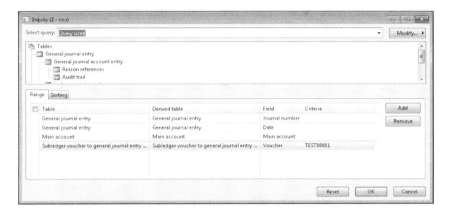

5. Click on **OK** to display the posted voucher:

How it works...

In the newly created job, first of all, we define ledger accounts where the posting will be done. Normally, this comes from the user input, but here for the demonstration purposes, we specify it in the code. We used the previously created `getLedgerDimension()` method to simulate the ledger account entry.

Next, we create a new `LedgerVoucher` object, which represents a collection of vouchers. Here, we call the `newLedgerPost()` constructor of the `LedgerVoucher` class. It accepts three mandatory and four optional arguments, which are listed as follows:

- Post detailed or summarized ledger transactions.
- The system module from which the transactions are originating.
- A number sequence code, which is used to generate the voucher number. In this example, we will set the voucher number manually. So, this argument can be left empty.
- The transaction type that will appear in the transaction log.
- The transaction text.
- A boolean value specifying whether this voucher should meet the approval requirements.
- A boolean value, defining whether the voucher could be posted without a posting type when posting inventory transactions.

Then, we create a new `LedgerVoucherObject` object, which represents a single voucher. We call the `newVoucher()` constructor of the `LedgerVoucherObject` class. It accepts only one mandatory and a number of optional parameters, which are listed as follows:

- The voucher number. Normally, this should be generated by using a number sequence but, in this example, we set it manually.
- The transaction date. The default is the session date.
- The module from which the transactions are originating.
- The ledger transaction type.
- A flag defining whether this is a correcting voucher. The default is `No`.
- The posting layer. The default is `Current`.
- The document number.
- The document date.
- The acknowledgment date.

The `addVoucher()` method of the `LedgerVoucher` class adds the created voucher object to the voucher.

Once the voucher is ready, we create two voucher transactions. The transactions are handled by the `LedgerVoucherTransObject` class. They are created by calling its `newTransactionAmountDefault()` constructor with the following mandatory arguments:

- The ledger voucher object.
- The ledger posting type.
- The ledger account number.

- ▶ The currency code.
- ▶ The amount in currency.
- ▶ The currency exchange rate helper.

Notice the last argument, which is a currency exchange rate helper, used when operating in currencies other that the main company currency.

We add the created transaction objects to the voucher by calling its `addTrans()` method. At this stage, everything is ready for posting.

Finally, we call the `end()` method on the `LedgerVoucher` object, which posts the transactions to the ledger.

See also

In this chapter:

- ▶ *Using a segmented entry control*

Changing an automatic transaction text

Every financial transaction in Dynamics AX can (and normally should) have a descriptive text. Some texts are entered by users, and some can be generated by the system. The latter option happens for automatically-generated transactions, where the user cannot interact with the process.

Dynamics AX provides a way to define text for automatically-generated transactions. The setup can be found in **Organizations administration | Setup | Default description**. Here, the user can create custom transaction texts for various automatic transaction types and languages. The text itself can have a number of placeholders—digits with a percent sign in front of them, which are replaced with actual values during the process. Placeholders can be from %1 to %6, and they are substituted with the following values:

- ▶ %1: the transaction date.
- ▶ %2: a relevant number, such as invoice, delivery note, etc.
- ▶ %3: the voucher number.
- ▶ %4 to %6: custom; depends on the module.

In this recipe, we will demonstrate how the existing automatic transaction text functionality can be modified and extended. One of the places where it is used is the automatic creation of vendor payment journal lines during the vendor payment proposal process. We will modify the system so that the text of the automatically-generated vendor payment lines will include the vendor names.

Getting ready

First, we need to make sure that the vendor payment transaction text is set up properly. Open **Organization administration | Setup | Default descriptions**, find a line with **Vendor - payment, vendor**, and change the text to **Vendor payment %2 to %5**, as shown in the following screenshot:

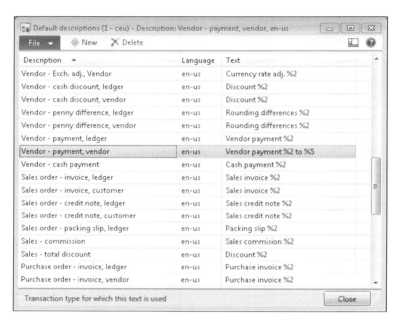

How to do it...

1. In the AOT, find the `CustVendPaymProposalTransferToJournal` class and add the following code to the bottom of the `getTransactionText()` method, right before its return command:

```
transactionTxt.setKey2(
    _custVendPaymProposalLine.custVendTable().name());
```

2. Open **Accounts payable | Journals | Payments | Payment journal** and create a new journal. Open journal lines, run **Payment proposal | Create payment proposal** from the action pane. Define the desired criteria and click on **OK**. On the newly opened **Vendor payment proposal** form, click on the **Transfer** button to transfer all proposed lines to the journal. Notice that the transaction text on each journal lines includes the vendor name, as shown in the following screenshot:

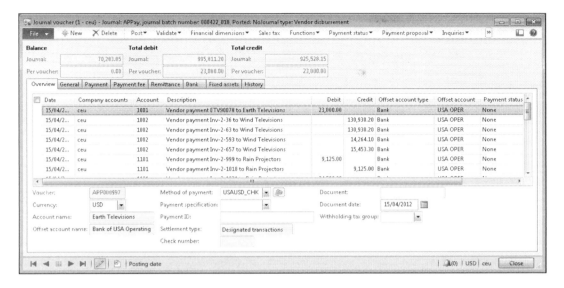

How it works...

The vendor payment proposal uses the `CustVendPaymProposalTransferToJournal` class to create the lines. The same class contains a method named `getTransactionText()`, which is responsible for formatting the text on each line. If we look inside it, we can see that the `TransactionTxt` class is used for this purpose. The class contains the following methods, which are used for substituting the placeholders from %1 to %6 in the defined text:

- ▶ %1: `setDate()`
- ▶ %2: `setFormLetter()`
- ▶ %3: `setVoucher()`
- ▶ %4: `setKey1()`
- ▶ %5: `setKey2()`
- ▶ %6: `setKey3()`

By looking at the code, we can see that only the %4 placeholder is used. So, we can occupy the %5 placeholder and fill it with the vendor name. To achieve this, we have to call the `setKey2()` method with the vendor name as an argument. In this way, every journal line created by the automatic vendor payment proposal will contain a vendor name in its description.

If more than three custom placeholders are required, it is always possible to add an additional one by creating a new setKey() method in the TransactionTxt class. For example, if we want to add placeholder %7, we have to do the following:

Add the following code to the class declaration of the TransactionTxt class:

```
str 20 key4;
```

Create a new method with the following code:

```
void setKey4(str 20 _key4)
{
    key4 = _key4;
}
```

Change the last line of the txt() method to the following:

```
return strFmt(
    txt,
    date2StrUsr(transDate, DateFlags::FormatAll),
    formLetterNum,
    voucherNum,
    key1,
    key2,
    key3,
    key4);
```

Now we can use the setKey4() method for substituting the %7 placeholder.

Notice that although even more placeholders could be added, it should be considered that the transaction text field has a finite number of characters, and the excessive text will be simply truncated.

Creating a purchase order

Purchase orders are used throughout the purchasing process to hold the information about the goods or services that a company buys from its suppliers. Normally, purchase orders are created from the user interface, but in automated processes, purchase orders can be also created from code.

In this recipe, we will learn how to create a purchase order from code. We will use a standard method provided by the application.

How to do it...

1. In the AOT, create a new job named `PurchOrderCreate` with the following code:

```
static void PurchOrderCreate(Args _args)
{
    NumberSeq  numberSeq;
    PurchTable purchTable;
    PurchLine  purchLine;

    ttsBegin;

    numberSeq = NumberSeq::newGetNum(
        PurchParameters::numRefPurchId());
    numberSeq.used();

    purchTable.PurchId = numberSeq.num();
    purchTable.initValue();
    purchTable.initFromVendTable(VendTable::find('1001'));

    if (!purchTable.validateWrite())
    {
        throw Exception::Error;
    }

    purchTable.insert();

    purchLine.PurchId = purchTable.PurchId;
    purchLine.ItemId  = '1205';

    purchLine.createLine(true, true, true, true, true, true);

    ttsCommit;

    info(strFmt(
        "Purchase order '%1' has been created",
        purchTable.PurchId));
}
```

2. Run the job to create a new purchase order.

3. Open **Procurement and sourcing | Common | Purchase orders | All purchase orders** to view the created purchase order:

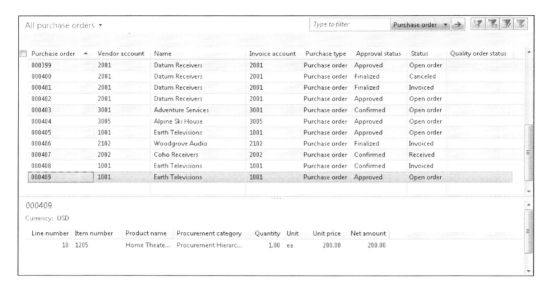

How it works...

In this recipe, we create a new job named `PurchOrderCreate`, which holds all of the code. Here, we start by getting the next purchase order number with the help of the `NumberSeq` class. We also call the `initValue()` and the `initFromVendTable()` methods to initialize various `purchTable` buffer fields. For demonstration purposes we specify the vendor account in the code. We insert the purchase order record into the table only if the validation in the `validateWrite()` method is successful.

Next, we create purchase order lines. Here, we assign the previously used purchase order number and then we set the item number. Again, for demonstration purposes we specify the item number in the code.

Finally, we call the `createLine()` method of the **PurchLine** table to create a new line. This is a very useful method, allowing us to quickly create purchase order lines. The method accepts a number of optional boolean arguments, which are listed as follows:

► Perform data validations before saving? The default is `false`.

► Initialize the line record from the **PurchTable** table? The default is `false`.

► Initialize the line record from the **InventTable** table? The default is `false`.

► Calculate inventory quantity? The default is `false`.

- ▶ Add miscellaneous charges? The default is `true`.
- ▶ Use trade agreements to calculate item price? The default is `false`.
- ▶ Do not copy inventory site and warehouse from the purchase order header? The default is `false`.
- ▶ Use purchase agreements to get item price? The default is `false`.

See also

In this chapter:

- ▶ *Posting a purchase order*

Posting a purchase order

In Dynamics AX, a purchase order goes through a number of statuses in order to reflect its current position within the purchasing process. This status can be updated either manually by using the user interface or programmatically from code.

In this recipe, we will demonstrate how a purchase order status can be updated from code. We will confirm the purchase order created in the previous recipe and will print the relevant document on the screen.

How to do it...

1. In the AOT, create a new job named `PurchOrderPost` with the following code (replace `000409` with your number):

```
static void PurchOrderPost(Args _args)
{
    PurchFormLetter purchFormLetter;
    PurchTable      purchTable;

    purchTable = PurchTable::find('000409');

    purchFormLetter = PurchFormLetter::construct(
        DocumentStatus::PurchaseOrder);

    purchFormLetter.update(
        purchTable,
        '',
        systemDateGet(),
        PurchUpdate::All,
        AccountOrder::None,
        NoYes::No,
        NoYes::Yes);
}
```

2. Run the job to post the specified purchase order and display the purchase order document:

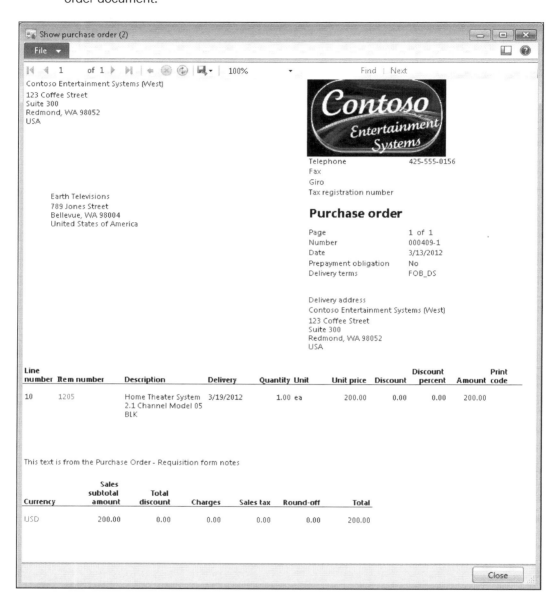

3. Open **Procurement and sourcing | Common | Purchase orders | All purchase orders**, and notice that the **Approval status** of the posted order is now different:

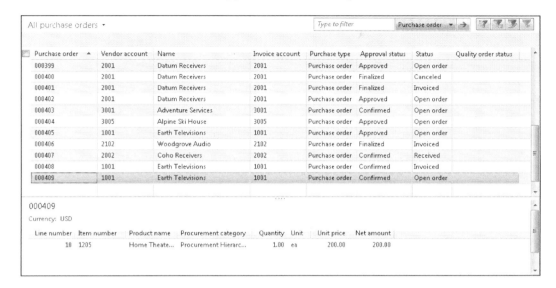

How it works...

In this recipe, we create a new job named `PurchOrderPost`, which holds all of the code.

First, we find a purchase order, which we are going to update. In this recipe, we use the purchase order created in the previous recipe. Here, we normally would replace this code with a user input or an output from some other function.

Next, we create a new `PurchFormLetter` object using its `construct()` constructor. The constructor accepts an argument of type `DocumentStatus`, which defines the type of the posting to be done. Here we use `DocumentStatus::PurchaseOrder` as a value, as we want to confirm the purchase order.

The last thing to do is to call the `update()` method of the `PurchFormLetter` object, which does the actual posting. It accepts a number of arguments, which are listed as follows:

▶ The purchase order header record. In this case, it is the **PurchTable** table.

▶ An external document number. It's not used in this demonstration, as it is not required when posting a purchase order confirmation.

▶ The transaction date. The default is the system date.

- ▶ The quantity to be posted. The default is `PurchUpdate::All`. Other options, such as `PurchUpdate::PackingSlip` or `PurchUpdate::ReceiveNow`, are not relevant when confirming a purchase order.

- ▶ Order summary update. This argument is not used at all. The default is `AccountOrder::None`.

- ▶ A boolean value defining whether a preview or actual posting should be done.

- ▶ A boolean value defining whether the document should be printed.

- ▶ A boolean value specifying whether printing management should be used. The default is `false`.

- ▶ A boolean value defining whether to keep the remaining quantity on order; otherwise it is set to zero. This argument is used when posting credit notes.

- ▶ A container of a number of **TmpFrmVirtual** records. This argument is optional, and is used only when posting purchase invoices.

There's more...

The same technique could be used to post a purchase packing slip, invoice, or update to any other status, which is available in a given context. In our example, let's replace the previous code listed here:

```
purchFormLetter = PurchFormLetter::construct(
    DocumentStatus::PurchaseOrder);
```

With the following code:

```
purchFormLetter = PurchFormLetter::construct(
    DocumentStatus::Invoice);
```

Also, replace the code:

```
purchFormLetter.update(
    purchTable,
    '',
    systemDateGet(),
    PurchUpdate::All,
    AccountOrder::None,
    NoYes::No,
    NoYes::Yes);
```

With the following code:

```
purchFormLetter.update(
    purchTable,
    '8001',
    systemDateGet(),
    PurchUpdate::All,
    AccountOrder::None,
    NoYes::No,
    NoYes::Yes);
```

Now, when you run the job, the purchase order should be updated to an invoice, and the invoice document should be displayed on the screen:

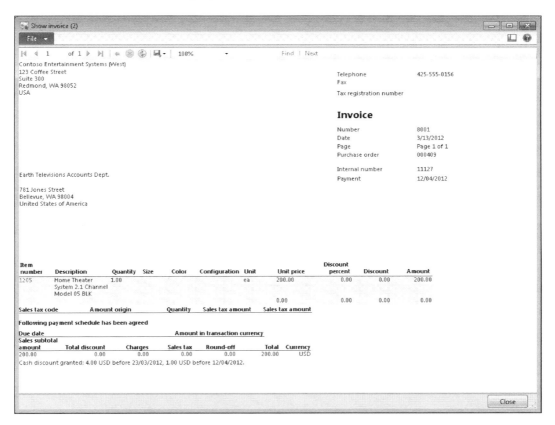

To check the updated purchase order, locate it in **Procurement and sourcing | Common | Purchase orders | All purchase orders**, and notice that its **Status** field is now different:

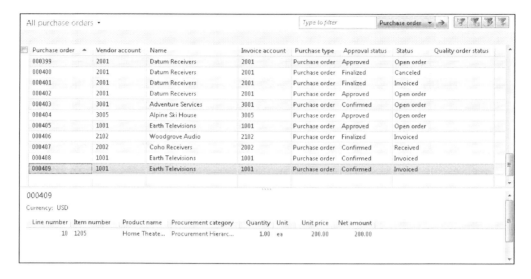

Creating a sales order

Sales orders are used throughout the sales process to hold the information about goods or services that a company sells to its customers. Normally, sales orders are created from the user interface, but in automated processes, sales orders can be also created from code.

In this recipe, we will learn how to create a sales order from code. We will use a standard method provided by the application.

How to do it...

1. In the AOT, create a new job named `SalesOrderCreate` with the following code:

```
static void SalesOrderCreate(Args _args)
{
    NumberSeq   numberSeq;
    SalesTable  salesTable;
    SalesLine   salesLine;

    ttsBegin;

    numberSeq = NumberSeq::newGetNum(
        SalesParameters::numRefSalesId());
```

```
        numberSeq.used();

        salesTable.SalesId = numberSeq.num();
        salesTable.initValue();
        salesTable.CustAccount = '1101';
        salesTable.initFromCustTable();

        if (!salesTable.validateWrite())
        {
            throw Exception::Error;
        }

        salesTable.insert();

        salesLine.SalesId = salesTable.SalesId;
        salesLine.ItemId  = '1205';

        salesLine.createLine(true, true, true, true, true, true);

        ttsCommit;

        info(strFmt(
            "Sales order '%1' has been created", salesTable.SalesId));
    }
```

2. Run the job to create a new sales order.
3. Open **Sales and marketing | Common | Sales orders | All sales orders** to view the newly created sales order:

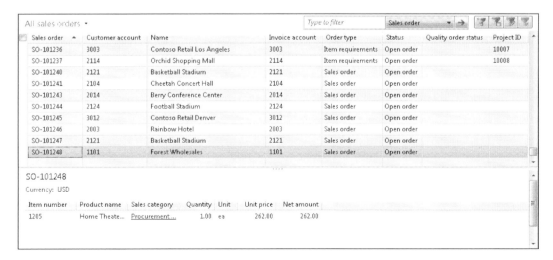

How it works...

In this recipe, we create a new job named `SalesOrderCreate`, which holds all of the code. The job starts by generating the next sales order number with the help of the `NumberSeq` class. We also call the `initValue()` and the `initFromCustTable()` methods to initialize various `salesTable` buffer fields. Notice that for `initFromCustTable()`, we first set the customer account and call the method afterwards, instead of passing the customer record as an argument. We insert the sales order record into the table only if the validation in the `validateWrite()` method is successful.

Next, we create purchase order lines. Here, we assign the previously used sales order number, and set the item number.

Finally, we call the `createLine()` method of the **SalesLine** table to create a new line. This is a very useful method allowing quickly create sales order lines. The method accepts a number of optional boolean arguments. The following list explains most of them:

- Perform data validations before saving? The default is `false`.
- Initialize the line record from the **SalesTable** table? The default is `false`.
- Initialize the line record from the **InventTable** table? The default is `false`.
- Calculate inventory quantity? The default is `false`.
- Add miscellaneous charges? The default is `true`.
- Use trade agreements to calculate item price? The default is `false`.
- Reserve the item? The default is `false`.
- Ignore customer credit limit? The default is `false`.

See also

In this chapter:

- *Posting a sales order*

Posting a sales order

In Dynamics AX, a sales order goes through a number of statuses in order to reflect its current position within the sales process. The status can be updated either manually using the user interface or programmatically from code.

In this recipe, we will demonstrate how a sales order status can be updated from code. We will register a packing slip for the sales order created in the previous recipe, and will print the relevant document on the screen.

How to do it...

1. In the AOT, create a new job named `SalesOrderPost` with the following code (replace `SO-101248` with your number):

    ```
    static void SalesOrderPost(Args _args)
    {
        SalesFormLetter salesFormLetter;
        salesTable        salesTable;

        salesTable = SalesTable::find('SO-101248');

        salesFormLetter = SalesFormLetter::construct(
            DocumentStatus::PackingSlip);

        salesFormLetter.update(
            salesTable,
            systemDateGet(),
            SalesUpdate::All,
            AccountOrder::None,
            NoYes::No,
            NoYes::Yes);
    }
    ```

2. Run the job to post the specified sales order, and display the packing slip document on the screen:

3. Open **Sales and marketing | Common | Sales orders | All sales orders**, and notice the updated sales order status:

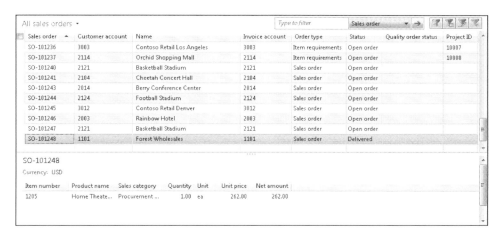

How it works...

In this recipe, we create a new job named `SalesOrderPost`, which holds all of the code.

First, we find a sales order, which we are going to update. In this recipe, we use the sales order created in the previous recipe. Here, we normally would replace this code with a user input or an output from some other function.

Next, we create a new `SalesFormLetter` object using its `construct()` constructor. The constructor accepts an argument of type `DocumentStatus`, which defines the type of the posting to be done. Here we use `DocumentStatus::PackingSlip` as a value, as we want to register a packing slip.

Finally, we call the `update()` of the `PurchFormLetter`, which does the actual posting. It accepts a number of arguments:

- ▸ The sales order header record, that is, the **SalesTable** table.
- ▸ The transaction date. The default is the system date.
- ▸ The quantity to be posted. The default is `SalesUpdate::All`.
- ▸ The order summary update. This argument is not used at all. The default is `AccountOrder::None`.
- ▸ A boolean value defining whether preview or actual posting should be done.
- ▸ A boolean value defining whether the document should be printed.
- ▸ A boolean value specifying whether printing management should be used. The default is `false`.

▶ A boolean value defining whether to keep the remaining quantity on order; otherwise it is set to zero. This argument is used when posting credit notes.

▶ A container of a number of **TmpFrmVirtual** records. This argument is optional and is used only when posting sales invoices.

There's more...

The `SalesFormLetter` class could also be used to do other types of posting, such as sales order confirmation, picking list, or invoice. For example, to invoice the previously used sales order, let's replace the code:

```
salesFormLetter = SalesFormLetter::construct(
    DocumentStatus::PackingSlip);
```

With the following code:

```
salesFormLetter = SalesFormLetter::construct(
    DocumentStatus::Invoice);
```

Now when you run the job, the sales order should be updated to an invoice, and the invoice document should be displayed on the screen:

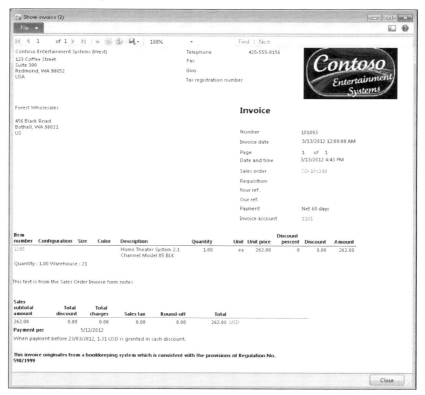

To check the updated sales order, find it in **Sales and marketing** | **Common** | **Sales orders** | **All sales orders** and notice that the **Status** field has now changed:

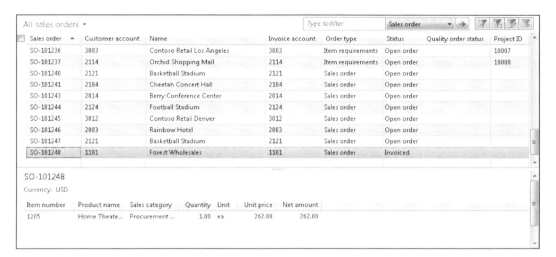

Creating an electronic payment format

Electronic payments, in general, can save time and reduce paperwork when making or receiving payments within a company. Dynamics AX provides a number of standard out of the box electronic payment formats. The system also provides an easy way of customizing the existing payment forms or creating new ones.

In this recipe, we will learn how to create a new custom electronic payment format. To demonstrate the principle, we will only output some basic information and will concentrate on the approach itself.

How to do it...

1. In the AOT, create a new class named `VendOutPaymRecord_Test` with the following code:

```
class VendOutPaymRecord_Test extends VendOutPaymRecord
{
}


public void output()
{
    str         outRecord;
    Name        companyName;
```

```
        BankAccount bankAccount;

        outRecord = strRep(' ', 50);

        companyName = subStr(
            custVendPaym.receiversCompanyName(), 1, 40);
        bankAccount = subStr(
            custVendPaym.receiversBankAccount(), 1, 8);

        outRecord = strPoke(outRecord, companyName, 1);
        outRecord = strPoke(outRecord, bankAccount, 43);

        file.write(outRecord);
    }
```

2. Create another class named VendOutPaym_Test with the following code:

```
class VendOutPaym_Test extends VendOutPaym
{
}

public PaymInterfaceName interfaceName()
{
    return "Test payment format";
}

public ClassId custVendOutPaymRecordRootClassId()
{
    return classNum(VendOutPaymRecord_Test);
}

protected Object dialog()
{
    DialogRunbase dialog;

    dialog = super();

    this.dialogAddFileName(dialog);

    return dialog;
}

public boolean validate(Object _calledFrom = null)
{
    return true;
```

```
}

public void open()
{
    #LocalCodePage

    file = CustVendOutPaym::newFile(filename, #cp_1252);

    if (!file || file.status() != IO_Status::Ok)
    {
        throw error(
            strFmt("File %1 could not be opened.", filename));
    }

    file.outFieldDelimiter('');
    file.outRecordDelimiter("\r\n");

    file.write('Starting file:');
}

public void close()
{
    file.write('Closing file');
}
```

3. Open **Accounts payable | Setup | Payment | Methods of payment** and create a
    new record as follows:

4. Open the **File formats** tab page, click on the **Setup** button, and move **Test payment format** from the right to the left:

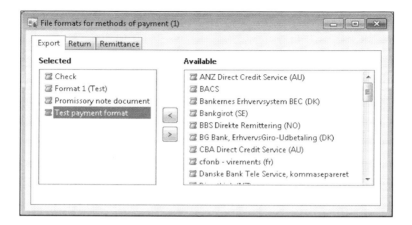

5. Then, go back to the **Methods of payment** form, and select this format in the **Export format** field as follows:

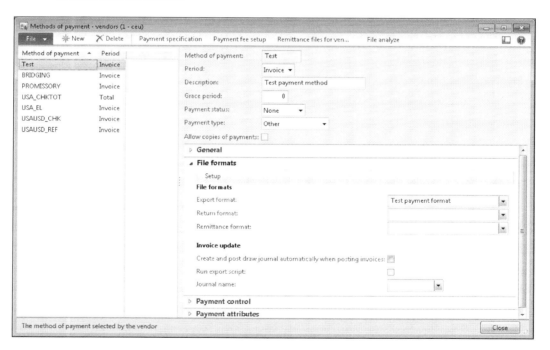

6. Close the **Methods of payment** form. Open **Accounts payable | Journals | Payments | Payment journal** and create a new journal:

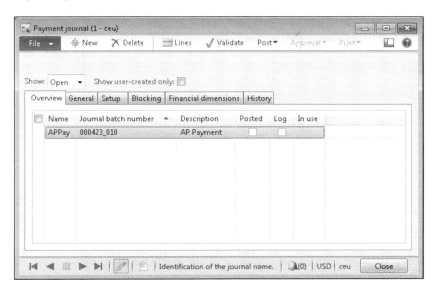

7. Click on the **Lines** button to open the journal lines. Create a new line and make sure you set the **Method of payment** to **Test**:

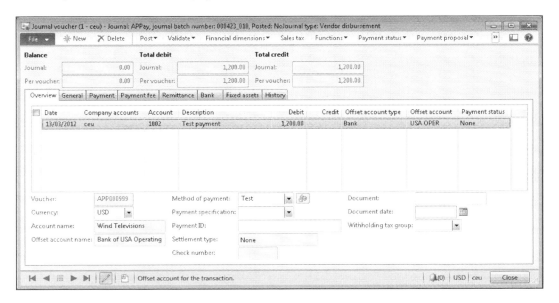

8. Next, click on **Functions | Generate payments**. Fill in the dialog fields as displayed in the following screenshot:

9. Click on **OK**, and choose the export file name:

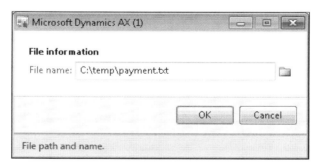

10. Click on **OK** to complete the process, and notice that the journal line's **Payment status** changed from **None** to **Sent**, which means that the payment file was generated successfully:

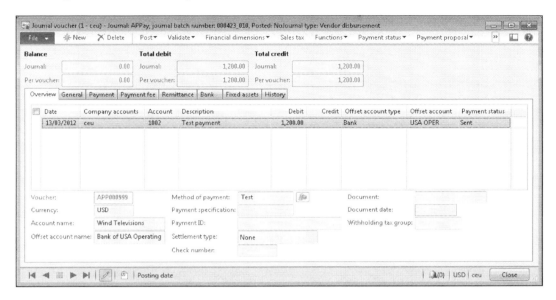

11. Open the created file with any text editor, for example Notepad, to check its contents:

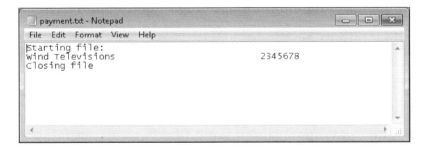

How it works...

In this recipe, we create two new classes, which are normally required for generating custom vendor payments. The electronic payments are presented as text files to be sent to the bank. The first one is the `VendOutPaymRecord_Test` class, which is responsible for formatting the payment lines, and the second one is the `VendOutPaym_Test` class, which generates the header and the footer sections, and creates the payment file itself.

The `VendOutPaymRecord_Test` class extends `VendOutPaymRecord`, and inherits all the common functionality. We only need to override its `output()` to define our own logic for formatting the payment lines. The `output()` is called once for each payment line.

Inside of the `output()` method, we use the `outRecord` variable, which we initially fill in with `50` blank characters using the global `strRep()` function, and then insert all required information into the predefined positions within the variable as per format requirements. Normally, here we should insert all the required information such as dates, account numbers, amounts, references, and so on. But, to keep this demonstration to a minimum, we only insert the company name and the bank account number.

In the same method, we use another variable named `custVendPaym` of type `CustVendPaym`, which already holds all the information we need. We only have to call some of its methods to retrieve it. In this example, to get the company name and the bank account number, we call `receiversCompanyName()` and the `receiversBankAccount()`, respectively. We trim the returned values using the global `substr()` function, and insert them into the first and 43rd positions of the `outRecord` variable using the global `strPoke()` function.

And finally, at the bottom of the `output()` method, we add the formatted text to the end of the payment file.

Another class that we create is `VendOutPaym_Test`. It extends the `VendOutPaym` class and also inherits all common functionality. We only need to override some of the methods that are specific to our format:

▶ The `interfaceName()` method returns a name of the payment format. Normally, this text is displayed in the user interface when configuring payments.

▶ The `custVendOutPaymRecordRootClassId()` method returns an ID of the class, which generates payment lines. It is used internally to identify which class to use when formatting the lines. In our case, it is `VendOutPaymRecord_Test`.

▶ The `dialog()` method is used only if we need to add something to the user screen when generating payments. Our payment is a text file, so we need to ask a user to specify the file name. We do that by calling the `dialogAddFileName()` method, which is a member method of the parent class. It will automatically add a file selection control, and we will not have to worry about things, such as a label or how to get its value from the user input. There are numerous other standard controls, which can be added to the dialog by calling various `dialogAdd...()` methods. Additional controls can also be added here by using the `addField()`, or similar methods of the dialog object directly.

▶ The `validate()` method is one of the methods which has to be implemented on each custom class. Normally, user input validation should go here. Our example does not have any validation, so we simply return `true`.

▶ In the `open()` method, we are responsible for initializing the file variable for further processing. Here, we use the `newFile()` constructor of the `CustVendOutPaym` class to create a new instance of the variable. After some standard validations, we set the field and the row delimiters, by calling its `outFieldDelimiter()` and `outRecordDelimiter()` methods, respectively. In this example, the values in each line should not be separated by any symbol, so we call the `outFieldDelimiter()` method with an empty string. We call the `outRecordDelimiter()` method with the new line symbol to define that every line ends with a line break. Note that the last line of this method writes a text to the file header. Here, we place some simple text, so that we can recognize it later when viewing the generated file.

▶ The last one is the `close()` method, which is used to perform additional actions before the file is closed. Here, we specify some text to be displayed in the footer of the generated file.

Now, this new payment format is ready to use. After some setup, we can start creating the vendor payment journals with this type of payment. Note the file generated in the previous section of this recipe—we can clearly see which text in the file comes from which place of the code. These places should be replaced with your own code to build custom electronic payment formats for Dynamics AX.

6
Integration with Microsoft Office

In this chapter, we will cover the following recipes:

- ▶ Creating an Excel file
- ▶ Reading an Excel file
- ▶ Creating a Word document from a template
- ▶ Creating a Word document with repeating elements
- ▶ Creating a Microsoft Project file
- ▶ Sending an e-mail using Outlook

Introduction

In most of the companies where Dynamics AX is used, people use Microsoft Office Suite too. The new Dynamics AX 2012 and Microsoft Office is now even closer—similar navigation, look and feel, out of the box integration, and so on.

In this chapter, we will pay special attention to the Microsoft Office applications, such as Excel, Word, Project, and Outlook. We will learn how to create and read various Office documents that could be used for exporting/importing business data for further distribution or analysis. We will also see how personalized documents can be created within Dynamics AX from predefined templates. The chapter also discusses about how to export Dynamics AX data as Microsoft Project plan and how to send emails from Dynamics AX using Outlook.

Creating an Excel file

The Microsoft Office Excel format is one of the formats that have been supported by Dynamics AX right from its early versions. Since Dynamics AX 2009, almost every form has the **Export to Excel** function, which quickly allows loading data on the screen into Excel for further analysis with powerful Excel tools. In Dynamics AX 2012, the new Microsoft Office Add-ins were introduced. They allow data exporting, refreshing, editing, and publishing back to Dynamics AX, in a very user-friendly manner.

But if the Add-ins are not installed, it is still possible to create an Excel document from code. Dynamics AX holds a set of standard application classes prefixed with `SysExcel`. Basically, those classes are `COM` wrappers for Excel, and they contain additional helper methods to make the developer's tasks easier.

In this recipe, we will demonstrate the use of the `SysExcel` classes. We will create a new Excel file from code, and will fill it with a customer list from the system.

How to do it...

Carry out the following steps in order to complete this recipe:

1. In the AOT, create a new job named `CreateExcelFile` with the following code:

```
static void CreateExcelFile(Args _args)
{
    CustTable            custTable;
    SysExcelApplication  excel;
    SysExcelWorkbooks    workbooks;
    SysExcelWorkbook     workbook;
    SysExcelWorksheets   worksheets;
    SysExcelWorksheet    worksheet;
    SysExcelCells        cells;
    SysExcelCell         cell;
    int                  row;

    excel = SysExcelApplication::construct();

    workbooks   = excel.workbooks();

    workbook    = workbooks.add();

    worksheets  = workbook.worksheets();

    worksheet   = worksheets.itemFromNum(1);

    cells       = worksheet.cells();
```

```
        cells.range('A:A').numberFormat('@');

        while select custTable
        {
            row++;
            cell = cells.item(row, 1);
            cell.value(custTable.AccountNum);
            cell = cells.item(row, 2);
            cell.value(custTable.name());
        }

        excel.visible(true);
    }
```

2. Run the job and check the list of customers on the screen:

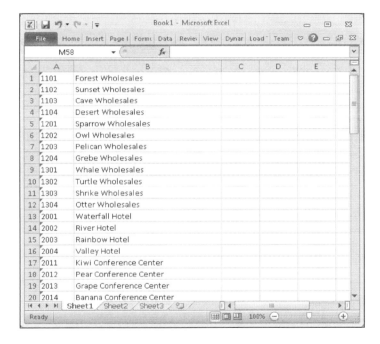

3. Save the list as a file for further use in the next recipe, say **C:\temp\customers.xlsx**.

How it works...

We start the code by creating the `SysExcelApplication` object, which represents
an instance of Excel. Next, we get a collection of Excel documents that are stored in the
`SysExcelWorkbooks` class. Initially, the collection is empty, so we have to create a new
document by calling the `add()` method of the `SysExcelWorkbooks` class.

Once the document is ready, we get a reference to a collection of sheets within the document, and then we get a reference to the first sheet in the collection. This is where we start adding the data.

Next, we get a reference to a collection of cells within the sheet. We use the `SysExcelCells` class for this. The first column in the sheet will contain a customer's account number, so we have to make sure it is formatted as text. To do that we address the first column by using the `A:A` range and setting its format to `@`.

To display all customers, we start looping through the **CustTable** table and fill customer account into the first column and customer name into the second one, for each row. In this way, we populate as many rows as we have customers in the system.

Finally, we set the Excel instance to show up on the screen by calling its `visible()` method. We do this after all data has been populated, to make sure the user cannot interfere with the process.

Note that we formatted only the first column of the sheet. This is to prevent automatic Excel formatting. Most of the time, customer accounts are expressed as numbers such as `1000`, `1001`, and so on, and although they are stored in the system as text, Excel will automatically display them as numbers. We do not have to format the second column as its data is unambiguous, and here we can rely on Excel's automatic formatting.

Reading an Excel file

In Dynamics AX, retrieving data from Excel files can be done with the help of the same `SysExcel` classes that we used for creating Excel files. The classes provide a simple interface for developers to access and read data in Excel files.

In this recipe, we will demonstrate how to read Excel files using the `SysExcel` classes. We will read the customer file created in the previous recipe and display its content in the Infolog.

How to do it...

Carry out the following steps in order to complete this recipe:

1. In the AOT, create a new job named `ReadExcelFile` with the following code (replace the file name with your own):

    ```
    static void ReadExcelFile (Args _args)
    {
        SysExcelApplication excel;
        SysExcelWorkbooks   workbooks;
        SysExcelWorkbook    workbook;
        SysExcelWorksheets  worksheets;
    ```

```
SysExcelWorksheet    worksheet;
SysExcelCells        cells;
COMVariantType       type;
int                  row;
CustAccount          account;
CustName             name;
#define.filename(@'C:\temp\customers.xlsx')

excel = SysExcelApplication::construct();

workbooks = excel.workbooks();

try
{
    workbooks.open(#filename);
}
catch (Exception::Error)
{
    throw error("File cannot be opened");
}

workbook   = workbooks.item(1);

worksheets = workbook.worksheets();

worksheet  = worksheets.itemFromNum(1);

cells      = worksheet.cells();

type = cells.item(row+1, 1).value().variantType();

while (type != COMVariantType::VT_EMPTY)
{
    row++;
    account = cells.item(row, 1).value().bStr();
    name    = cells.item(row, 2).value().bStr();
    info(strFmt('%1 - %2', account, name));
    type = cells.item(row+1, 1).value().variantType();
}
excel.quit();
}
```

2. Run the job to display the contents of the file in the Infolog, as shown in the following screenshot:

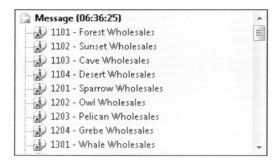

How it works...

We start the code by creating the `SysExcelApplication` object, which represents an instance of Excel. Next, we get a collection of Excel documents that are stored in the `SysExcelWorkbooks` class. Initially, the collection is empty and we open the previously created file as the first document in the collection, by calling the `open()` method of the `SysExcelWorkbooks` class. Then, we get a reference to the opened document, which is expressed as the `SysExcelWorkbook` class.

Once the document is ready, we get a reference to a collection of sheets within the document, and then we get a reference to the first sheet in the collection. This is where our data is located.

Next, we get a reference to a collection of cells within the sheet. We use the `SysExcelCells` class for this. We also use a `do while` statement to go through all the rows until the first cell of the next row is empty. Inside the statement, we read the customer account from the first cell and customer name from the second cell in each row, and output them to the Infolog. The `value()` method of the `SysExcelCells` class returns an object of type `COMVariant`, and we call its `bStr()` method to retrieve the textual data.

Note that the `COMVariant` class is used for storing various types of data when dealing with external objects. It could be of any type, such as string, integer, decimal, and so on. In cases when it is not known what type of data to expect in a cell, we may call the `variantType()` method to check what kind of data is stored in the cell and, depending on the result, we may use `bStr()`, `int()`, `float()`, or other relevant methods of the `COMVariant` class.

The last thing to do is to close the instance of Excel.

Creating a Word document from a template

Microsoft Office Word can present Dynamics AX data in a variety of formats. One way is to use Word templates which can combine predefined formats with Dynamics AX data to generate nice looking business documents. Another way of formatting extracted Dynamics AX data using Office documents is the newly introduced Microsoft Office Add-ins.

But if Add-ins are not installed, Dynamics AX still allows Word documents to be created from code. Although there are no standard helper classes for Word as we have for Excel, Word documents can still be created using a very similar approach by calling COM components directly.

In this recipe, we will create a simple Word document from a template. We will use the COM component model to read the Word template and fill it in with data from the system.

Getting ready

Before we start with the code, we have to create a new Word template and save it as a file named **letter.dotx**. Add some text and four bookmarks (use the **Insert | Links | Bookmark** button). as per the following list:

- ▸ **Customer**, one space after the text **To:**
- ▸ **User**, in the next line after the text **Kind Regards**
- ▸ **Company**, in the next line after the text **User**
- ▸ **Phone**, one space after the text **Tel.:**

The document should look identical to the following screenshot:

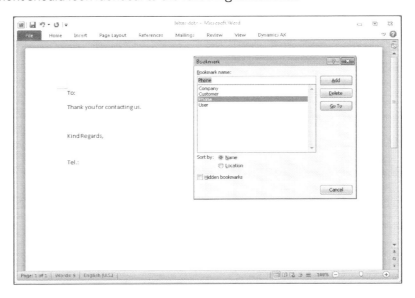

How to do it...

Carry out the following steps in order to complete this recipe:

1. In the AOT, create a new job named `CreateWordDocument` with the following code:

```
static void CreateWordDocument(Args _args)
{
    Filename    template;
    CustTable   custTable;
    COM         word;
    COM         documents;
    COM         document;
    COM         bookmarks;
    COM         bookmark;
    COM         range;

    void processBookmark(str _name, str _value)
    {
        if (!bookmarks.exists(_name))
        {
            return;
        }
        bookmark = bookmarks.item(_name);
        range    = bookmark.range();
        range.insertAfter(_value);
    }

    #define.Word('Word.Application')
    #define.template(@'C:\temp\letter.dotx');

    custTable = CustTable::find('1101');

    try
    {
        word = new COM(#Word);
    }
    catch (Exception::Internal)
    {
        if (word == null)
        {
            throw error("Microsoft Word is not installed");
        }
    }

    documents = word.documents();
    document  = documents.add(#template);
    bookmarks = document.bookmarks();

    processBookmark(
```

```
        'Customer',
        custTable.name());

    processBookmark(
        'User',
        HcmWorker::find(
            DirPersonUser::current().worker()).name());

    processBookmark(
        'Company',
        CompanyInfo::find().Name);

    processBookmark(
        'Phone',
        CompanyInfo::find().phone());

    word.visible(true);
}
```

2. Run the job to see the results. Note the data from the system inserted in the template near each bookmark:

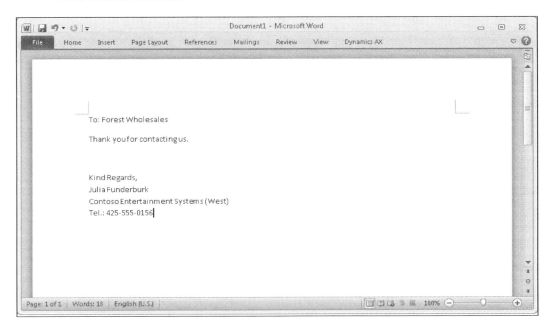

How it works...

In this recipe, we start by declaring various COM objects and their collections, a collection of documents, and so on. We also declare a local function for inserting a value into a document near a predefined bookmark.

Next, we create a new instance of Word, get a reference to the document collection, and create a new document from the template. Then, we get a reference to the bookmark collection and start inserting the values into the document with the help of the previously defined function.

Finally, once the document is finished, we display it on the screen.

Creating a Word document with repeating elements

Microsoft Office Word documents created from Dynamics AX code, besides simple data output, can have more complex structures, such as a dynamic number of repeating elements. For example, a collection letter document can have a variable list of overdue invoices for different customers.

In this recipe, we will create a Word document with repeating elements. For this demonstration, we will display the contents of the **LedgerParameters** table in a dynamically generated Word table.

Getting ready

For this example, we need to prepare a new Word template and save it as a file named **table.dotx**. The template should contain one bookmark named **TableName** at the top, and one table beneath with a single row and two columns, as follows:

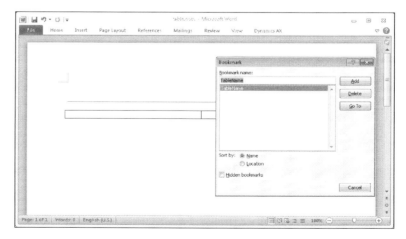

How to do it...

Carry out the following steps in order to complete this recipe:

1. In the AOT, create a new job named `CreateWordTable` with the following code:

```
static void CreateWordTable(Args _args)
{
    TableId            tableId;
    COM                word;
    COM                documents;
    COM                document;
    COM                bookmarks;
    COM                bookmark;
    COM                tables;
    COM                table;
    COM                rows;
    COM                row;
    COM                cells;
    COM                cell;
    COM                range;
    Query              query;
    QueryRun           queryRun;
    Common             common;
    TmpSysTableField   fields;
    DictField          dictField;
    int                i;

    void processBookmark(str _name, str _value)
    {
        if (!bookmarks.exists(_name))
        {
            return;
        }
        bookmark = bookmarks.item(_name);
        range    = bookmark.range();
        range.insertAfter(_value);
    }

    #define.Word('Word.Application')
    #define.template(@'C:\temp\table.dotx');

    tableId = tableNum(LedgerParameters);

    try
    {
        word = new COM(#Word);
```

```
}
catch (Exception::Internal)
{
    if (word == null)
    {
        throw error("Microsoft Word is not installed");
    }
}

documents = word.documents();
document  = documents.add(#template);
bookmarks = document.bookmarks();
processBookmark(
    'TableName',
    tableId2pname(tableId));

tables = document.tables();
table  = tables.Item(1);
rows   = table.rows();

query = new Query();
query.addDataSource(tableId);

queryRun = new QueryRun(query);
queryRun.next();

common = queryRun.get(tableId);

fields = TmpSysTableField::findTableFields(
    null, tableId);

while select fields
{
    dictField = new DictField(
        tableId,
        fields.FieldId);

    if (dictField.isSystem())
    {
        continue;
    }

    i++;

    row   = rows.item(i);
    cells = row.cells();
```

```
cell   = cells.item(1);
range = cell.range();
range.insertAfter(fields.FieldLabel);

cell   = cells.item(2);
range = cell.range();
range.insertAfter(
    strFmt('%1', common.(fields.FieldId)));

row = rows.add();
}

row.delete();

word.visible(true);
}
```

2. Run the job to generate the document containing a list, the **LedgerParameters** table field, and their values:

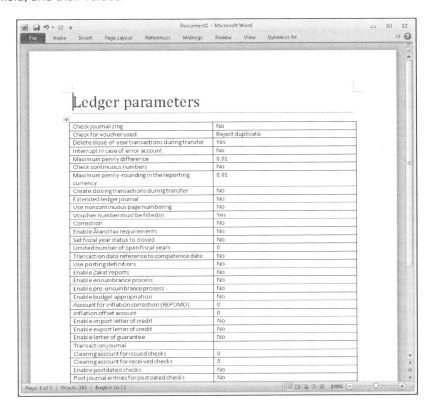

How it works...

In this recipe, in a way quite similar to what we did previously, we declare COM objects representing various elements, such as the Word application itself, a document collection, and bookmarks. We also declare objects representing table, row, cell, and their collections, respectively, and a local helper function for inserting a value into a document near a predefined bookmark.

After the declaration section, we create a new instance of Word, get a reference to the document collection, and create a new document from the template. Then, we get a reference to the bookmark collection and insert the selected table name as a document title with the help of the previously defined function.

Next, we get a reference to a table collection and then a reference to the first and only table in the collection. This is the table we inserted into the template previously. Then, we prepare a query for retrieving data from the selected table and get the first record in the returned result set. The **LedgerParameters** table is a configuration table and normally contains a single record per company. We also get a list of its fields with the help of the `findTableFields()` method of the **TmpSysTableField** table. The field information is inserted into the temporary table for further use.

Lastly, we insert each field's name into the first column of the table in the document and its respective value into the second column. Here, we exclude any system fields, such as **RecId**, **dataAreaId**, **createdBy**, and others. Once the document is finished, we display it on the screen.

Creating a Microsoft Project file

Microsoft Project files are one of the many files that can be created in Dynamics AX by using the COM component model. Microsoft Project files can be very useful when it comes to presenting some kind of scheduling information, such as a project plan or a production schedule.

In this recipe, we will create a new Microsoft Project file from code. We will output a project's forecast data as a project plan in Microsoft Project.

Getting ready

For this recipe, we need to set up some data. Open **Project management and accounting | Common | Projects | All projects**, select any of the open projects and click on **Plan | Forecast | Hour forecasts** in the action pane. In the open **Hour forecasts** form, create several forecast lines similar to the ones in the following screenshot:

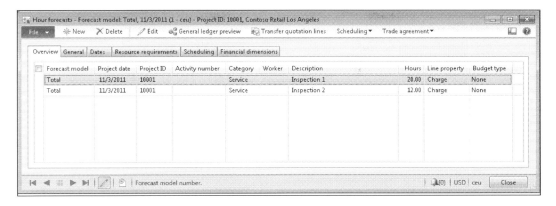

To update scheduling, click on **Scheduling | Scheduling** in the action pane of the **Hour forecasts** form, and then click on the **OK** button to accept the default parameters and run scheduling:

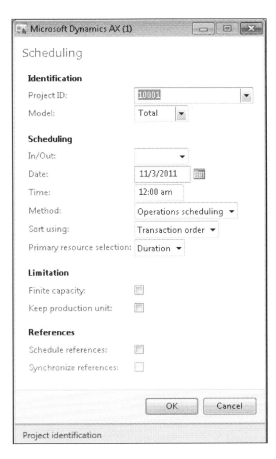

Now, the information in the **Scheduling** tab of the **Hour forecasts** form should look identical to the following screenshot:

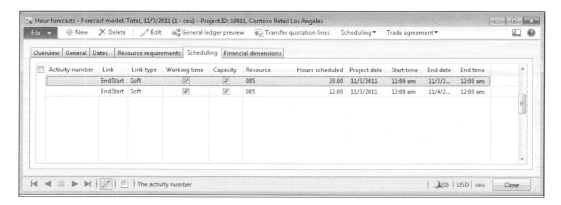

How to do it...

Carry out the following steps in order to complete this recipe:

1. In the AOT, create a new job named `CreateProjectFile` with the following code (replace the project number and the forecast model with your own):

```
static void CreateProjectFile(Args _args)
{
    ProjTable        projTable;
    ProjForecastEmpl forecastEmpl;
    COM              msproject;
    COM              projects;
    COM              project;
    COM              tasks;
    COM              task;
    int              n;
    #define.MSProject('MSProject.Application')

    projTable = ProjTable::find('10001');

    try
    {
        msproject = new COM(#MSProject);
    }
    catch (Exception::Internal)
    {
        if (msproject == null)
        {
```

```
            throw error(
                "Microsoft Project is not installed");
        }
    }

    projects = msproject.Projects();
    project  = projects.Add();

    tasks = project.Tasks();

    task = tasks.Add();
    task.Name(ProjTable.Name);
    task.OutlineLevel(1);

    while select forecastEmpl
        where forecastEmpl.ProjId  == projTable.ProjId
          && forecastEmpl.ModelId == 'Total'
    {
        task = tasks.Add();
        task.OutlineLevel(2);
        task.Name(forecastEmpl.Txt);
        task.Start(forecastEmpl.SchedFromDate);
        task.Duration(forecastEmpl.SchedTimeHours*60);
        if (n)
        {
            task.LinkPredecessors(tasks.UniqueID(n));
        }
        n = task.UniqueID();
    }

    msproject.visible(true);
}
```

2. To test the code, run the job. Note the forecasted project hours displayed as a Microsoft Project plan:

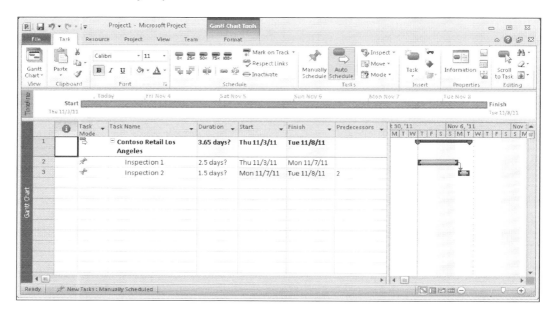

How it works...

In this recipe, we use very similar approach used previously to create other Microsoft Office documents. We declare the project and task objects, and their collections, respectively. Then, we create a new instance of the Microsoft Project application, get a reference to the collection of projects, which is initially empty, and create a new project.

Once the project is ready, we get a reference to the collection of tasks and start adding individual tasks. The first task is a parent task and we set its name to the name of the selected project.

Next, we go through all project hour forecast records and start adding each line as a new task in the document. Here, we set various task properties, such as name, start date, and duration. We also define every task to be dependent on the previous one by calling the LinkPredecessors() method with the previous task number as an argument.

Finally, once the document is ready, we display it on the screen.

Sending an e-mail using Outlook

In Dynamics AX, e-mails can be sent in several ways. One of them is to use Microsoft Office Outlook. The benefit of using Outlook is that the user can review e-mails and modify if required, before they are actually sent. Also, all the sent e-mails can be stored in the user's Outlook folders.

In this recipe, we will send an e-mail using Outlook. We will incorporate customer data from the system into a template to create the e-mail's text.

Getting ready

Before we start with the code, we need to create a new e-mail template. This is standard Dynamics AX functionality and can be found in **Organization administration | Setup | E-mail templates**. Open the **E-mail templates** form and create the following record:

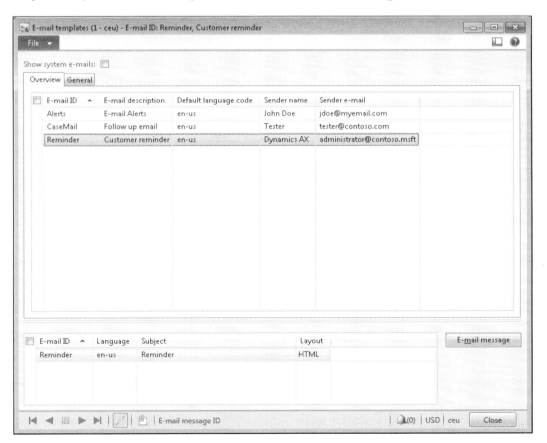

Next, click on the **E-mail message** button and enter the e-mail body, as shown in the following screenshot:

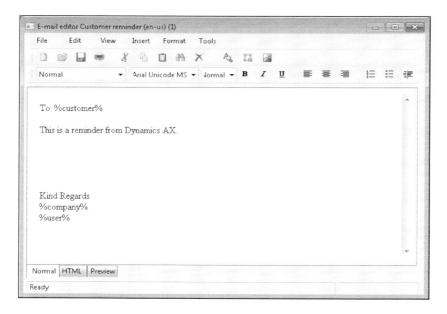

How to do it...

Carry out the following steps in order to complete this recipe:

1. In the AOT, create a new job named `SendCustReminderEmail` with the following code (replace the customer account number with your own):

```
static void SendCustReminderEmail(Args _args)
{
    CustTable custTable;
    Map       mappings;

    custTable = custTable::find('1101');

    mappings = new Map(Types::String, Types::String);

    mappings.insert(
        'customer',
        custTable.name());

    mappings.insert(
        'company',
        CompanyInfo::find().Name);

    mappings.insert(
```

```
        'user',
        HcmWorker::find(
            DirPersonUser::current().worker()).name());

    SysINetMail::sendEMail(
        'Reminder',
        custTable.languageId(),
        custTable.email(),
        mappings);
}
```

2. Run the job, and click on the **Allow** button once Microsoft Outlook displays the following security warning:

3. To review the results, open Outlook and look for the newly created message in either the **Outbox** or **Sent Items** folders. Note that all placeholders were replaced with actual values from the system:

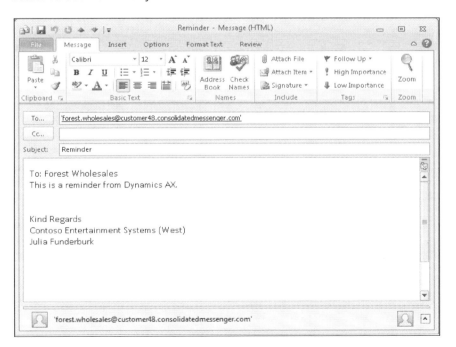

How it works...

In this recipe, we prepare a number of key-value mappings, which will be inserted into the e-mail template. Then, we use the `sendEMail()` method of the `SysINetMail` class to send an e-mail using Outlook. The method accepts the following arguments:

- ▸ The name of the template.
- ▸ Customer language code.
- ▸ Customer e-mail address.
- ▸ The prepared mapping.

Note that, depending on the version of Outlook, the **To** field may not be populated automatically with the customer's email. This is due to a MAPI compatibility issue.

7
Using Services

In this chapter, we will cover the following recipes:

- ▶ Consuming the system query service
- ▶ Consuming the system metadata service
- ▶ Consuming an existing document service
- ▶ Creating a document service
- ▶ Consuming a document service
- ▶ Using an enhanced document service
- ▶ Creating a custom service
- ▶ Consuming a custom service
- ▶ Consuming an external service

Introduction

Dynamics AX provides many out of the box services—programmable objects that can be used to communicate with application components or third-party applications. In order to meet complex business requirements, the existing services can also be customized or new services can be created from scratch.

The services are divided into three categories: non-customizable built-in system services, document services, which provide a standard approach for communicating between systems, and custom services, which allow any X++ logic to be exposed as a service.

In this chapter, various scenarios of creating and consuming all three types of services will be presented. The recipes in this chapter will demonstrate how services can be exposed and consumed using different techniques. All examples, one way or another, will use the system currency information.

Consuming the system query service

The query service is one of the built-in system services in Dynamics AX. The service provides a set of operations allowing any AOT or dynamic query to be executed. The results are returned as an ADO.NET `DataSet` object. The query service cannot be customized and is hosted on the Application Object Server at a fixed address.

In this recipe, we will create a .NET console application that will connect to the query service. The application will retrieve a list of currencies in the system, with the help of a dynamically created query.

How to do it...

Carry out the following steps in order to complete this recipe:

1. In Visual Studio, create a new Visual C# Console Application project named `ConsumeSystemQueryService`.

2. Add a new service reference named `QueryService`, to the project (replace `SEA-DEV:8101` with your address):

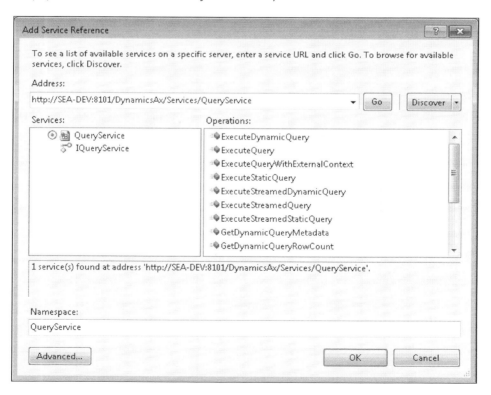

3. Add the following code to the top section of the `Program.cs` file:

```
using ConsumeSystemQueryService.QueryService;
using System.Data;
```

4. Add the following code to the `Main()` method:

```
QueryServiceClient serviceClient;
QueryMetadata query;
QueryDataSourceMetadata currencyDataSource;
QueryDataFieldMetadata field1, field2;
Paging paging = null;
DataSet result;

query = new QueryMetadata();
query.QueryType = QueryService.QueryType.Join;
query.AllowCrossCompany = true;
query.DataSources = new QueryDataSourceMetadata[1];

currencyDataSource = new QueryDataSourceMetadata();
currencyDataSource.Name = "Currency";
currencyDataSource.Enabled = true;
currencyDataSource.FetchMode = FetchMode.OneToOne;
currencyDataSource.Table = "Currency";
currencyDataSource.DynamicFieldList = false;
currencyDataSource.Fields = new QueryFieldMetadata[2];
query.DataSources[0] = currencyDataSource;

field1 = new QueryDataFieldMetadata();
field1.FieldName = "CurrencyCode";
field1.SelectionField = SelectionField.Database;
currencyDataSource.Fields[0] = field1;

field2 = new QueryDataFieldMetadata();
field2.FieldName = "Txt";
field2.SelectionField = SelectionField.Database;
currencyDataSource.Fields[1] = field2;

serviceClient = new QueryServiceClient();
result = serviceClient.ExecuteQuery(query, ref paging);

foreach (DataRow row in result.Tables[0].Rows)
{
    Console.WriteLine(String.Format("{0} - {1}", row[0], row[1]));
}

Console.ReadLine();
```

5. Run the program to see the results, as shown in the following screenshot:

```
file:///c:/users/administrator/documents/visual studio 2010/Projects/ConsumingSystemQueryServi...
TWD - New Taiwan Dollar
TZS - Tanzanian Shilling
UAH - Hryvnia
UGX - Uganda Shilling
USD - US Dollar
UYI - Uruguay Peso en Unidades Indexadas
UYU - Peso Uruguayo
UZS - Uzbekistan Sum
VEF - Bolivar Fuerte
VND - Dong
VUV - Vatu
WST - Tala
XAF - CFA Franc BEAC
XAG - Silver
XAU - Gold
XCD - East Caribbean Dollar
XDR - SDR
XOF - CFA Franc BCEAO
XPD - Palladium
XPF - CFP Franc
XPT - Platinum
YER - Yemeni Rial
ZAR - Rand
ZWD - Zimbabwe Dollar
```

How it works...

We start the recipe by creating a new Visual C# Console Application project and add a new service reference. The address is set to the standard query service address. The format of the query service address is as follows:

```
net.tcp://<hostname:port>/DynamicsAx/Services/QueryService
```

`hostname` and `port` define an Application Object Server address.

Next, we allow the use of the types in a namespace, so we do not have to qualify them later in the code.

All the code goes into the `Main()` method of the application. In the code, we create a new query with the help of the `QueryMetadata` class, add a new data source based on the `QueryDataSourceMetadata` class, and define two fields in the data source that will be retrieved from the database. The query, data source and field classes, and their properties are very similar to the `Query`, `QueryBuildDataSource`, and `QueryBuildFieldList` classes in Dynamics AX.

Finally, we call the query service with the created query as an argument. The service returns a `DataSet` object, so we go through each row in the first table and display its fields on the screen.

Consuming the system metadata service

The metadata service is another system service that allows clients to get information about the AOT object metadata, such as table and field properties, labels, and others. The metadata services are not customizable and are hosted on the Application Object Server, at a fixed address.

In this recipe, we will create a .NET console application that will connect to the metadata service. The application will retrieve a few properties of the **Currency** and **ExchangeRate** tables.

How to do it...

Carry out the following steps in order to complete this recipe:

1. In Visual Studio, create a new Visual C# Console Application project named `ConsumeSystemMetadataService`.

2. Add a new service reference named `MetadataService` to the project (replace `SEA-DEV:8101` with your address):

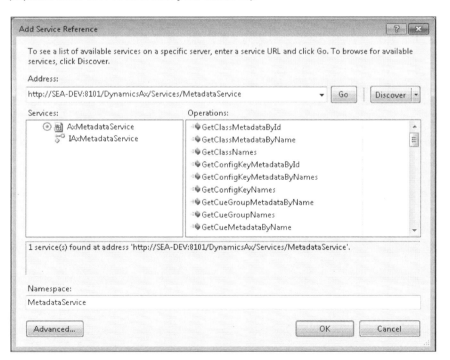

3. Add the following code to the top section of the `Program.cs` file:

```
using ConsumeSystemMetadataService.MetadataService;
```

4. Add the following code to the `Main()` method:

```
AxMetadataServiceClient serviceClient;
TableMetadata[] tables;

serviceClient = new AxMetadataServiceClient();
serviceClient.Open();

tables = serviceClient.GetTableMetadataByName(
    new string[] { "Currency", "ExchangeRate" });

for (int i = 0; i < tables.Length; i++)
{
    Console.WriteLine(
        String.Format("{0}: {1}, {2}",
        tables[i].Name,
        tables[i].TitleField1.Name,
        tables[i].TitleField2.Name));
}

Console.ReadLine();

serviceClient.Close();
```

5. Run the program to see the results, as shown in the following screenshot:

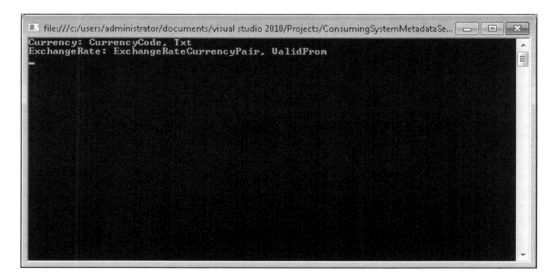

How it works...

In this recipe, we first create a new Visual C# Console Application project and then add a new service reference. The address is set to the standard metadata service address. The format of the metadata service address is follows:

```
net.tcp://<hostname:port>/DynamicsAx/Services/MetadataService
```

`hostname` and `port` define an Application Object Server address.

Next, we allow the use of the type in a namespace, so we do not have to qualify it later in the namespace.

All the code resides in the `Main()` method of the application. Here, we create and open the client object. Then we call the `GetTableMetadataByName()` method—one of the many available operations. This method accepts a list of field names and returns the information about them in an instance of the `TableMetadata` class.

Finally, we display on the screen **TitleField1** and **TitleField2** properties of each object in the returned result and close the client object.

Consuming an existing document service

In Dynamics AX, document services allow data to be exchanged with external systems by sending and receiving XML documents, such as customers, sales orders, vendors, and many others.

In this recipe, we will explore how data could be retrieved from the system using one of the existing services. We will create a .NET console application that will get a currency description from the system using the **read** operation.

How to do it...

Carry out the following steps in order to complete this recipe:

1. In the AOT, locate the **CurrencyServices** service group.
2. Choose the **Deploy Service Group** option from the right-click context menu. A number of messages should be displayed in the Infolog about successful deployment.

3. Open **System administration | Setup | Services and Application Integration Framework | Inbound ports** to check the newly deployed service (note the **WSDL URI** value):

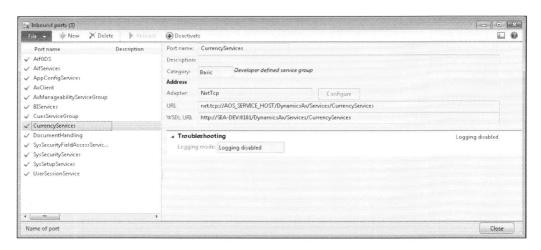

4. In Visual Studio, create a new Visual C# Console Application project named ConsumeExistingDocumentService.

5. Add a new service reference named CurrencyServices to the project.

6. Copy the address from the **WSDL URI** field into the **Address** field:

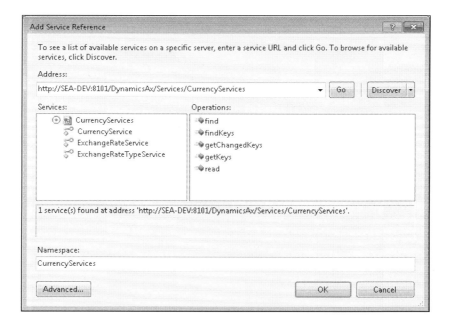

7. Add the following code to the top section of the `Program.cs` file:

```
using ConsumeExistingDocumentService.CurrencyServices;
```

8. Add the following code to the `Main()` method:

```
CurrencyServiceClient serviceClient;
AxdLedgerCurrency currency;

KeyField keyField = new KeyField();
keyField.Field = "CurrencyCode";
keyField.Value = "LTL";

EntityKey keys = new EntityKey();
keys.KeyData = new KeyField[1] { keyField };

serviceClient = new CurrencyServiceClient();
currency = serviceClient.read(null, new EntityKey[1] { keys });

Console.WriteLine(
    String.Format("{0} - {1}",
    currency.Currency[0].CurrencyCode,
    currency.Currency[0].Txt));

Console.ReadLine();
```

9. Run the program to see the results, as shown in the following screenshot:

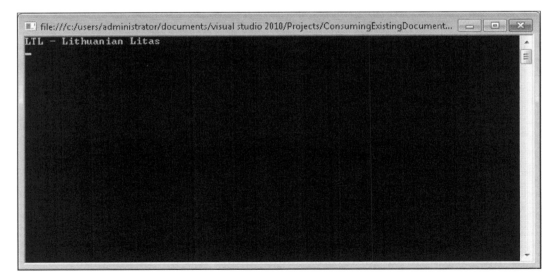

How it works...

We start this recipe by deploying the **CurrencyServices** service group. This action reads the group's configuration, creates a basic port record in the **Inbound ports** form, and then activates it. The existing service will be overridden.

Then we create a new Visual C# Console Application project, add the newly deployed service as a new reference, and allow the use of the type in a namespace.

The `Main()` method starts by defining and creating a new `KeyField` instance. Here, we set the information that will be used for searching—field name and its value. Then the key field is added to the table key list, which normally holds a number of elements matching the number of fields in the table's primary key.

Next, we create the service client object and call its **read** operation with the table key list as an argument. The result is an `AxdLedgerCurrency` object, which represents the **Currency** table.

Lastly, we display some of the field values on the screen.

There's more

The previous example returns only one value matching the key provided. It could be slightly modified to return multiple results, depending on the query provided. Let's replace the code in the `Main()` method with the following code:

```
CriteriaElement criteriaElement = new CriteriaElement();
criteriaElement.DataSourceName = "Currency";
criteriaElement.FieldName = "CurrencyCode";
criteriaElement.Value1 = "A??";
criteriaElement.Operator = Operator.Equal;

QueryCriteria query = new QueryCriteria();
query.CriteriaElement =
    new CriteriaElement[1] { criteriaElement };

CurrencyServiceClient serviceClient = new CurrencyServiceClient();
AxdLedgerCurrency currency = serviceClient.find(null, query);

if (currency.Currency != null)
{
    for (int i = 0; i < currency.Currency.Length; i++)
    {
        Console.WriteLine(
            String.Format("{0} - {1}",
```

```
            currency.Currency[i].CurrencyCode,
            currency.Currency[i].Txt));
    }
}

    Console.ReadLine();
```

The difference is that we now we use the **find** operation, which executes the provided query and returns the results. In the code we defined a query with a single data source, with a filter on the **CurrencyCode** field to find all currencies starting with the letter A. The program's results now are as shown in the following screenshot:

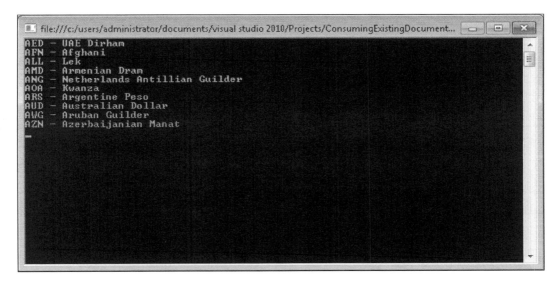

Creating a document service

In Dynamics AX, new document services can be created using the **AIF Document Service Wizard**. The developer has to provide a table and a query representing the document service, and the wizard generates all objects required to run the service. Document services created by the wizard can be further customized to meet more complex requirements.

In this recipe, we will use the **AIF Document Service Wizard** to create a new document service for exposing currency information. Dynamics AX already contains out-of-the-box currency document service, but for demonstration purposes we will create another one.

How to do it...

Carry out the following steps in order to complete this recipe:

1. In the AOT, create a new query named **CurrencyQuery**.

2. Add a new data source to the newly created query with the following properties:

Property	Value
Name	Currency
Table	Currency
Update	Yes

3. In the data source, change the properties of the **Fields** node as follows:

Property	Value
Dynamic	Yes

4. Open the **AIF Document Service Wizard** form, which can be found either in **Tools | Wizards** or in the **Add-Ins** section of the right-click context menu, on the query in the AOT. In the latter case, the wizard will start from the second page with the query name already filled in. In any case, once the query name is entered click on the **Next** button:

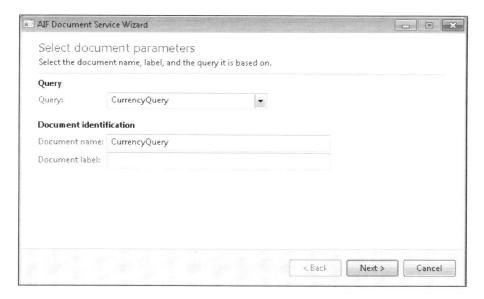

5. On the next page, leave the default names, select the service operations, as in the following screenshot, and click on the **Next** button:

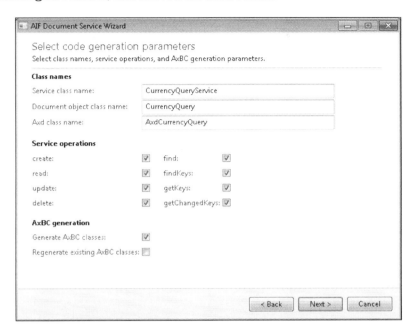

6. On the following page, review what will be generated by the system and click on the **Generate** button:

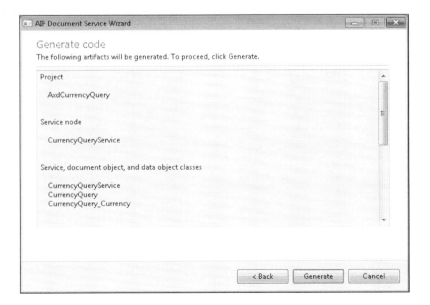

7. On the last page, click on the **Finish** button to complete the wizard:

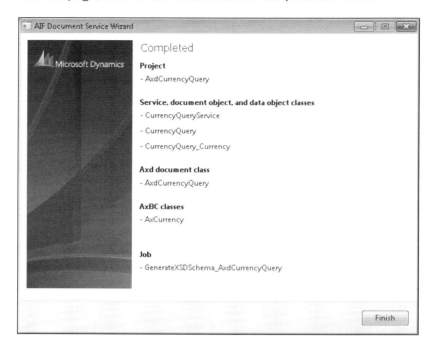

8. To review the newly created objects, locate and open the **AxdCurrencyQuery** private development project:

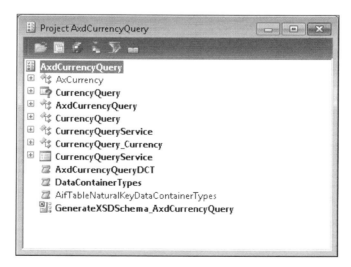

9. Compile the project to ensure that there are no errors.

10. In the AOT, create a new service group named **BasicCurrencyServices**.

11. In the service group, create a new service node with the following properties:

Property	Value
Name	CurrencyQueryService
Service	CurrencyQueryService

12. Deploy the service group by selecting the **Deploy Service Group** option from the service group's right-click context menu. The Infolog should display a number of messages about successful deployment.

13. Open **System administration | Setup | Services and Application Integration Framework | Inbound ports**, to view the newly deployed service:

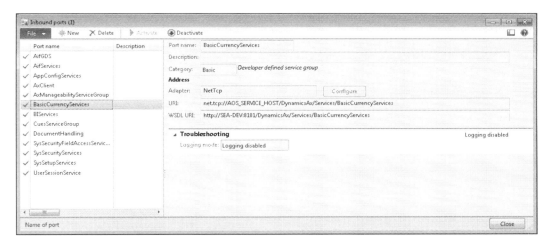

How it works...

We start the recipe by creating a new query. This query will be used by the service to return data. The query contains only one data source linked to the **Currency** table. Although, in this recipe, we will only be retrieving the data, setting the **Update** property of the data source to **Yes** would allow modifying the data too. We also set the **Fields** node to be dynamic, to make sure any field added to the table later will automatically appear in the query.

Once the query is ready, we start the wizard. On the second page we specify the query name and document name. On the third page we select the operations to be implemented. And on the two final pages, we review which objects will be created and finish the wizard. The wizard creates a new private development project with all the generated objects in it. At this point everything is ready, and we only need to create a new service group, add our service, and publish the group.

If everything is successful, we should see a new entry in the **Inbound ports** form. It is activated automatically and we can use the address specified in the **WSDL URI** field to access the service.

Consuming a document service

In Dynamics AX, document services normally provide a number of predefined operations, such as **create**, **delete**, **read**, **find**, **findKeys**, and others. Each operation is responsible for some particular action, for example, **create** allows creating a new document, **delete** allows deleting a document, and so on. The **read** operation was demonstrated in the *Consuming an existing document service* recipe.

In this recipe, we will create a .NET console application to demonstrate how the **find** operation can be used. We will consume the service created in the *Creating a document service* recipe to list all currencies in the system.

How to do it...

Carry out the following steps in order to complete this recipe:

1. In Visual Studio, create a new Visual C# Console Application project named `ConsumeBasicDocumentService`.

2. Add a new service reference named `BasicCurrencyServices` to the project.

3. Copy the address from the **WSDL URI** field, from the *Creating a document service* recipe, into the **Address** field:

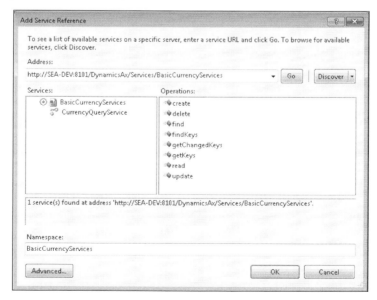

4. Add the following code to the top section of the `Program.cs` file:

```
using ConsumeBasicDocumentService.BasicCurrencyServices;
```

5. Add the following code to the `Main()` method:

```
CriteriaElement criteriaElement = new CriteriaElement();
criteriaElement.DataSourceName = "Currency";
criteriaElement.FieldName = "CurrencyCode";
criteriaElement.Value1 = "";
criteriaElement.Operator = Operator.NotEqual;

QueryCriteria query = new QueryCriteria();
query.CriteriaElement = new CriteriaElement[1] {
    criteriaElement };

CurrencyQueryServiceClient serviceClient = new
CurrencyQueryServiceClient();
AxdCurrencyQuery currency = serviceClient.find(null, query);

if (currency.Currency != null)
{
    for (int i = 0; i < currency.Currency.Length; i++)
    {
        Console.WriteLine(
            String.Format("{0} - {1}",
            currency.Currency[i].CurrencyCode,
            currency.Currency[i].Txt));
    }
}

Console.ReadLine();
```

6. Run the program to display the results as shown in the following screenshot:

How it works...

In this recipe, we first create a new Visual C# Console Application project and then add a new service reference pointing to the address from the previous recipe. Then, we allow the use of the type in a namespace.

The code in the `Main()` method creates a new query based on the **Currency** table and a filter on the **CurrencyCode** field. Here, we set the filter to not empty, that is, return all records from the table.

To get the results we call the **find** operation, which accepts the query as an argument and returns the `AxdCurrencyQuery` document. The last thing to do is to display all the records in the document on screen.

See also

In this chapter:

▶   *Creating a document service*

Using an enhanced document service

In Dynamics AX, services can be exposed using basic or enhanced integration ports. Normally, simple services are exposed using basic ports. Conversely, enhanced ports are used in more complex scenarios. Enhanced ports offer additional capabilities compared to the basic integration ports. Enhanced ports can restrict returned data, execute complex pre-processing and post-processing rules, can be hosted on Internet Information Services, and so on.

In this recipe, we will demonstrate how to create and consume a document service using an enhanced integration port. We will use the document filtering feature of the enhanced port to restrict the range of data being exposed.

How to do it...

Carry out the following steps in order to complete this recipe:

1.   Open **System administration | Setup | Services and Application Integration Framework | Inbound ports** and create a new record as follows:

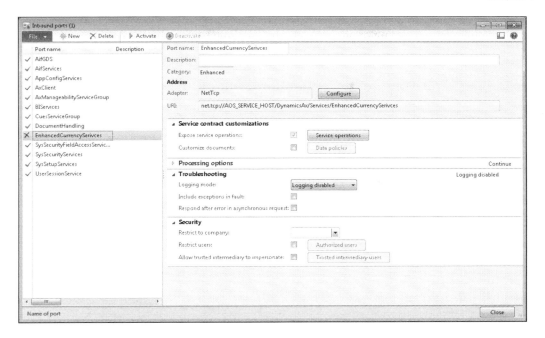

2. Click on the **Service operations** button to open the **Select service operations** form.

3. Select all of the **CurrencyQueryService** service operations that were previously created in the *Creating a document service* recipe:

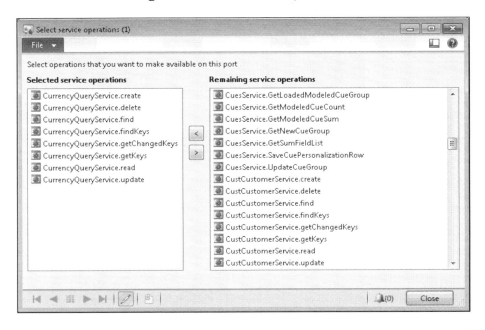

4. Close the **Select service operations** form.

5. On the **Inbound ports** form, expand the **Processing Options** tab page and open the **Document filters** form by clicking on the **Document filters** button.

6. On the opened form, click on the **Add** button, type **Currencies starting with B** into the **Description** field, and save the record. The form should look as follows:

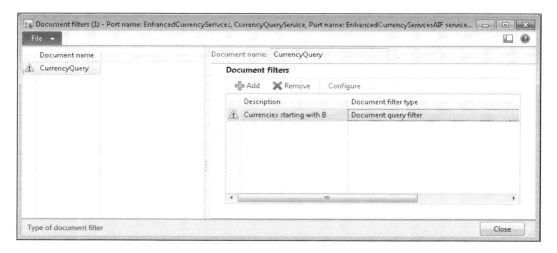

7. Click on the **Configure** button while the newly created record is selected, and specify **B??** in the **Criteria** field, as follows:

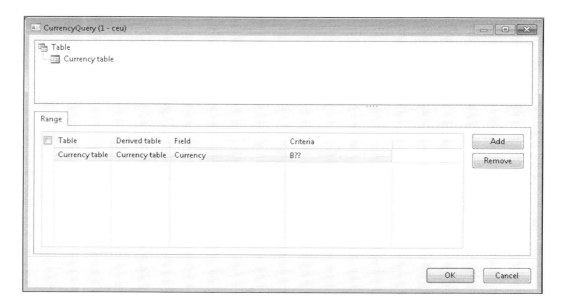

8. Click on **OK** to close the query configuration form and then click on **Close** to close the **Document filter** form.

9. On the **Inbound ports** form, make sure the **EnhancedCurrencyServices** record is selected and click on the **Activate** button. The status should change as follows (note the value in the **WSDL URI** field):

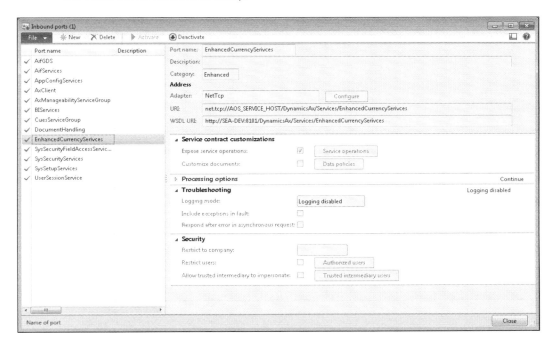

10. In Visual Studio, create a new Visual C# Console Application project named `ConsumeEnhancedDocumentService`.

11. Add a new service reference named `EnhancedCurrencyServices` to the project.

12. Copy the address from the **WSDL URI** field into the **Address** field:

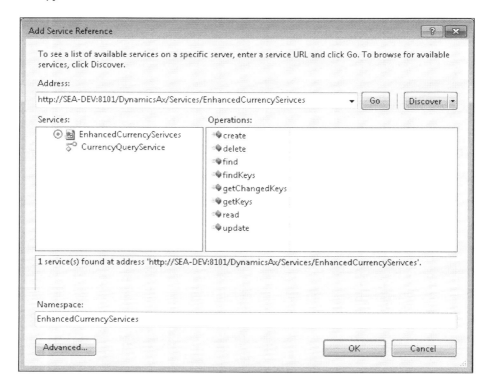

13. Add the following code to the top section of the `Program.cs` file:

```
using ConsumeEnhancedDocumentService.EnhancedCurrencyServices;
```

14. Add the following code to the `Main()` method:

```
CurrencyQueryServiceClient serviceClient =
    new CurrencyQueryServiceClient();
EntityKeyPage keyPage = serviceClient.getKeys(null, null);

for (int i = 0; i < keyPage.EntityKeyList.Length; i++)
{
    Console.WriteLine(keyPage.EntityKeyList[i].KeyData[0].Value);
}

Console.ReadLine();
```

15. Run the program to display the results as shown in the following screenshot:

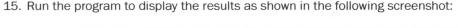

How it works...

In this recipe, no X++ code is required. In the **Inbound ports** form, we created a new entry and selected the operations created in one of the previous recipes. Note that the **Category** field for manually created ports is set to **Enhanced**, meaning that the additional features are available. One of them is document filtering. To demonstrate its use, we create a new filter to limit the returned results to only currencies starting with B. Once everything is ready, we activate the service.

At this stage the service is ready. Next, we create a new Visual C# Console Application project and add a new service reference pointing to the address of the newly created port. We also allow the use of the type in a namespace.

In the Main() method, we create a new service client object and call its getKeys() operation. Document filters applied on enhanced ports are used only in the getChangedKeys() and getKeys() operations, so our operation returns only entity keys that match the applied filters.

The last thing to do is to go through the results and display them on the screen.

See also

In this chapter:

▸ *Creating a document service*

Creating a custom service

A custom service in Dynamics AX allows any X++ logic to be exposed as a service. Custom services are normal X++ classes decorated with attributes, which allow any existing methods to be exposed as service operations without writing any additional code.

In this recipe, we will create a new custom service with a single, simple operation. The operation will accept currency code and return the currency description.

How to do it...

Carry out the following steps in order to complete this recipe:

1. In the AOT, create a new class named CustomCurrencyService with the following code:

```
class CustomCurrencyService
{
}

[SysEntryPointAttribute]
public CurrencyName getCurrencyName(CurrencyCode _currencyCode)
{
    return Currency::find(_currencyCode).Txt;
}
```

2. Set the class properties as follows:

Property	Value
RunOn	Server

3. In the AOT, create a new service with the following properties:

Property	Value
Name	CustomCurrencyService
Class	CustomCurrencyService

4. Expand the newly created service and choose the **Add Operation** option from the **Operations** node's right-click context menu.

5. On the **Add service operations** form, select the **getCurrencyName** line by marking the **Add** checkbox and clicking on **OK**:

6. The service in the AOT should look like the following screenshot:

7. In the AOT, create a new service group named **CustomCurrencyServices**.

8. In the service group, create a new service node reference with the following properties:

Property	Value
Name	CustomCurrencyService
Service	CustomCurrencyService

9. Deploy the service group by selecting the **Deploy Service Group** option from its right-click context menu. The Infolog should display a number of messages about successful deployment.

10. Open **System administration | Setup | Services and Application Integration Framework | Inbound ports** to check the newly deployed service:

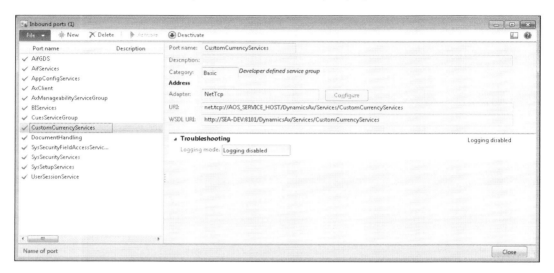

11. To verify the service, open the address specified in the **WSDL URI** field in a browser:

```xml
<?xml version="1.0" encoding="utf-8" ?>
- <wsdl:definitions name="CustomCurrencyServices" targetNamespace="http://tempuri.org/" xmlns:wsdl="http://schemas.xmlsoap.org/wsdl/"
    xmlns:wsx="http://schemas.xmlsoap.org/ws/2004/09/mex" xmlns:wsa10="http://www.w3.org/2005/08/addressing"
    xmlns:tns="http://tempuri.org/" xmlns:soap12="http://schemas.xmlsoap.org/wsdl/soap12/" xmlns:wsu="http://docs.oasis-
    open.org/wss/2004/01/oasis-200401-wss-wssecurity-utility-1.0.xsd" xmlns:wsp="http://schemas.xmlsoap.org/ws/2004/09/policy"
    xmlns:wsap="http://schemas.xmlsoap.org/ws/2004/08/addressing/policy"
    xmlns:msc="http://schemas.microsoft.com/ws/2005/12/wsdl/contract"
    xmlns:wsa="http://schemas.xmlsoap.org/ws/2004/08/addressing" xmlns:wsam="http://www.w3.org/2007/05/addressing/metadata"
    xmlns:wsaw="http://www.w3.org/2006/05/addressing/wsdl" xmlns:soap="http://schemas.xmlsoap.org/wsdl/soap/"
    xmlns:i0="http://tempuri.org" xmlns:xsd="http://www.w3.org/2001/XMLSchema"
    xmlns:soapenc="http://schemas.xmlsoap.org/soap/encoding/">
  + <wsp:Policy wsu:Id="NetTcpBinding_CustomCurrencyService_policy">
    <wsdl:import namespace="http://tempuri.org" location="http://sea-dev:8101/DynamicsAx/Services/CustomCurrencyServices?
      wsdl=wsdl0" />
    <wsdl:types />
  + <wsdl:binding name="NetTcpBinding_CustomCurrencyService" type="i0:CustomCurrencyService">
  - <wsdl:service name="CustomCurrencyServices">
    - <wsdl:port name="NetTcpBinding_CustomCurrencyService" binding="tns:NetTcpBinding_CustomCurrencyService">
        <soap12:address location="net.tcp://sea-dev:8201/DynamicsAx/Services/CustomCurrencyServices" />
      - <wsa10:EndpointReference>
          <wsa10:Address>net.tcp://sea-dev:8201/DynamicsAx/Services/CustomCurrencyServices</wsa10:Address>
        - <Identity xmlns="http://schemas.xmlsoap.org/ws/2006/02/addressingidentity">
            <Upn>AX_AOS_Service@contoso.com</Upn>
          </Identity>
        </wsa10:EndpointReference>
      </wsdl:port>
    </wsdl:service>
  </wsdl:definitions>
```

How it works...

In Dynamics AX, any class can be a custom service. Here, we create a new one with a single method that accepts currency code and returns the currency name. To enable the method as a service operation, we specify the `SysEntryPointAttribute` attribute at the top of the method, which will ensure that the method is available in the service operation list when creating service nodes. We also set the class to run on the server.

Next, we create a new service node and add the newly created operation to it. In order to deploy it, we also have to create a new service group that includes the created service. Once deployed, a new record is created in the **Inbound ports** form.

If everything is successful the service will be ready to be consumed, which is explained in the next recipe.

See also

In this chapter:

> ▸ *Consuming a custom service*

Consuming a custom service

Custom services are consumed in a way quite similar to any other Dynamics AX service. The difference is that each custom service can have a totally different set of operations, where the system or document services always expose the same list operations.

In this recipe, we will create a .NET console application to demonstrate how to consume a custom service. We will use the service created in the *Creating a custom service* recipe, which returns a description of the provided currency.

How to do it...

Carry out the following steps in order to complete this recipe:

1. In Visual Studio, create a new Visual C# Console Application project named `ConsumeBasicCustomService`.

2. Add a new service reference named `CustomCurrencyServices` to the project.

3. Copy the address from the **WSDL URI** field, from the *Creating a custom service* recipe, into the **Address** field:

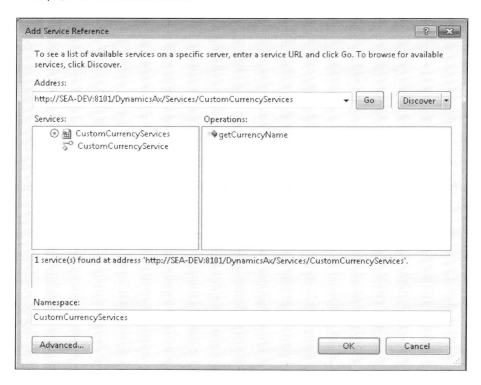

4. Add the following code to the top section of the `Program.cs` file:

    ```
    using ConsumeBasicCustomService.CustomCurrencyServices;
    ```

5. Add the following code to the `Main()` method:

    ```
    CustomCurrencyServiceClient serviceClient =
        new CustomCurrencyServiceClient();
    string currencyName = serviceClient.getCurrencyName(null, "EUR");
    Console.WriteLine(currencyName);
    Console.ReadLine();
    ```

6. Run the program to display the results as shown in the following screenshot:

How it works...

We start this recipe by creating a new Visual C# Console Application project and adding a new service reference pointing to the address from the previous recipe. Then, we allow the use of the type in a namespace.

The code in the `Main()` method is very similar to the other recipes. Here, we create a new service client object and call its `getCurrencyName()` operation to find the currency name.

See also

In this chapter:

- *Creating a custom service*

Consuming an external service

In Dynamics AX, external services can be used in a variety of scenarios for retrieving information from external providers. This could be currency exchange rates, address information, logistics data, and many others. Such external services can be consumed directly from X++ code, with the help of Visual Studio.

In this recipe, we will demonstrate how external services can be consumed from X++ code. For demonstration purposes, we will use the service created in the *Creating a custom service* recipe, and we will assume that this service is an external service.

How to do it...

Carry out the following steps in order to complete this recipe:

1. In Visual Studio, create a new Visual C# Class Library project named `ExtSrv`.

2. Add a new service reference named `CurServices`, to the project.

3. Copy the address from the **WSDL URI** field, from the *Creating a custom service* recipe, into the **Address** field:

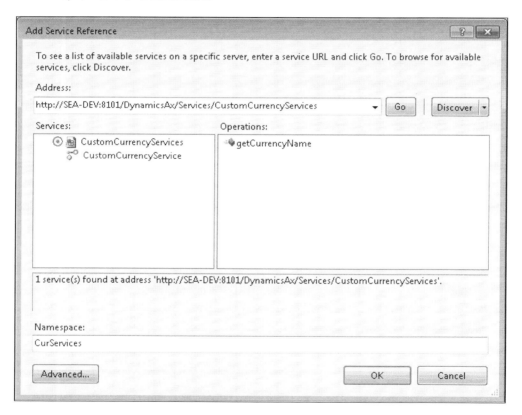

4. In Visual Studio, add the project to the AOT by selecting the **Add ExtSrv to AOT** option from the **File** menu.

5. Open the **Properties** window from the **View** menu, change the following properties of the project, and save the project:

Property	Value
Deploy to Client	Yes
Deploy to Server	Yes

6. In Visual Studio, the project should look as follows:

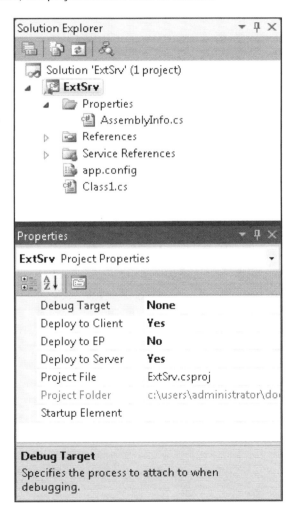

7. Restart the Dynamics AX client and verify that the `ExtSrv` project exits in the AOT under the **Visual Studio Projects | C Sharp Projects** node:

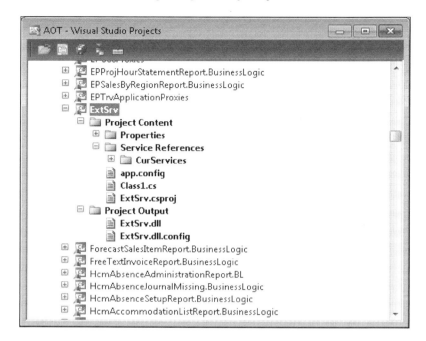

8. Create a new job named `ConsumeExternalService` with the following code:

```
static void ConsumeExternalService(Args _args)
{
    ClrObject serviceClientType;
    ExtSrv.CurServices.CustomCurrencyServiceClient serviceClient;
    System.Exception ex;

    try
    {
        serviceClientType = CLRInterop::getType(
            "ExtSrv.CurServices.CustomCurrencyServiceClient");
        serviceClient = AifUtil::CreateServiceClient(
            serviceClientType);
        info(serviceClient.getCurrencyName(null, "USD"));
    }
    catch (Exception::CLRError)
    {
        ex = CLRInterop::getLastException();
        info(ex.ToString());
    }

}
```

9. Run the job to display the results:

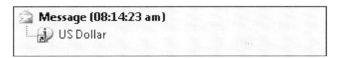

How it works...

In this recipe, we create a new Visual C# Class Library project and add a new service reference pointing to the address from the previous recipe.

Next, we add the project to the AOT and then change the deployment properties to make sure the service is available for X++ code running on both tiers.

To demonstrate how to consume the service, we create a new job. We start the job by defining the service reference created in Visual Studio. Then, we create the service client object and call its getCurrencyOperation() operation, as if it was a regular X++ method.

See also

In this chapter:

▶   *Creating a custom service*

8
Improving Development Efficiency

In this chapter, we will cover the following recipes:

- ► Creating an editor template
- ► Modifying the Tools menu
- ► Modifying the right-click context menu
- ► Searching for an object in a development project
- ► Modifying the Personalization form
- ► Modifying the application version

Introduction

Dynamics AX has its own integrated development environment called MorphX, which contains various tools for designing, modifying, compiling, and debugging code. Besides that, the system allows us to modify existing tools and create new tools for improving development experience and efficiency.

This chapter contains several recipes for this purpose. It explains how code editor templates can be created, how the **Tools** and the right-click context menus can be modified, and how to search within development projects for the AOT objects. The chapter also discusses how we can modify the **Personalization** form and change the application version.

Creating an editor template

Editor templates allow developers to reuse commonly used blocks of code. Dynamics AX provides a number of out of the box code templates for creating `construct()`, `main()`, and `parm()` methods, various statements such as `if`, `else`, `switch`, code comments, and others. The existing templates can also be modified, or new templates can be created.

In this recipe, we will create a new code template for the `find()` method, which is normally created on most of the tables. The template will only be available for table methods and will automatically detect the current table's name and use its primary key to determine the method's arguments.

How to do it...

Carry out the following steps in order to complete this recipe:

1. In the AOT, locate the `xppSource` class and create a new method with the following code:

```
public Source findMethod(TableName _tableName)
{
    str             method;
    DictTable       dictTable;
    DictIndex       dictIndex;
    DictField       dictField;
    FieldName       fieldName;
    DictType        dictType;
    DictEnum        dictEnum;
    int             fieldCount;
    int             i;
    container       fields1;
    container       fields2;
    container       fields3;
    IdentifierName varName;
    IdentifierName varType;

    method =
        'public static %1 find' +
            '(%2, boolean _forUpdate = false)%5' +
        '{%5' +
        '    %1 table;%5' +
        '%5' +
        '    if (%3)%5' +
        '    {%5' +
        '        if (_forUpdate)%5' +
```

```
'                    table.selectForUpdate(_forUpdate);%5' +
'%5' +
'            select firstOnly table%5' +
'                where %4;%5' +
'        }%5' +
'        return table;%5' +
'}';

dictTable = new DictTable(tableName2id(_tableName));

dictIndex = dictTable.indexObject(
    dictTable.replacementKey() ?
        dictTable.replacementKey() :
        dictTable.primaryIndex());

if (dictIndex)
{
    fieldCount = dictIndex.numberOfFields();

    for (i = 1; i <= fieldCount; i++)
    {
        dictField = new dictField(
            dictTable.id(),
            dictIndex.field(i));
        fieldName = dictField.name();
        varName = '_' + strLwr(subStr(fieldName,1,1)) +
            subStr(fieldName,2,strLen(fieldName)-1);

        if (dictField.typeId())
        {
            dictType = new DictType(dictField.typeId());
            varType  = dictType.name();
        }
        else if (dictField.enumId())
        {
            dictEnum = new DictEnum(dictField.enumId());
            varType  = dictEnum.name();
        }
        else
        {
            throw error(
                strfmt(
                    "Field '%1' type is not defined",
                    fieldName));
        }

        fields1 += strFmt('%1 %2',
```

```
                        varType,
                        varName);
                fields2 += varName;
                fields3 += strFmt(
                    'table.%1 == %2',
                    fieldName,
                    varName);
            }
        }

        source = strFmt(
            method,
            _tableName,
            con2Str(fields1,', '),
            con2Str(fields2, ' && '),
            con2Str(fields3, #newLine + strRep(' ', 14) + '&& '),
            #newLine);

        return source;
    }
```

2. In the AOT, locate the `EditorScripts` class, and create a new method with the following code:

```
public void template_method_find(Editor _editor)
{
    TreeNode   objNode;
    xppSource xpp;
    Source     template;

    objNode = EditorScripts::getApplObjectNode(_editor);

    if (!objNode)
    {
        return;
    }

    _editor.gotoLine(1);
    _editor.firstLine();
    while (_editor.moreLines())
    {
        _editor.deleteLines(1);
        _editor.nextLine();
    }

    xpp      = new xppSource();
    template = xpp.findMethod(objNode.AOTname());
    _editor.insertLines(template);
}
```

3. In the same class, find the `isApplicableMethod()` method, and add the following code to the bottom of the `switch` statement:

```
case methodStr(EditorScripts, template_method_find):
    return (_aotNode &&
        _aotNode.treeNodeType().id() == #NT_DBTABLE);
```

4. To test the template, in the AOT, create a new table or locate any table which does not have the `find()` method, for example **CustCollectionsPool**.

5. Create a new table method, then right click anywhere in the code editor and choose **Scripts | template | method | find** from the context menu (alternatively, type **find** anywhere in the editor and click on the *TAB* key):

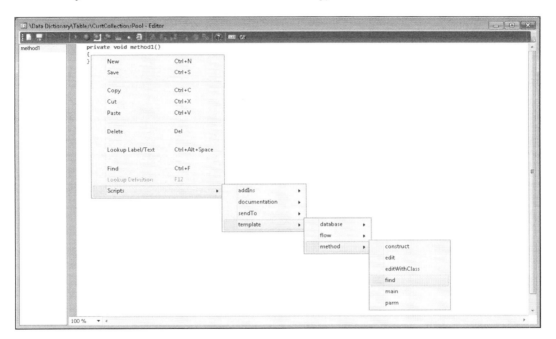

6. The following code should be generated:

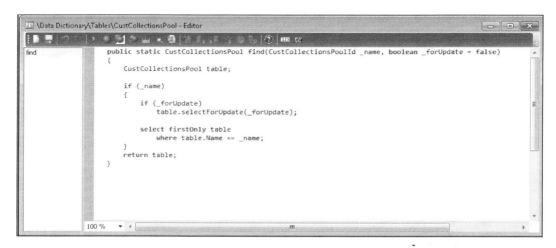

How it works...

Code templates are located in the `xppSource` class of a standard application. We start the recipe by creating a new method in the class that holds all the code for generating the `find()` method template. The method accepts table name as an argument as this is the only thing we need to create the `find()` method.

Right after the variable declaration section, we initialize the `method` variable containing static code for the `find()` method. The placeholders, `%1`, `%2`, and others, will be dynamically replaced with the following table information:

- ▸ `%1` – The table name.
- ▸ `%2` – The list of arguments that depend on a number of fields in the table's primary key. The list contains pairs of type and argument, separated by commas.
- ▸ `%3` – The list of fields in the `if` statement. The list consists of the method's arguments separated by `&&`. The statement is used to improve the method's performance, so that no database query is executed if any of the primary fields are empty.
- ▸ `%4` – The list of fields in the `where` clause. The list consists of table fields from the primary key and corresponding arguments.
- ▸ `%5` – A new line symbol.

The method returns a dynamically generated code for the `find()` method, for a given table.

In this recipe, to simplify the demonstration, the `findMethod()` method was created using a simple string formatting function, `strFmt()`. Alternatively, the template code could be formatted using various helper methods of the `xppSource` class such as `beginBlock()`, `endBlock()`, `indent()`, and others. For more information, explore the other methods in the same class.

The next step is to create a link in the right-click context menu for the newly created template. This is done by creating a relevant method in the `EditorScripts` application class. The method name is `template_method_find()`, which represents a location in the right-click menu, that is, **template | method | find**. In this method, first we clear any existing code in the editor, and then we call the previously created method of the `xppSource` class to insert the generated code into the editor.

The last thing is to modify the `isApplicableMethod()` method in the same class, to make sure the **find** option is only available for table methods.

Modifying the Tools menu

In the AOT, Dynamics AX contains the menus section, which holds all the user menus. Although most of them correspond to a specific module, there are several special system menus. For example, the **MainMenu** menu is a top menu that holds references to all module menus and allows navigation throughout the system. The **GlobalToolsMenu** menu represents **File | Tools** in the user workspace and contains shortcuts to commonly used user functions. The **DevelopmentTools** menu represents the **Tools** menu in the development workspace and contains tools for a developer.

In this recipe, we will demonstrate how system menus can be modified. We will add a link to the **Online users** form in the **DevelopmentTools** menu.

How to do it...

Carry out the following steps in order to complete this recipe:

1. In the AOT, locate the **DevelopmentTools** menu.
2. Add a new separator to the top of the menu.
3. Add a new menu item to the top of the same menu with the following properties:

Property	Value
MenuItemType	Display
MenuItemName	SysUsersOnline

4.   The **DevelopmentTools** menu should look as shown in the following screenshot:

5.   To test the menu, restart the client and note the newly added **Online users** option under the **Tools** menu:

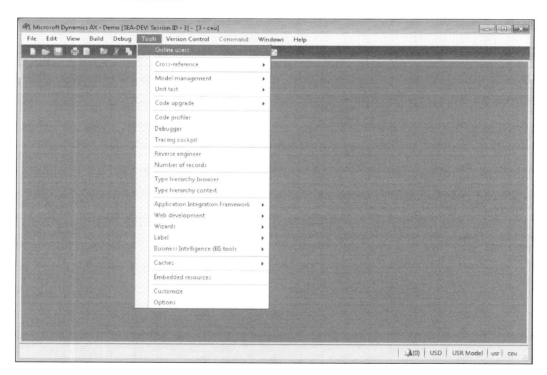

How it works...

In this recipe, we only need to add the desired menu item to the **DevelopmentTools** menu. The menu item is available the next time you log in to Dynamics AX, under the **Tools** menu.

Modifying the right-click context menu

In the development workspace, many developer tools can be accessed from the right-click context menu in the AOT. Some of the tools, such as **Export**, **Delete**, **Restore**, and others, are common for all AOT objects. Some of the options are only available for specific objects, for example, the **Compile** function is only available for classes, tables, and other objects that contain code.

In this recipe, we will demonstrate how to modify the right-click context menu. We will add two new options for development project nodes, allowing setting and clearing any selected project as a startup project.

How to do it...

Carry out the following steps in order to complete this recipe:

1. In the AOT, create a new action menu item with the following properties:

Property	Value
Name	DevProjectStartupUpdateSet
Label	Set as startup project

2. Create one more action menu item with the following properties:

Property	Value
Name	DevProjectStartupUpdateClear
Label	Clear startup project

3. In the AOT, create a new class with the following code:

    ```
    class DevProjectStartupUpdate
    {
    }

    public static void main(Args _args)
    {
        UserInfo        userInfo;
        SysContextMenu  contextMenu;
    ```

```
        IdentifierName projectName;

        if (!_args.menuItemName() ||
            !SysContextMenu::startedFrom(_args))
        {
            return;
        }

        contextMenu = _args.parmObject();

        switch (_args.menuItemName())
        {
            case menuitemActionStr(DevProjectStartupUpdateSet):
                projectName =
                    contextMenu.getFirstNode().treeNodeName();
                break;
            case menuitemActionStr(DevProjectStartupUpdateClear):
                projectName = '';
                break;
            default:
                return;
        }

        ttsBegin;

        select firstOnly forUpdate userInfo
            where userInfo.id == curUserId();

        userInfo.startupProject = projectName;

        if (!userInfo.validateWrite())
        {
            throw Exception::Error;
        }

        userInfo.update();

        ttsCommit;
    }

    public static boolean isStartupProject(
        IdentifierName _projectName,
        UserId _userId = curUserId())
    {
        return (select firstOnly UserInfo
            where UserInfo.id == _userId
                && UserInfo.startupProject == _projectName).RecId ?
            true :
            false;
    }
```

4. For the both menu items, set the properties as follows:

Property	Value
ObjectType	Class
Object	DevProjectStartupUpdate

5. Add the newly created menu items to the **SysContextMenu** menu, as shown in the following screenshot:

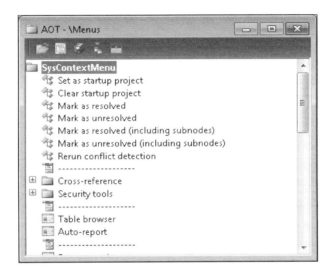

6. In the AOT, find the SysContextMenu class, open its verifyItem() method, and locate the following code at the bottom of the method:

```
case menuitemActionStr(SysXppILIncrementalBuild):
case menuitemActionStr(SysXppILFullBuild):
    // enable for AOT root node only
    return firstNode.treeNodeType().id() == 1;
```

7. Add the following code right after the code mentioned in the previous step:

```
case menuitemActionStr(DevProjectStartupUpdateSet):
    if (firstNode.handle() != classNum(ProjectNode) ||
        !match(#pathProjects, firstNode.treeNodePath()))
    {
        return 0;
    }
    return !DevProjectStartupUpdate::isStartupProject(
        firstNode.treeNodeName());
```

```
case menuitemActionStr(DevProjectStartupUpdateClear):
    if (firstNode.handle() != classNum(ProjectNode) ||
        !match(#pathProjects, firstNode.treeNodePath()))
    {
        return 0;
    }
    return DevProjectStartupUpdate::isStartupProject(
        firstNode.treeNodeName());
```

8. To test the results, open the project window, select any project, and choose the newly created **Add-Ins | Set as startup project** option from the right-click context menu as follows:

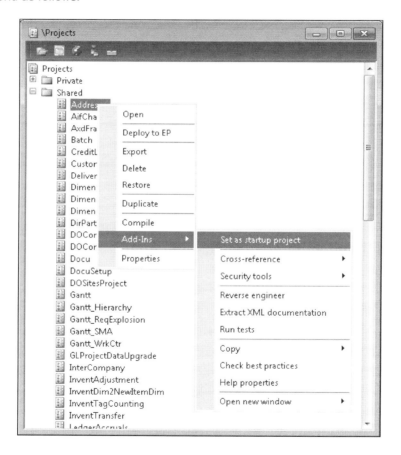

9. Open the **Options** form from the **Tools** menu, you will see that the previously selected project is set as **Startup project** in the **Development** tab:

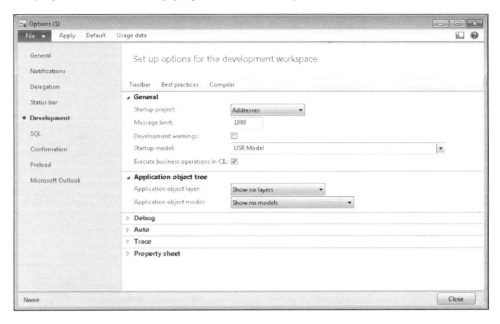

10. To clear the startup project in the project window, select the same project again and choose the **Add-Ins | Clear startup project** option from the right-click context menu:

How it works...

We start this recipe by creating two new menu items. One of them is used for setting the currently selected project as the startup project, and the other one is used for clearing the current project from the startup project, if it was set before. Each of the menu items points to the class that, depending on the caller menu item, will update the **UserInfo** table with the startup project or will clear it. The same class also contains the isStartupProject() helper method, which is used later to determine if the given project is already defined as a startup project.

Next we add the newly created menu items to the **SysContextMenu** menu, which is actually the right-click menu for the AOT. In order to ensure that the menu items are displayed only for project nodes, we modify the verifyItem() method of the standard SysContextMenu class. At the top level, this method has a switch statement with three cases, one for each type of menu item: display, action, and output. Inside each case, there is another switch statement with cases for individual menu items located in the **SysContextMenu** menu—an item is displayed in the menu if a case returns 1 and is not visible if 0 is returned.

We add two additional cases for our menu items under the action case. The menu item for setting the startup project will appear only if the currently selected project is not already specified in the **UserInfo** table. It is the opposite for the menu item for clearing the startup project, that is, it is only shown if the current project is specified in the **UserInfo** table.

Searching for an object in a development project

In Dynamics AX, any development changes to the application normally have to be organized in development projects. The same object could belong to one or more projects, but Dynamics AX does not provide an easy way to determine this.

In this recipe, we will create a class for searching the development projects. The class is only for demonstration purposes but could easily be converted to a standalone tool or integrated into the right-click menu.

How to do it...

Carry out the following steps in order to complete this recipe:

1. In the AOT, create a new class with the following code:

```
class DevProjectSearch
{
}

private boolean findChildren(
```

```
        TreeNode _parent,
        UtilElementType _type,
        IdentifierName _name)
{
    TreeNode         child;
    TreeNodeIterator iterator;
    #TreeNodeSysNodeType

    iterator = _parent.AOTiterator();

    child = iterator.next();

    while (child)
    {
        if (child.treeNodeType().id() == #NT_PROJECT_GROUP)
        {
            return this.findChildren(child, _type, _name);
        }
        else if (child.AOTname() == _name &&
                 child.treeNodePath() &&
                 child.utilElement().recordType == _type)
        {
            return true;
        }
        child.treeNodeRelease();
        child = iterator.next();
    }
    return false;
}

public void find(UtilElementType _type, IdentifierName _name)
{
    TreeNode    projects;
    ProjectNode project;

    projects = SysTreeNode::getSharedProject();

    if (!projects)
    {
        return;
    }

    project = projects.AOTfirstChild();
```

```
        while (project)
        {
            if (this.findChildren(
                    project.loadForInspection(),
                    _type,
                    _name))
            {
                info(project.AOTname());
            }
            project = project.AOTnextSibling();
        }

    }
```

2. To test the class, create a new job with the following code:

```
static void TestDevProjectSearch(Args _args)
{
    DevProjectSearch search;

    search = new DevProjectSearch();
    search.find(UtilElementType::Table, tableStr(CustTable));
}
```

3. Run the job to display the results in the Infolog, as follows:

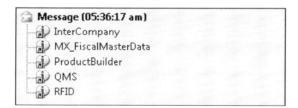

How it works...

In this recipe, we create a new class with several methods. One of them is `findChildren()` and is used for a recursive search operation within the AOT node. It accepts a `TreeNode` object, element type, and element name. In this method, we go through all the children of the argument object and check if any of them matches the element type and name. If any of the child nodes contain more nodes within, we use the same `findChildren()` method to determine if any of its children matches the element type and name.

The second method is named `find()` and is used for the actual search for the given element type and name. The method goes through all of the shared development projects and calls the `findChildren()` method to determine whether the given element is in one of its nodes.

The class can be called from anywhere in the system, but in this recipe we create a new job, define and instantiate the class, and use the `find()` method to search for the **CustTable** table in all shared projects.

See also

In this chapter:

> ► *Modifying the right-click context menu*

Modifying the Personalization form

The **Personalization** form allows users to customize their most often used forms to fit their needs. Users can hide or move form controls, change labels, and so on. This setup is available for any Dynamics AX form and can be opened from the right-click context menu by selecting the **Personalize** option.

For developers, this form can be very useful too. For example, it contains the very handy **System name** field, which displays the name of the currently selected table field or method, so that you do not need to search in the AOT. The **Information** tab provides details about the form itself, the caller object, and the menu item used, and it allows opening those objects instantly in the AOT view. The last tab page, **Query**, shows information about the tables used in the form's query, which is also very useful to facilitate quick understanding of the underlying data structure.

In this recipe, we will demonstrate how to enhance the **Personalization** form. We will add a new button to the last tab, which will open the selected table in the AOT.

How to do it...

Carry out the following steps in order to complete this recipe:

1. Open the **SysSetupForm** form in the AOT and find the following code in its `fillQueryTreeQueryDatasource()` method:

    ```
    formTreeItem = new FormTreeItem(
        nodeText, imagelist.image(#ImageDataSource), -1, null);
    ```

2. Replace it with the following code:

```
formTreeItem = new FormTreeItem(
    nodeText,
    imagelist.image(#ImageDataSource),
    -1,
    queryBuildDataSource.table());
```

3. Add a new `ButtonGroup` control to the **QueryPage** tab with the following properties:

Property	Value
Name	ButtonGroup1

4. Add a new `Button` control to the created button group and set its properties as follows:

Property	Value
Name	EditTable
AutoDeclaration	Yes
Text	Edit

5. Override the `clicked()` event method of the button with the following code:

```
void clicked()
{
    FormTreeItem formTreeItem;
    TableId       tableId;
    TreeNode      treeNode;
    #AOT

    formTreeItem = QueryTree.getItem(
        QueryTree.getSelection());

    tableId = formTreeItem.data();

    if (!tableId || !tableId2name(tableId))
    {
        return;
    }

    treeNode = infolog.findNode(
        #TablesPath +
        #AOTDelimiter +
        tableid2name(tableId));

    if (!treeNode)
    {
        return;
    }

    treeNode.AOTnewWindow();
}
```

6. On the **QueryTree** control, override the `selectionChanged()` event method with the following code:

```
public void selectionChanged(
    FormTreeItem _oldItem,
    FormTreeItem _newItem,
    FormTreeSelect _how)
{
    super(_oldItem, _newItem, _how);

    EditTable.enabled(
        tableid2name(_newItem.data()) ? true : false);
}
```

7. To test the changes, open any form, for example, **Main accounts** located in the **General ledger**, and open the **Personalization** form by right-clicking anywhere on the form and selecting the **Personalize** option:

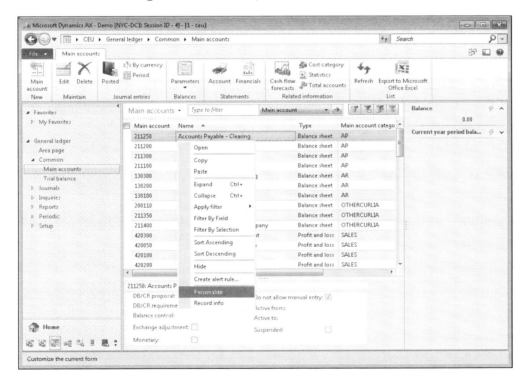

8. Go to the **Query** tab and select one of the tables displayed:

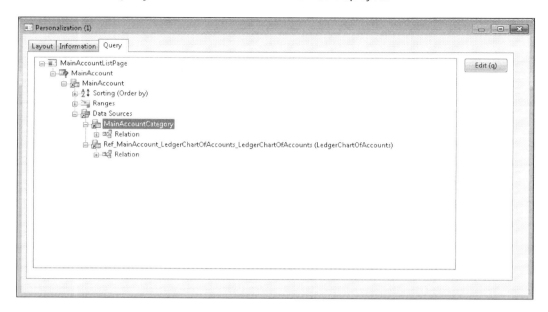

9. Click the newly created **Edit** button to open the selected table in the AOT:

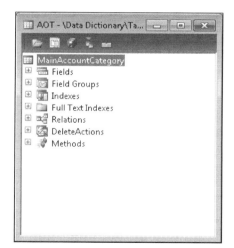

How it works...

First, we modify the creation of the query tree control. Normally, each tree node can hold some data. The query tree in the **SysSetupForm** form does not have any data associated with its nodes, so we have to modify the code and store the table number in each node that represents a table.

Next, we add a new button and override its `clicked()` method. In this method, we get the table number stored in the currently selected node—this is what we stored earlier—and search for that table in the AOT. We display it in a new AOT window, if found.

Finally, we override `selectionChanged()` on the **QueryTree** control to make sure the button's status is updated upon node selection. In other words, the **Edit** button is enabled if the current tree node contains some data, otherwise it is disabled.

In this way, we have modified the **Personalization** form to provide the developer with quick access to the underlying tables directly in the AOT.

Modifying the application version

Dynamics AX releases are identified with two main numbers—**Kernel version** and **Application version**. The numbers indicate the major Dynamics AX release, and if there are any service packs, cumulative updates, or individual hotfixes installed. Version numbers can be viewed in the **About Microsoft Dynamics AX** dialog, which can be accessed from the **Help** menu. This dialog can also be modified to contain additional versions for solution developers to control their releases.

In this recipe, we will learn how to modify the system to include additional version numbers in the **About Microsoft Dynamics AX** dialog. For demonstration purposes, we will add a new custom version line to this dialog.

How to do it...

Carry out the following steps in order to complete this recipe:

1. In the AOT, find the `ApplicationVersion` class and create a new method with the following code:

    ```
    static str usrAppl()
    {
        return '1.0.0';
    }
    ```

2. In the AOT, locate the **SysAbout** form and add a new **StaticText** control with the following properties to the bottom of **DetailGrp | MainGrp | RightGroup | VersionInfoGroup**:

Property	Value
Name	CustomVersion
AutoDeclaration	Yes
Width	Column width
Text	

3. The form in the AOT should look as shown in the following screenshot:

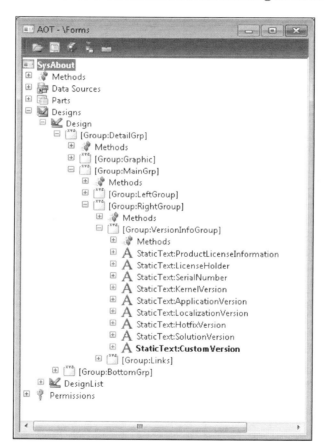

4. Add the following code to the variable declaration section of the form's `run()` method:

    ```
    str usrVersionNumber = ApplicationVersion::usrAppl();
    ```

5. Add the following code to the same method, right before `element.unLock(true)`:

    ```
    element.unLock(true):

    if (usrVersionNumber)
    {
        CustomVersion.text('Custom version: ' + usrVersionNumber);
    }
    ```

6. Open **Help | About Microsoft Dynamics AX** and note the newly created **Custom version** control:

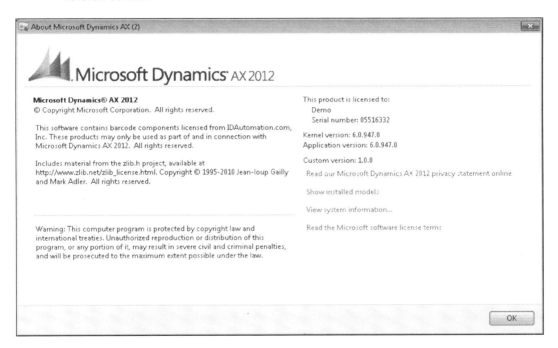

How it works...

The `ApplicationVersion` class is the place where the application version numbers are stored. For example, the `applBuildNo()` method returns the current application version. By modifying this class, Dynamics AX developers can modify original or add custom version numbers. This class is called from the **SysAbout** form, which is actually the **About Microsoft Dynamics AX** dialog.

In this recipe, first we create a new method in the `ApplicationVersion` class, which returns our version number. Normally, the number should be updated with every new release.

Next, we modify the **SysAbout** form by adding a new control. Then we modify the form's `run()` method to ensure that the number in the previously created method is displayed on the form.

Now, the **About Microsoft Dynamics AX** dialog contains a new line showing our custom version number.

9

Improving Dynamics AX Performance

In this chapter, we will cover the following recipes:

- ▶ Calculating code execution time
- ▶ Writing efficient SQL statements
- ▶ Caching a display method
- ▶ Using Dynamics AX Trace Parser
- ▶ Using SQL Server Database Engine Tuning Advisor

Introduction

It is quite common for many larger Dynamics AX installations to suffer from performance issues. This could be caused by insufficient hardware, incorrect configuration, ineffective code, lack of user training, and many other reasons.

This chapter discusses how the system's performance could be improved by following several simple rules. This is not a complete guide for troubleshooting Dynamics AX performance issues, but a compilation of must-know information for developers.

Calculating code execution time

While working on improving an existing code, there is always the question of how to measure the results. There are numerous ways of doing that, for example, visually assessing the improvements, getting feedback from users, using the code profiler, or some other tool to measure execution times, and so on.

In this recipe, we will discuss how to measure the code execution time using a very simple method, just by temporarily adding a few lines of code. In this way, the execution time of the old code can be compared with the execution time of the new one to show whether any improvements were made.

How to do it...

Carry out the following steps in order to complete this recipe:

1. In the AOT, create a new job with the following code:

    ```
    static void GetExecutionTime(Args _args)
    {
        int start;
        int end;

        start = WinAPI::getTickCount();

        sleep(1000); // pause for 1000 milliseconds

        end = WinAPI::getTickCount();

        info(strFmt("%1", end - start));
    }
    ```

2. Run the job to see how many milliseconds it takes to execute the code:

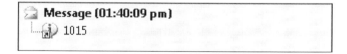

How it works...

In this recipe, the main element is the `getTickCount()` method of the standard `WinAPI` class. The method returns the `TickCount` property of the .NET environment, which is a 32-bit integer containing the amount of time, in milliseconds, that has passed since the last time the computer was started.

We place the first call to the `getTickCount()` method before the code we want to measure, and we place the second call right after the code. In this way, we know when the code was started and when it was finished. The difference between the times is the code execution time in milliseconds.

Normally, using such a technique to calculate the code execution time does not provide very useful information, as we cannot exactly tell whether it is right or wrong. It is much more beneficial to measure the execution time before and after we optimize the code. In this way, we can clearly see if any improvements were made.

There's more...

The approach described in the previous section could be successfully used for measuring long-running code, such as various calculations or complex database queries. But, it may not be possible to assess code that takes only a few milliseconds to execute. The code improvement may not be noticeable, as it could be greatly affected by variances caused by current system conditions. In such a case, the code in question could be executed a number of times, so the execution times can be properly compared.

To demonstrate this, we can modify the previously created job as follows:

```
static void GetExecutionTime(Args _args)
{
    int start;
    int end;
    int i;

    start = WinAPI::getTickCount();

    for (i = i; i <= 100; i++)
    {
        sleep(1000); // pause for 1000 milliseconds
    }

    end = WinAPI::getTickCount();

    info(strFmt("%1", end - start));
}
```

Now, the execution time will be much longer, and therefore easier to compare.

Writing efficient SQL statements

In Dynamics AX, SQL statements can often become performance bottlenecks. Therefore, it is very important to understand how Dynamics AX handles database queries and follow all the best practice recommendations in order to keep your system healthy.

In this recipe, we will discuss some of the best practices to use when writing database queries. For demonstration purposes, we will create a sample method with several scenarios and will discuss each of them. The method will locate the **CustGroup** table record of the given customer account.

How to do it...

Carry out the following steps in order to complete this recipe:

1. In the AOT, locate the **CustGroup** table and create the following method:

```
public static CustGroup findByCustAccount(
    CustAccount _custAccount,
    boolean     _forupdate = false)
{
    CustTable custTable;
    CustGroup custGroup;

    if (_custAccount)
    {
        select firstOnly CustGroup from custTable
            where custTable.AccountNum == _custAccount;
    }

    if (custTable.CustGroup)
    {
        if (_forupdate)
        {
            custGroup.selectForUpdate(_forupdate);
        }

        select firstOnly custGroup
            where custGroup.CustGroup == custTable.CustGroup;
    }

    return custGroup;
}
```

2. On the same table, create another method with the following code:

```
public static CustGroup findByCustAccount2(
    CustAccount  _custAccount,
    boolean      _forupdate = false)
{
    CustTable custTable;
    CustGroup custGroup;

    if (_custAccount)
    {
        if (_forupdate)
        {
            custGroup.selectForUpdate(_forupdate);
        }

        select firstOnly custGroup
            exists join custTable
            where custGroup.CustGroup  == custTable.CustGroup
                && custTable.AccountNum == _custAccount;
    }

    return custGroup;
}
```

How it works...

In this recipe, we have two different versions of the same method. Both methods are technically correct, but the second one is more efficient. Let's analyze each of them.

In the first method, we should pay attention to the following points:

▸ Check that the `_custAccount` argument is not empty; this will avoid running an unnecessary database query.

▸ Use the `firstOnly` keyword in the first SQL statement to disable the effect of the read-ahead caching. If there were no `firstOnly` keyword, the statement would retrieve a block of records, return the first one, and ignore the others. In this case, even though the customer account is a primary key and there is only one match, it is always recommended to use the `firstOnly` keyword in `find()` methods.

▸ In the same statement, specify the field list—the **CustGroup** field—we want to retrieve, instructing the system not to fetch any other fields that we are not planning to use. In general, this could also be done on the AOT query objects by setting the **Dynamic** property of the **Fields** node to **No** on the query data sources, and manually adding only the required fields. This can also be done in forms by setting the **OnlyFetchActive** property to **Yes** on the form data sources.

▸ Execute the `selectForUpdate()` method only if the `_forupdate` argument is set. The `if` statement is more efficient than calling the `selectForUpdate()` method with an argument `false`.

The second method already uses all of the discussed principles, plus one additional, as follows:

> ▸ Both SQL statements are combined into one using an `exists` join. One of the benefits is that only a single trip is made to the database. Another benefit is that no fields are retrieved from the customer table because of the `exists` join. This makes the statement even more efficient.

Caching a display method

In Dynamics AX, display methods are widely used to show additional information on forms or reports that come from different data sources, including special calculations, formatting, and more.

Display methods are shown as physical fields and are executed each time the form is redrawn. This means that the more complex the method is, the longer it takes to display it on the screen. Normally, it is recommended to keep the code in display methods to a minimum.

The performance of display methods can be improved by caching them. This is when display method's return value is retrieved from a database or calculated only once, and subsequent calls are made to the cache.

In this recipe, we will create a new cached display method. We will also discuss a few scenarios to learn how to properly use caching.

How to do it...

Carry out the following steps in order to complete this recipe:

1. In the AOT, locate the **CustGroup** table and create a new display method with the following code:

    ```
    display Description displayPaymTermDescription()
    {
        return (select firstOnly Description from PaymTerm
            where PaymTerm.PaymTermId == this.PaymTermId).Description;
    ```

2. Add the newly created method to the table's **Overview** group, right beneath the **PaymTermId** field, as shown in the following screenshot:

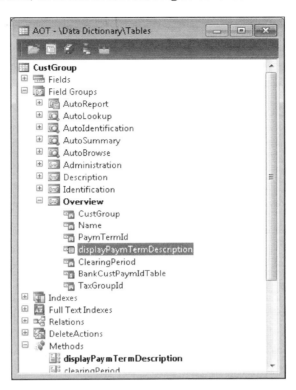

3. In the AOT, find the **CustGroup** form and override the init() method of its **CustGroup** data source with the following code:

```
public void init()
{
    super();
    this.cacheAddMethod(
        tableMethodStr(CustGroup,displayPaymTermDescription));
}
```

4. To test the display method, open **Accounts receivable | Setup | Customers | Customer groups**:

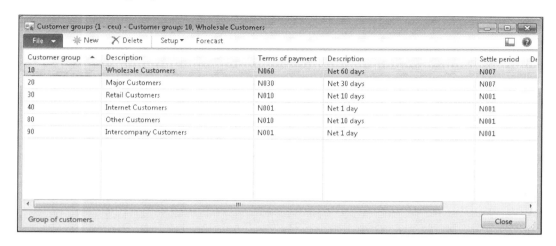

How it works...

In this recipe, we create a new display method on the **CustGroup** table to show the description of the **Terms of payment** defined on a customer group record. In the method, we use a query to retrieve only the **Description** field from the **PaymTerm** table. Here, we could have used the find() method of the **PaymTerm** table, but that would have decreased the display method's performance, as it returns the whole **PaymTerm** record, while we only need a single field. We also add the method that we created to the **Overview** group on the table, to ensure that it automatically appears on the overview screen of the **Customer group** form.

In order to cache the display method, we override the init() method of the **CustGroup** data source and call its cacheAddMethod() method to make sure the method's return values are stored in the cache.

The cacheAddMethod() method instructs the system's caching mechanism to load the method's values into the cache for the records visible on the screen, plus some subsequent records. It is important that only display methods that are visible on the **Overview** tab page are cached. Display methods located on different tab pages does not properly utilise the caching mechanism. They normally show a value from a single record at a time and therefore three is no point to cache subsequent records as they not displayed on the screen anyway.

Speaking about display method caching, the best option, of course, is not to place any display methods on the overview screen, or at least keep the number of display fields to a minimum. It is also advised not to create display methods on the forms directly as they cannot be reused elsewhere.

Alternatively, in this recipe, we could have used the `SysClientCacheDataMethodAttribute` attribute by adding it to the top of the display method, as shown in the following code:

```
[SysClientCacheDataMethodAttribute]
display Description displayPaymTermDescription()
{
    return (select firstOnly Description from PaymTerm
        where PaymTerm.PaymTermId == this.PaymTermId).Description;
}
```

In this case, the method will automatically be cached on any form where it is used without any additional code. Note that this is only acceptable if the display method is only shown on the overview screen.

Using Dynamics AX Trace Parser

Dynamics AX has a feature that allows generating trace files of the client and server activity. It collects lots of useful information, such as user sessions, call trees, SQL statements, execution durations, and much more. Such trace files can be analyzed with a tool called Dynamics AX Trace Parser, which displays all the trace information within the informative graphical user interface and allows developers to see what is happening behind the scenes and make appropriate decisions.

In this recipe, we will demonstrate how to use Dynamics AX Trace Parser. We will create and run a simple class containing a simple SQL statement while running AX tracing. Then, we will analyze the generated trace using Trace Parser.

How to do it...

Carry out the following steps in order to complete this recipe:

1. In the AOT, create a new class with the following code:

   ```
   class CustTransTracing
   {
   }
   ```

```
public static void main(Args _args)
{
    CustTrans custTrans;

    select count(RecId) from custTrans
        where custTrans.Approved;
}
```

2. Change the following property of the class:

Property	Value
RunOn	Server

3. Open **Tools | Tracing cockpit**. Mark the **Bind parameters** checkbox and accept the default values for the rest of the parameters as follows:

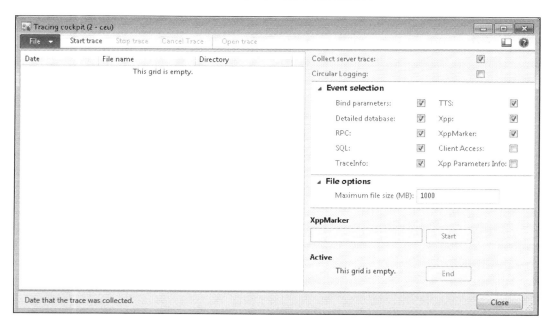

4. Click on **Start trace** and then save the trace file to, say, **C:\temp\trace.etl**.
5. Go back to the created class and run it.

6.   Now, in the **Tracing cockpit** form, click on **Stop trace**:

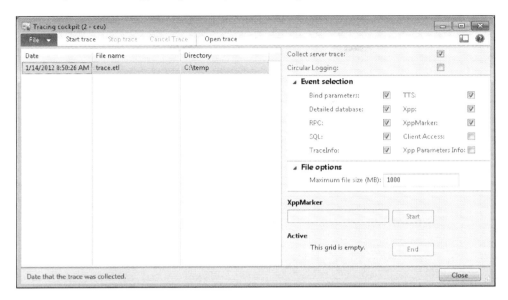

7.   Open **Microsoft Dynamics AX 2012 Trace Parser**, import the previously saved trace file, and select your session in the **Session** field at the top:

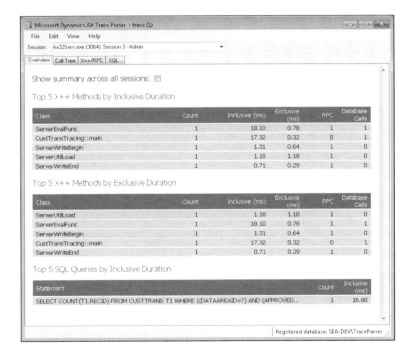

8. Open the **SQL** tab page. The query should be displayed here. If there are too many records, apply the filter by typing **CustTrans** into the **Name Filter** field and marking the **Show Tables** checkbox to find your query:

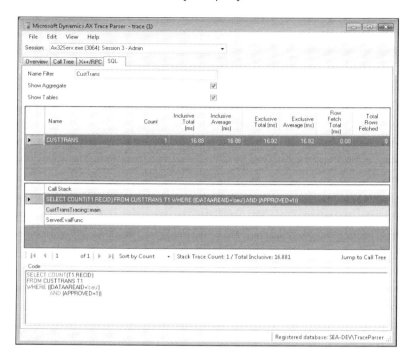

9. Click on **Jump to Call Tree** to display the query in the call stack:

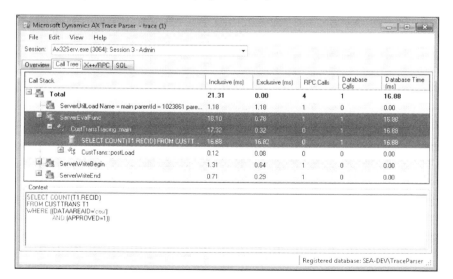

How it works...

The goal of this recipe is to demonstrate how we can trace X++ code and X++ SQL statements converted to actual database queries.

For this purpose, we created a simple class with a `main()` method containing a single SQL statement.

Then, we start tracing, run the class, and stop tracing, which generates a trace file with all the information we need. Note that tracing can also be started and stopped from the code by calling the `start()` and `stop()` methods of the `xClassTrace` class.

The next step is to open the file using Trace Parser. The tool provides a lot of information, but for the purpose of this recipe, we only search for our SQL statement on the **SQL** tab page. On this tab page we see the details of our query, along with its tracked execution times. We can see the class and method name that this SQL statement was called from. We can also see what the actual SQL statement, which has been executed on the database, looks like. Such information is very useful to understand how Dynamics AX converts X++ code into SQL queries.

Additionally, it is possible to locate the SQL statement in the call stack by clicking on the **Jump to Call Tree** button. This view shows the code in question in the context of other processes.

Note that the statement we used contains a non-indexed field in its `where` clause, which makes it inefficient. In the next recipe we will demonstrate how we can improve it.

See also

In this chapter:

► _Using SQL Server Database Engine Tuning Advisor_

Using SQL Server Database Engine Tuning Advisor

SQL Server Database Engine Tuning Advisor allows developers to analyze and improve database queries. Database Engine Tuning Advisor examines query usage and recommends how it can be improved. Though most of the time the results of this tool are accurate, before making any database changes it is recommended to confirm them manually or by using another technique.

In this recipe, we will use Database Engine Tuning Advisor to analyze the query captured by Trace Parser from the previous recipe.

How to do it...

Carry out the following steps in order to complete this recipe:

1. Open **SQL Server Management Studio** and connect to the server where your Dynamics AX database resides.

2. Select the Dynamics AX database, create a new query, and copy the SQL statement from Trace Parser from the previous recipe. Execute the query to ensure it is error free:

3. Right-click anywhere in the query window, and from the context menu select **Analyze Query in Database Engine Tuning Advisor**, and then click on **Start Analysis** and wait for the results:

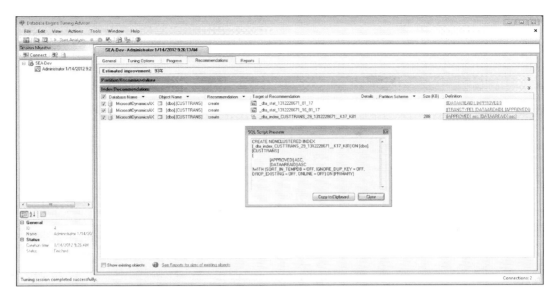

How it works...

The goal of this recipe is to demonstrate how we can use suggestions from Database Engine Tuning Advisor to improve the performance of SQL statements in Dynamics AX. As an example, we use the SQL statement from the previous recipe that contains a non-indexed field in its where clause.

Database Engine Tuning Advisor can be opened from the **Tools** menu of SQL Server Management Studio, or directly from the right-click context menu of the query window. In the latter case, it will automatically analyze a query specified in the query window.

Once the analysis is completed, **Database Engine Tuning Advisor** displays a list of recommendations, which can be reviewed by clicking on the value in the **Definition** column of the **Recommendations** tab page.

In this recipe, the tuning advisor suggests creating database statistics and a new index. The index here is the most important element. In the **SQL Script Preview** window, we can see which fields are included in the index and we can create this index in Dynamics AX.

Normally, after creating indexes, we have to run Database Engine Tuning Advisor to verify whether the estimated query performance was improved.

See also

In this chapter:

- *Using Dynamics AX Trace Parser*

Index

V

validate() method 138, 205, 250
validateWrite() method 111, 144, 230, 238
value() method 117, 258
valueNot() method 117
valueUnlimited() method 117
variantType() method 258
VendTableSqlBuilder class 35
VendTable table 161
verifyItem() method 319, 322
View details link
about 105
adding 105-107
visible() method 256

W

where clause 31
while loop 51
WinAPI class 334
windowType() method 79

WindowType property 79
wizard
about 134
creating 135-144
working 143
Word document
creating, from template 259-261
creating, repeating elements used 262-266
working 262
writeExp() method 48
write() method 111

X

XBRL 41
X++ code 7, 58
XML 41
XML file
data, exporting to 42-44
data, importing from 44-46
xppSource class 310

Thank you for buying
Microsoft Dynamics AX 2012
Development Cookbook

About Packt Publishing

Packt, pronounced 'packed', published its first book "*Mastering phpMyAdmin for Effective MySQL Management*" in April 2004 and subsequently continued to specialize in publishing highly focused books on specific technologies and solutions.

Our books and publications share the experiences of your fellow IT professionals in adapting and customizing today's systems, applications, and frameworks. Our solution-based books give you the knowledge and power to customize the software and technologies you're using to get the job done. Packt books are more specific and less general than the IT books you have seen in the past. Our unique business model allows us to bring you more focused information, giving you more of what you need to know, and less of what you don't.

Packt is a modern, yet unique publishing company, which focuses on producing quality, cutting-edge books for communities of developers, administrators, and newbies alike. For more information, please visit our website: www.PacktPub.com.

About Packt Enterprise

In 2010, Packt launched two new brands, Packt Enterprise and Packt Open Source, in order to continue its focus on specialization. This book is part of the Packt Enterprise brand, home to books published on enterprise software – software created by major vendors, including (but not limited to) IBM, Microsoft and Oracle, often for use in other corporations. Its titles will offer information relevant to a range of users of this software, including administrators, developers, architects, and end users.

Writing for Packt

We welcome all inquiries from people who are interested in authoring. Book proposals should be sent to author@packtpub.com. If your book idea is still at an early stage and you would like to discuss it first before writing a formal book proposal, contact us; one of our commissioning editors will get in touch with you.

We're not just looking for published authors; if you have strong technical skills but no writing experience, our experienced editors can help you develop a writing career, or simply get some additional reward for your expertise.

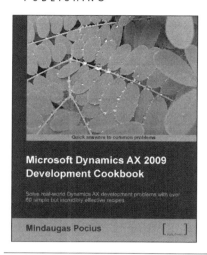

Microsoft Dynamics AX 2009 Development Cookbook

ISBN: 978-1-847199-42-3   Paperback: 352 pages

Solve real-world Dynamics AX development problems with over 60 simple but incredibly effective recipes

1. Develop powerful, successful Dynamics AX projects with efficient X++ code

2. Proven AX recipes that can be implemented in various successful Dynamics AX projects

3. Covers general ledger, accounts payable, accounts receivable, project, CRM modules and general functionality of Dynamics AX

Microsoft Dynamics AX 2009 Programming: Getting Started

ISBN: 978-1-847197-30-6   Paperback: 348 pages

Get to grips with Dynamics AX 2009 development quickly to build reliable and robust business applications

1. Develop and maintain high performance applications with Microsoft Dynamics AX 2009

2. Create comprehensive management solutions to meet your customer's needs

3. Best-practices for customizing and extending your own high-performance solutions

4. Thoroughly covers the new features in AX 2009 and focuses on the most common tasks and issues

Please check **www.PacktPub.com** for information on our titles

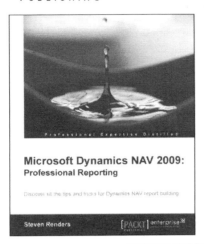

Microsoft Dynamics NAV 2009: Professional Reporting

ISBN: 978-1-84968-244-2   Paperback: 352 pages

Discover all the tips and tricks for Dynamics NAV report building

1. Get an overview of all the reporting possibilities, in and out of the box

2. Understand the new architecture and reporting features in Microsoft Dynamics NAV 2009

3. Full of illustrations, diagrams, and tips with clear step-by-step instructions and real-world examples

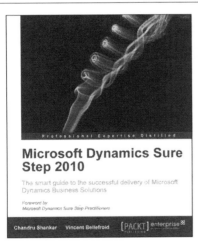

Microsoft Dynamics Sure Step 2010

ISBN: 978-1-84968-110-0   Paperback: 360 pages

The smart guide to the successful delivery of Microsoft Dynamics Business Solutions

1. Learn how to effectively use Microsoft Dynamics Sure Step to implement the right Dynamics business solution with quality, on-time and on-budget results

2. Leverage the Decision Accelerator offerings in Microsoft Dynamics Sure Step to create consistent selling motions while helping your customer ascertain the best solution to fit their requirements

3. Understand the review and optimization offerings available from Microsoft Dynamics Sure Step to further enhance your business solution delivery during and after go-live

Please check **www.PacktPub.com** for information on our titles